John Ashbery

in conversation with

Mark Ford

John Ashbery

in conversation with

Mark Ford

BETWEEN THE LINES BTL BETWEEN THE LINES

First published in 2003 by

BETWEEN THE LINES **BTL** BETWEEN THE LINES

9 Woodstock Road
London N4 3ET
UK

T : + 44 (0)20 8374 5526   F : + 44 (0)20 8374 5736   E-mail : btluk@aol.com
Website: http://www.interviews-with-poets.com

Design and typography: Philip Hoy

Printed and bound by T.J. International Ltd.,
Padstow, Cornwall PL28 8RW, UK

BTL publishes unusually wide-ranging and unusually deep-going interviews with some of today's most accomplished poets.

Some would deny that any useful purpose is served by putting to a
writer questions which are not answered by his or her books. For them,
what Yeats called "the bundle of accident and incoherence that sits down
to breakfast" is best left alone, not asked to interrupt its cornflakes, or to
set aside its morning paper, while someone with a tape recorder inquires
about its life, habits and attitudes.

If we do not share this view, it is not because we endorse Sainte-Beuve's
dictum, *tel arbre, tel fruit — as the tree, so the fruit —* but because we
understand what Geoffrey Braithwaite was getting at when the author of
Flaubert's Parrot had him say:

> But if you love a writer, if you depend upon the drip-feed
> of his intelligence, if you want to pursue him and find
> him – despite edicts to the contrary – then it's impos-
> sible to know too much.

The first eleven volumes, featuring W.D. Snodgrass, Michael Ham-
burger, Anthony Thwaite, Anthony Hecht, Donald Hall, Thom Gunn,
Richard Wilbur, Seamus Heaney, Donald Justice, Ian Hamilton and
Charles Simic, respectively, are already available; the next, featuring Mark
Strand, is now being prepared. (Further details about the series are given
overleaf.)

As well as the interview, each volume contains a sketch of the poet's
life and career, a comprehensive bibliography, archival information, and
a representative selection of quotations from the poet's critics and re-
viewers. More recent volumes also contain uncollected poems. It is hoped
that the results will be of interest to the lay reader and specialist alike.

— OTHER VOLUMES FROM BTL —

W.D. SNODGRASS
in conversation with
Philip Hoy

MICHAEL HAMBURGER
in conversation with
Peter Dale

ANTHONY THWAITE
in conversation with
Peter Dale and Ian Hamilton

ANTHONY HECHT
in conversation with
Philip Hoy

DONALD HALL
in conversation with
Ian Hamilton

THOM GUNN
in conversation with
James Campbell

RICHARD WILBUR
in conversation with
Peter Dale

SEAMUS HEANEY
in conversation with
Karl Miller

DONALD JUSTICE
in conversation with
Philip Hoy

IAN HAMILTON
in conversation with
Dan Jacobson

— FORTHCOMING —

MARK STRAND
in conversation with
Philip Hoy

CONTENTS

LIST OF ILLUSTRATIONS

9

ACKNOWLEDGEMENTS

The editors would like to thank the following people for their help with this volume: Olivier Brossard, Marcella Durand, Juno Gemes, Danny Gillane, Gustavo Hoffman, Richard Jackson, Shunk Kender, David Kermani, Richard Kostelanetz, Scott R. LaClaire (of the *Georgia Review*), Herbert Leibowitz (of *Parnassus*), George Montgomery, Danny Mulligan (of Farrar, Straus and Giroux), Harry Redl, and Elisabeth Sifton (of Farrar, Straus and Giroux).

John Ashbery

Photograph courtesy of
Juno Gemes

©

A Note on John Ashbery

John Lawrence Ashbery was born in Rochester, New York, on July 28th 1927, the first son of Chester Frederick (a farmer) and Helen Ashbery (a biology teacher). He went to school in Rochester and in his home town of Sodus, and at the age of sixteen was sent as a boarder to Deerfield Academy in Massachusetts. After graduating from there, in 1945, he entered Harvard University, where he studied English.

Ashbery had been writing poetry since his schooldays, and while at Deerfield had even had two of his poems accepted by the prestigious magazine, *Poetry*. Two years after he went to college he submitted work to *The Harvard Advocate*, the recently revived undergraduate magazine, whose editors were Robert Bly, Donald Hall and Kenneth Koch. The poems were quickly published, and just a few months later their author found himself installed as the fourth member of the magazine's editorial board. According to Hall, he rapidly became the *Advocate*'s leading light.

Ashbery obtained his BA in 1949, and went to Columbia University to study for his MA. He graduated from there in 1951, and found work in publishing, becoming a copywriter, first for Oxford University Press and then for the McGraw Hill Book Company. Poems of his continued to appear in magazines, amongst them *Furioso*, *Poetry New York* and *Partisan Review,* but as well as pursuing his literary interests, Ashbery was now mixing in New York's artistic circles, frequenting the galleries, and getting to know the painters. Then, in 1953, thanks to its director, John Myers, the city's influential Tibor de Nagy Gallery published a slender chapbook of Ashbery's poems, complete with illustrations by the artist Jane Freilicher. *Turandot and Other Poems* seems not to have attracted much notice, but Alfred Corn subsequently included its publication in a list of the most important events 'in the history of twentieth century avant-garde art'.

Three years later, by which time he was in Paris on a Fulbright fellowship, Ashbery's first full collection was chosen by W.H. Auden for inclusion in Yale University Press's Younger Poets Series. Reviewing *Some Trees* for *Poetry*, Frank O'Hara wrote of Ashbery's 'faultless music' and 'originality of perception', and pronounced it 'the most beautiful first book to appear in America since *Harmonium*'. Not everyone felt so enthusiastic, however. William Arrowsmith, writing for *The Hudson Review*, declared that he had 'no idea most of the time what Mr Ashbery is talking about ... beyond the communication of an intolerable vagueness that looks as if it was meant for precision,' and added, for good measure: 'What does come through is an impression of an impossibly fractured brittle world, depersonalized and discontinuous, whose characteristic emotional gesture is an effete and cerebral whimsy.'

Ashbery's period as a Fulbright fellow came to an end in 1957, but life in Paris had been so much to his liking that, after another year in the US – a year in which he took graduate classes at New York University and worked as an instructor in elementary French – he returned, avowedly to pursue research for a doctoral dissertation on the writer Raymond Roussel. He was to remain in France for several years, supporting himself by writing for a number of different journals. He had started to review for the magazine *ArtNews* during his year in New York, and continued with this once back in Paris. Then, in 1960, he became art critic for the *New York Herald Tribune* (international edition), and, in 1961, art critic for *Art International* as well. Nor were these his only such commitments. In the same year that he started writing for the *New York Herald Tribune*, he joined with Kenneth Koch, Harry Mathews, and James Schuyler and founded the literary magazine, *Locus Solus.* That folded in 1962, but the following year he got together with Anne Dunn, Rodrigo Moynihan and Sonia Orwell, and founded *Art and Literature,* a quarterly review he worked on until he went back to living in the US, in 1966.

When not writing reviews, or engaged in editorial work, Ashbery still found time to write poetry. It was poetry of a very different kind to that he had published in *Some Trees*, however, and readers familiar with the first book will have been altogether unprepared for the 'violently experimental' character of the second (unless they had been keeping an eye on *Big Table* and *Locus Solus,* the magazines in which some of these poems first appeared). Reactions to *The Tennis Court Oath* were generally hostile. James Schevill told readers of the *Saturday Review*: 'The trouble with Ashbery's work is that he is influenced by modern painting to the point where he tries to apply words to the page as if they were abstract, emotional colors and shapes ... Consequently, his work loses coherence ... There is little substance to the poems in this book.' And Mona Van Duyn told readers of *Poetry*: 'If a state of continuous exasperation, a continuous frustration of expectation, a continuous titillation of the imagination are sufficient response to a series of thirty-one poems, then these have been successful. But to be satisfied with such a response I must change my notion of poetry.' Even so devoted an admirer of Ashbery as Harold Bloom thought the book a 'fearful disaster' and confessed to being baffled at how its author could have 'collapse[d] into such a bog' just six years after *Some Trees.*

Ashbery has said that when he was working on the poems that went into *The Tennis Court Oath* he was 'taking language apart so I could look at the pieces that made it up', and that after he'd done this he was intent on 'putting [the pieces] back together again'. *Rivers and Mountains*, published in the year that he settled back in the US, was the first of his books to follow, and marked what several of his critics regard as his real arrival as a poet, with poems such as "These Lacustrine Cities", "Clepsydra" and "The Skaters" all demonstrating for the first time what one of them has called the 'astonishing range and flexibility of Ashbery's voice'. The volume was nominated for the National Book Award.

Ashbery had gone back to the US after being offered the job of executive editor of *ArtNews*. Four years later, in 1969, the Black Sparrow Press published his long poem "Fragment", with illustrations by the painter Alex Katz. Writing about this seven years on, Bloom declared that it was, for him, Ashbery's 'finest work'. By then, it should be noted, the poem had plenty of rivals, since *The Double Dream of Spring* (which included "Fragment") had appeared in 1970, *Three Poems* had appeared in 1972, and *The Vermont Notebook* and *Self-Portrait in a Convex Mirror* had appeared in 1975. All of these books had won Ashbery admiring notices, and *Three Poems* had also secured him the Modern Poetry Association's Frank O'Hara Prize, but it was *Self-Portrait in a Convex Mirror* that proved to be the breakthrough, carrying off all three of America's most important literary prizes – the National Book Award, the National Book Critics Circle Award, and the Pulitzer Prize. John Malcolm Brinnin's notice for the *New York Times Book Review* can be taken as representative: '[A] collection of poems of breathtaking freshness and adventure in which dazzling orchestrations of language open up whole areas of consciousness no other American poet has even begun to explore ...'

ArtNews was sold in 1972, and Ashbery had to find himself another job. A Guggenheim Fellowship sustained him for some months, but then, in 1974, he took up the offer of a teaching post at Brooklyn College – a part of the City University of New York – where he co-directed the MFA program in creative writing. Though he has confessed to not liking teaching very much, he has been doing it ever since (with one extended break between 1985 and 1990, made possible by the award of a MacArthur Foundation fellowship). He left Brooklyn College in 1990, was Charles Eliot Norton Professor of Poetry at Harvard between 1989 and 1990, and from then until now has been Charles P. Stevenson, Jr. Professor of Languages and Literature at Bard College at Annandale-on-Hudson, New York.

Just as Ashbery's art reviewing and editorial work seemed not to affect his creative output during the Sixties and early Seventies, so his teaching work seems not to have affected it during the decades since. In fact, he has been remarkably prolific, averaging a new collection once every eighteen months. *Self-Portrait in a Convex Mirror* was followed by: *Houseboat Days* (1977), *As We Know* (1979), *Shadow Train* (1981), *A Wave* (1984), *April Galleons* (1987), *Flow Chart* (1991), *Hotel Lautréamont* (1992), *And the Stars Were Shining* (1994), *Can You Hear, Bird* (1995), *Wakefulness* (1998), *Girls on the Run* (1999), *Your Name Here* (2000), *As Umbrellas Follow Rain* (2001) and *Chinese Whispers* (2002) (to mention only his book-length collections). He has also published

Three Plays (1978), *Reported Sightings* (a selection of his art reviews) (1989) and *Other Traditions* (revised versions of the Charles Eliot Norton Lectures he gave in 1989 and 1990).

This large body of work has won Ashbery numerous admirers, amongst them some of today's most prominent critics. It has also won him numerous honours, awards and prizes, a partial list of which would include (apart from those already mentioned) two Ingram Merrill Foundation grants (1962, 1972), *Poetry* magazine's Harriet Monroe Poetry Award (1963) and Union League Civic and Arts Foundation Prize (1966), two Guggenheim fellowships (1967, 1973), two National Endowment for the Arts publication awards (1969, 1970), the Poetry Society of America's Shelley Memorial Award (1973), *Poetry* magazine's Levinson Prize (1977), a National Endowment for the Arts Composer/Librettist grant (with Elliott Carter) (1978), a Rockefeller Foundation grant for playwriting (1979-1980), the English Speaking Union Award (1979), membership of the American Academy and Institute of Arts and Letters (1980), fellowship of the Academy of American Poets (1982), the New York City Mayor's Award of Honour for Arts and Culture, Bard College's Charles Flint Kellogg Award in Art and Letters, membership of the American Academy of Arts and Sciences (1983), *American Poetry Review*'s Jerome J. Shestack Poetry Award (1983, 1995), *Nation* magazine's Lenore Marshall Award, the Bollingen Prize, Timothy Dwight College/Yale University's Wallace Stevens fellowship (1985), the MLA Common Wealth Award in Literature (1986), the American Academy of Achievement's Golden Plate Award (1987), Chancellorship of the Academy of American Poets (1988-1989), Brandeis University's Creative Arts Award in Poetry (Medal) (1989), the Bavarian Academy of Fine Arts (Munich)'s Horst Bienek Prize for Poetry (1991), *Poetry* magazine's Ruth Lilly Poetry Prize, the Academia Nazionale dei Lincei (Rome)'s Antonio Feltrinelli International Prize for Poetry (1992), the French Ministry of Education and Culture (Paris)'s Chevalier de L'Ordre des Arts et Lettres (1993), the Poetry Society of America's Robert Frost Medal (1995), the Grand Prix des Biennales Internationales de Poésie (Brussels), the Silver Medal of the City of Paris (1996), the American Academy of Arts and Letters's Gold Medal for Poetry (1997), *Boston Review of Books*'s Bingham Poetry Prize (1998), the State of New York/ New York State Writers Institute's Walt Whitman Citation of Merit (2000), Columbia County (New York) Council on the Arts Special Citation for Literature, the Academy of American Poets's Wallace Stevens Award, Harvard University's Signet Society Medal for Achievement in the Arts (2001), the New York State Poet Laureateship (2001-2002), and France's Officier de la Légion d'Honneur (2002).

Ashbery lives in the Chelsea district of New York City and in Hudson, New York.

A Note on Mark Ford

Mark Ford was born in Nairobi, Kenya, in 1962. He went to school in London, and attended Oxford and Harvard Universities. He wrote his doctorate at Oxford University on the poetry of John Ashbery, and has published widely on nineteenth- and twentieth-century American writing. From 1991-1993 he was Visiting Lecturer at Kyoto University in Japan. He currently teaches in the English Department at University College London, where he is a Senior Lecturer. He has published two collections of poetry, *Landlocked* (Chatto & Windus, 1992;1998) and *Soft Sift* (Faber & Faber, 2001/Harcourt Brace, 2003). He has also written a critical biography of the French poet, playwright and novelist, Raymond Roussel, *Raymond Roussel and the Republic of Dreams* (Faber & Faber, 2000/Cornell University Press, 2001). He is a regular contributor to the *Times Literary Supplement* and the *London Review of Books*.

The Conversation

What follows is an edited version of exchanges between John Ashbery and Mark Ford which were recorded at the former's apartment in the Chelsea district of Manhattan during February 2002.

I thought we might start chronologically: you were born on July 28th, 1927. Does that make you a Leo?

Yes, with Virgo rising. I was born at 8.20 am, and there was a thunderstorm at the time, which may be significant.

That was in Rochester?

Yes. My parents lived near a small farming community about thirty miles east of Rochester, called Sodus. My father and his father had bought some farmland near Lake Ontario, where they grow a lot of fruit, mainly apples, cherries and peaches. There is a narrow band along the edge of Lake Ontario where fruit is grown. Just a few miles south the climate and the crops are different.

Did he plant the fruit trees himself?

Yes, with his own hands, like Johnny Appleseed! His father had owned a rubber stamp factory in Buffalo, which I can't imagine was very prosperous – at least I don't think they produced them in mass quantities. For whatever reason, the Ashbery family wanted to leave the city, and they bought this farm in 1915.

Was your mother keen on farming as well?

No. She was from the city and her father was a professor of Physics at the University of Rochester. In fact he was quite famous locally and did the first x-ray experiments in the US outside of New York City. This fact was often alluded to solemnly in family conversations. I think we sometimes omitted the 'outside of New York City' when doing so. I knew he was the grand old man of our family, but was surprised when his obituary appeared in the *New York Times* when he died in 1954.

This is Henry Lawrence.

19

Yes. He was the head of the Physics Department for forty years, and was a friend of George Eastman.

Of Kodak?

Yes – I think I met George Eastman when I was about four years old when my grandfather took me to a reception at his mansion, which is still there, and is now a famous photography museum.

Did your grandfather invest in Kodak?

No. He did, but not early enough. Eastman wanted him to and offered to lend him money to do so, but my grandfather was suspicious of this newfangled gadget so he didn't do so at a time when he could have made a killing. He was very frugal. He was born in a very pretty little village, Pultneyville, on Lake Ontario. He was poor, and attended a one-room schoolhouse, and somehow managed to educate himself.

How did your parents meet?

At a dance one night in or near this village, where my mother's family used to spend the summer. In fact she probably was well on the way to becoming an old maid. She was thirty-two when they married, and my father was thirty-four. I think her sorority sisters at the University of Rochester – who were family friends – always thought she had married beneath herself, but it was probably lucky she managed to catch somebody when she was already thirty-two. Although she was very pretty at that time, she was very shy, extremely shy, some of which has rubbed off on me.

Was she more intellectual than your father?

No, not at all. Neither was intellectual. She studied Biology in college, and taught Biology at High School at Albion, a small town west of Rochester. But her father, my grandfather, read a great deal in addition to books about Physics. He had the works of Dickens, Thackeray, George Eliot, Huxley, Tyndall, all of which he actually read, and I think he read Greek also – plus the works of Tennyson, Browning, Jean Ingelow and Shakespeare. He had a wonderful Victorian edition of Shakespeare – which I still have – including ghoulish steel-engraved illustrations of things like skulls with snakes slithering from their eye-sockets. Actually I read Shakespeare from about the age of ten or eleven. I didn't understand much, but I also had Lamb's *Tales from Shakespeare* as a trot.

Your first schools were in Rochester rather than Sodus: why was that?

Until I was about seven I lived mainly with my grandparents, which I much preferred, since it was in the city, and there were lots of kids to play with. In Sodus there was no kindergarten, so I went to kindergarten in Rochester, and part of first grade. Then my grandfather retired in 1934, and moved to the cottage they had in Pultneyville, which they'd had remodelled, or as we'd now say, winterised. After that I still used to spend almost every weekend with them – my grandfather would come and pick me up at the school in Sodus on Friday and drive me to their house, about six miles away and my parents would come and get me on Sunday.

Why did you spend so much time with them?

Well, I didn't get along with my father. He had a violent temper. He could be very, not brutal, but he used to wallop me a great deal, often for no reason I could detect, so I felt always as though I were living on the edge of a live volcano – although, on the other hand, when he wasn't being that way, he could be very nice. But my grandfather was much nicer. I resembled him physically much more than anyone in the family. He had this wonderful smell of wool and pipe tobacco – I suppose the sort of 'old man's smell' that makes Japanese girls faint with disgust.

He sounds somewhat like an eminent Victorian.

Yes. He was born in 1864, and my grandmother in 1867. I felt very happily plugged into the Victorian era at their place – despite my familiarity with *Hard Times* and *Oliver Twist* ... Also my parents quarrelled a great deal, though I never knew about what exactly.

Was the farm successful?

Not really. It was the Depression. I think one reason I lived so much with my grandparents when I was young was because I was a mouth to feed, and by that time I had a little brother; it was a way of saving money. I remember my father once opened a store in Rochester where he sold apples from the farm. I don't think that lasted very long, but I guess it was typical of the times – people were selling apples on street corners all over. A very early memory is being in the store and smelling the apples.

How old were you when your brother Richard was born?

I was three and a half. In fact one of my earliest datable memories is of my mother coming back from the hospital after she'd given birth to my brother, and my father carrying her up the stairs to her room, like a romantic hero, *à la Gone with the Wind*, though this was long before that movie was made, and my going up to her room after and doing a little dance to entertain her, a sort of jig, I guess ... And the other thing that I remember and can date was my grandfather coming home and telling my grandmother that George Eastman had died. In fact he'd committed suicide. That was in 1932, I think.

Snow features pretty often in your poetry. Does this come from your childhood?

No doubt. My father's farm was about a mile from Lake Ontario, just due south, and often snowbound. Even three miles further south it would not be snowing, while we were up to our necks in it.

How did you amuse yourself? Did you have neighbours?

There were some. But I didn't see much of them.

Did you have the book you allude to in "The Skaters", Three Hundred Things a Bright Boy Can Do?

No, I didn't have that one, but I did have *The Book of Knowledge*, which had similar advice on Things to Make and Things to Do. I don't think I ever actually did any of them because they required objects like hollowed-out elder branches, and I never knew quite where to find such things! But in the summer, when I spent as much time as possible with my grandparents, I had a whole group of friends whose parents came from Rochester and vacationed by the lake.

Your first poem was "The Battle", which you wrote when you were how old?

Eight. Actually, one influence on it might have been the movie of *A Midsummer's Night's Dream*, made in 1935, with Mickey Rooney as Puck. I remember boning up on Lamb's version before seeing this movie in which there were lots of fairies sliding down moonbeams and so on.

Well, your poem – which is about a conflict between fairies and bunnies – has the lines:

> *The fairies are riding upon their snowflakes,*
> *And the tall haystacks are great sugar mounds.*
> *These are the fairies' camping grounds.*

Very Shakespearean ...

Yes! And at the time it seemed quite perfect to me. It even ended up being read by the best-selling author in America at the time, Mary Roberts Rinehart. She mainly wrote mystery stories, a number of which featured a female detective named Tish. She was very famous and lived on 5th Avenue – though I'd never been to New York City, I'd heard of 5th Avenue. Anyway, her son married my mother's cousin, and on Christmas day, so the story goes, this poem was read aloud in her apartment to great acclaim. Alas, I wasn't there, and in fact didn't get to New York City until I was seventeen years old.

Yet despite this early triumph, you were more interested in music and painting while you were growing up?

Well, I'd always drawn ever since I was old enough to hold a pencil, and I took piano lessons also from an early age. Then my school at Sodus dropped its art department, so I was given special dispensation to take Friday afternoon off to go into Rochester to an art class for children at the art museum there.

Was it in Rochester that you used to see Mary Wellington, the girl you were in love with?

No. She used to come and stay with her grandmother in Pultneyville – which is a rather elegant place with pretty, early nineteenth-century houses right along the lake. Mary's grandmother had a cottage there, and next door to us was another girl called Carol, the daughter of one of my mother's college friends, whom I also liked very much. I could never make up my mind which one I liked best, though things never really got very far physically. It wasn't until I was about thirteen that I actually kissed a girl

– and that was about the last time too! Not that I didn't like it … And another girl who used to come and stay was Eleanor (I must be sounding like Marcel on the beach at Balbec in *A l'ombre des jeunes filles en fleurs!*). She was nicknamed Barney after the famous racing driver Barney Oldfield …

Doesn't he feature in the novel you co-wrote with Jimmy Schuyler, A Nest of Ninnies?

Yes, Jimmy dropped him in. Anyway, I had a big crush on Barney; we'd go to the movies and hold hands, and then nothing else would happen, and neither of us would ever allude to this. But my biggest crush was on a girl named Frances, whom none of my friends knew. She was in my art class. She was so beautiful that I felt a painful sensation like an electric shock whenever I saw her. Though I barely knew her, I asked her one day if she'd like to visit the current show at the museum – an exhibition of Van Gogh reproductions! – and while we looked at the pictures I told her I loved her. She seemed quite horrified and was quite distant with me after that. We were both about thirteen. I would occasionally keep tabs on her through a girlfriend of hers who eventually moved to New York and edited an art magazine with Hilton Kramer, so I knew she had attended Goucher College. Years later when I gave a reading there, I mentioned her to an older teacher who remembered her and showed me her photo in a yearbook, mentioning that she had died. It was strange to see her picture for the first time and to learn at the same moment that she was dead.

Were your dates with Barney the beginning of your obsession with the movies? How often did you go?

Never as much as I wanted to. We went quite often in the summer at the movie theatre near Pultneyville, and in the village of Sodus there was a movie theatre which I went to, but this would end up quite an expedition, because my parents would have to come in to drop me off and then pick me up and drive me home. Then there was a largish town nearby called Newark, which had an almost first-run movie theatre. My father was very fond of musicals so we'd tool over to see the latest Busby Berkeley.

What kind of painter were you? Were you a Surrealist?

Well, I wanted to paint Surrealist pictures but they didn't really come out the way I meant, and I was told I had to be a realist painter first ...

You were greatly impressed by the pictures reproduced in Life *magazine of the 1936 show at the Museum of Modern Art, "Fantastic Art, Dada, and Surrealism".*

Yes.

When did you first come across the American Surrealist magazine, View?

Not, I think, until I was at Deerfield Academy, that is sometime after 1943; but I had a cousin, Wallace, in Buffalo, my father's brother's son, who was the only intellectual in the family, and he once brought me a copy of a poetry magazine called *Upstate*, edited by John Bernard Myers, whom of course I wasn't to meet for years. I think there was something by Auden in it, and Wallace knew I liked Auden. There was one issue that was devoted to Latin American poetry, in particular Octavio Paz, who was the first Surrealist poet I came across.

And that inspired you?

Well, I was already by that time experimenting a bit. There were other kinds of Surrealist American poets, and the early Randall Jarrell – poets such as Oscar Williams, and Charles Henri Ford, whose 93rd birthday, I think, is in a couple of days.*

Were you seen as a prodigy in your family, with your successes in spelling bee competitions, and on radio as a Quiz Kid?

Sort of – first of all with my successful poem, my pocket-career as poet. Then I was the spelling-bee champion of the county, and got to go to the New York State Fair to take part in the state-wide contest in which, however, I didn't fare too well. Then the following year I won this Quiz Kid competition – *Quiz Kids* was a very famous program on the radio. I picked up an entry form in Sibley's, the main department store in Rochester, and went back there for the early rounds. I kept winning, until I reached the finals, which were very exciting – they were held on the stage of the RKO Palace, the grandest movie palace of the city – it got torn down, alas, in the Fifties ... Anyway, I won, and got to go to Chicago, with my mother and grandmother. That was my first proper long trip – we went by train, in a Pullman, and stayed in a hotel. I'd never stayed in a hotel

*Charles Henri Ford died on September 27, 2002 (Eds).

before – I'd only dreamed of things like that. Unfortunately I tanked on the program ...

Was it all fixed, as in the movie Quiz Show*?*

When I got to Chicago they asked me what I was interested in and I said eighteenth-century French painters, so they gave me a question related to that, which I answered.

Was it fingers on the buzzers?

You raised your hand. There was a warm-up period before we were actually on the air, during which I answered a whole bunch of questions, not realizing the more seasoned 'kids' weren't wasting their arms on these. I knew the answers to a few questions in the contest proper, but I didn't get my arm up in time.

When exactly was this?

December, 1941. In fact it was just a few days after Pearl Harbour, and much of the half-hour program was used up by the latest news bulletins from the Pacific, which annoyed me no end.

Were you very different from your brother, Richard?

Yes. He was interested in sports and life on the farm, and he would probably have taken it over from my father. He would probably have been straight, and married and had children, and not been the disappointment that I undoubtedly was to my parents.

In a recent poem, "The History of My Life", included in your 2000 collection, Your Name Here, *you seem to allude quite directly to aspects of your childhood:*

> *Once upon a time there were two brothers.*
> *Then there was only one: myself.*
>
> *I grew up fast, before learning to drive,*
> *even ...*

Childhood memories in fact figure pretty often in your work ...

I guess, in an abstract kind of way. But while writing about it I'm not aware that that's what I'm doing. Then on finishing a poem – immediately on finishing it in the case of "The History of My Life" – I realize that that's what I've done, but while I was writing it I thought I was just writing another poem. Then I start asking myself, 'How did *that* happen?'

Later in the poem you describe yourself as becoming 'weepy for what had seemed / like the pleasant early years'. You quite often sound this backward-looking or nostalgic note, with varying degrees of irony, of course – I'm thinking of the end of "Daffy Duck in Hollywood", 'Always invoking the echo, a summer's day', which, it suddenly occurs to me, itself invokes the end of Roussel's "La Vue", '[le] souvenir vivace et latent d'un été / Déjà mort, déjà loin de moi, vite emporté'.

Summers were particularly important to me, not just the way summer is for everybody, but that was when I had my social life when I was a kid. I was sort of an outcast among the other kids in Sodus. I was considered a sissy. I didn't like sports. So I didn't really have many close friends, except one very good friend who was a nerd like me.

What did your brother Richard die of?

Leukaemia.

Was it very sudden?

I think it was about six months or thereabouts – I don't know how sudden that is. He became ill in January, then was hospitalised several times in Rochester. Nobody told me much about it. It never occurred to me that he had a fatal disease – or even that children got fatal diseases. He was finally released from the hospital when, I guess, they realised they couldn't do any more for him, so he could spend his last days with my parents. I was sent away to stay with the son of yet other friends of my parents in Rochester. I stayed at their house almost a month in the end. Then I was allowed home and found my brother had just died.

Did that change things in the family a lot?

It did. There was enough age difference between my brother and me so we weren't actually that close. I loved him but also considered him a pest. The house was certainly much quieter ... Also, I realized my parents were now pinning all their hopes on me.

It was in 1943, wasn't it, that you won a current affairs competition sponsored by Time *magazine?*

Yes; the contest itself was no big thing; they had them weekly in every school. But that was when I won the prize of a book and chose the *Modern British and American Poetry* anthology, edited by Louis Untermeyer. I had a choice of four books – and although I wasn't very interested in poetry then, it was the one that seemed the most promising.

Untermeyer was a close friend of Frost's, wasn't he, and his anthology heavily influenced by Frost's ideas about poetry?

He may well have been, but Frost would have been in any anthology at that time. In fact we even read him at high school – that was about as modern as poetry in school ever got. We read Elinor Wylie also.

And Ella Wheeler Wilcox?

No, I think she had already lost whatever fame she had had.

Did you like Frost?

Yes, but I hadn't at that time read any other modern poetry, so I had nothing to judge him by.

That same year you went to Deerfield Academy, a rather posh boarding school in Western Massachusetts. How did that come about?

Through a friend of my mother's, Mrs Wells. The Wells had a summer place on the lake near our farm. They had three sons who all went to Deerfield, and Mrs Wells persuaded my parents that I should go to a better school than the one in Sodus, which wasn't great (although I did study Latin and French there) and actually paid my tuition, although I wasn't told this at the time. I was interviewed at Deerfield, accepted, and then told I'd been given a scholarship. This wasn't true. Just before I was about to graduate I happened to see a file card in the office with my name on it, on which was written 'Tuition paid by Mrs. Wells.'

Was it a scholarly place? Did it groom you for Harvard?

Deerfield was very upper class – like most boarding schools in America. The emphasis was more on athletics at that time. I mean there were good teachers but it wasn't very scholarly. They had an artist-in-residence, who was a kind of afterthought, which meant there was a studio where we went and painted, but this was slightly frowned upon by the headmaster, a kind of benevolent despot; he taught there from about 1902 to, I don't know, 1972, and turned it into a very prestigious school. It had been a local public school (as we call them) in the eighteenth century, and according to the terms of its charter, there had to be a certain number of young girls from the village enrolled as well. So there were these girls, about a dozen of them, who were really ignored by everyone else in the school. It was strange: there were about three hundred or more horny jocks, whom you'd think would be slavering at the sight of these girls, but they weren't. I guess it was some kind of class thing. They were just conditioned not to see them.

Were you pleased to go?

I wanted to get out of the house, but I wasn't quite sure about Deerfield. I was sort of at the lowest level of the food-chain when I got there. Obviously I was not of the same class, economically and socially, as most of the students, though there were some other charity cases like me. I was mostly invisible. In fact, though, I won some kind of award from them in the Eighties for distinguished something or other. That was the first, or maybe only the second time they gave it. Ironical when you consider my status when I was there.

And did you write a lot at Deerfield?

I'd already been writing, and I continued to do so. Actually I published some of my first poems in the *Deerfield Scroll*, a school newspaper.

And it was while you were at Deerfield that someone sent your poems under a pseudonym to Poetry, *who published them?*

Yes, it was during my second year there. I roomed for a semester with a boy named Haddock, who also wrote poetry of a sort I suppose you could call Surrealist. That year there was a poet in residence, also a kind of afterthought, an elderly gent from Amherst, called David Morton, who I think was a friend of Robert Frost's, and was somewhat known at the time. Both Haddock and I showed him our poems, but Haddock submitted his first, including a bunch of mine; Morton liked them and sent them on to *Poetry* magazine in Chicago, which then chose to publish two that I had written. I didn't know about this. When I showed Morton these same poems he looked at me rather oddly and said dismissively, 'Well, yes, these are very nice,' and gave them back. I only found out about all this the following December by which time both Haddock and I were at Harvard. I bought the December issue of *Poetry* and there were my poems under the pseudonym Joel Michael Symington.

Were you pleased the poems had been accepted?

No! I was horrified. First of all because I realised that not only David Morton, but the editors of *Poetry* probably thought *I* was a plagiarist, because I had sent these same poems to *Poetry*, and got them back with the briefest of rejection notes that said simply, '*Sorry.*' I thought I'd be blacklisted at what was effectively the major American poetry magazine for the rest of my life – there were really very few other places to publish poetry at that time.

So what was the first poem that came out under your own name?

I published a number of poems in *The Harvard Advocate* over the next few years, and in my last year at Harvard I had two in a magazine called *Furioso*, based at Carleton College in Minnesota.

What was it like arriving at Harvard?

It was an improvement over Deerfield, just as Deerfield had been an improvement over home. I'd always wanted to live in a metropolis and Boston was the closest I'd come so far to that. I arrived just before the end of World War Two, in July 1945, about a month before Hiroshima. In fact there was practically nobody there. Most college-age men were in the armed services, and until the following year it was pretty under-populated.

You were too young to fight?

Yes, my eighteenth birthday was that summer. I was going to be called up and I did go for a physical exam, but by the time that happened the war had ended and they weren't interested in taking on a lot of new recruits, especially types like me.

When did you meet Kenneth Koch?

In 1947, in my junior year.

And he helped you get elected to the board of The Harvard Advocate?

Yes. The magazine had been closed a long time, partly because of the war, though there were rumours of a homosexual scandal there, after which the alumnus who funded it said he would continue to do so, but there had to be a rule stipulating that no homosexuals be allowed on the board. Kenneth didn't know I was gay at that time, and whenever I suggested my election might infringe against this law, he'd say, 'No, no, don't be ridiculous!' So, anyway, despite such qualms I was eventually elected – and it turned out that half the people on the board were also gay.

What other poets were around at that time?

Well, there was Robert Bly and Donald Hall, and Kenneth, who were all on the staff of the *Advocate*, and there was Adrienne Rich, and Robert Creeley, with whom I took a course in the eighteenth-century novel, and of course Frank O'Hara, but I didn't meet him until about six weeks before I graduated.

Did you take any classes in modern poetry?

My freshman year I had a poetry workshop – which was pretty unusual for Harvard in those days, or for any college. Creeley and the future novelist John Hawks were in the class. And my senior year I took a course on Wallace Stevens with F.O. Matthiessen, who was a very inspiring teacher. He got me interested in Stevens, whom until then I hadn't really been able to 'dig'. My favourite poet for a long time had been Auden.

Did you meet Auden while you were at Harvard?

Yes. He came to give a reading. I was in the front row, and rushed up at the end with my *Collected Poems* and had it autographed. In fact, I've still got it. Then I went to a party given by George Montgomery, a photographer, who somehow knew Auden – he had gay New York connections. He gave a party in his rooms for Auden, whom I met properly then. Actually on this occasion he sort of started coming on to me; but much as

I was intrigued by the idea, because I loved his poetry so much, I couldn't quite, well, bite the bullet ...

Did you know Chester Kallman at this time?

No, I didn't get to know him until several years later when I was in New York and after I'd met Jimmy Schuyler. This first Auden reading would have been in about 1947. I think I also met him another time when he gave another reading at Harvard, and then I wrote my Honours thesis on him.

Did you feel you were making significant breakthroughs with poems like "The Painter" or "Some Trees" which were written the year after, in 1948?

Yes, I think I was quite pleased with them.

Were you consciously trying to write in a manner that was different from that of High Modernist American poets of the previous generation – T.S. Eliot, say, or Marianne Moore?

No, no – well, I eventually wanted to if I could, but really I was just fascinated by their work – though in fact not at that time that of Eliot so much. It was really only later in life that I suddenly realized how good he was. But, yes, Moore very much, and Elizabeth Bishop and also Delmore Schwartz.

There are a number of poets who were writing in the Thirties and Forties, like Schwartz, or Paul Goodman, or John Wheelwright, or David Schubert, whom you feel have been overlooked by standard accounts of twentieth-century American poetry. Why is it these writers have been so neglected?

I think the war probably played a big part in this. A poet like Randall Jarrell, whose early work I had liked, went off to war and began writing dreary war poetry. And the new poets who began publishing after the war, like Robert Lowell, were very serious and depressing, and not, to me anyway, verbally engaging. I remember giving a reading at the ICA in London, after which I was 'in conversation' with Peter Ackroyd. Somebody asked me, 'Why is it that you don't like Robert Lowell? Do you find him too serious?', to which I replied, 'Yeah, I guess so.' But, as Peter pointed out to me afterwards, what I should have replied is that I found him too hysterical ... In fact I also think something similar happened in England; before the war there were the bright young things of the Thirties like Auden, MacNeice, Spender, Prince and Nicholas Moore. After it, there was the boring New Apocalypse, with the likes of Henry Treece and George Barker, and in art, there was, say, Henry Moore, whom I've always found very dull. I suppose people had got fed up with experimentation and were too tired to want anything jarring.

Did you become interested in the work of Hart Crane?

I like his quieter moments. I don't really go for his attempts at the epic, but I like the small lyrics in *White Buildings*. Some of *The Bridge* is good, especially the part where he mimics the cacophony of Manhattan, but at other times it sounds pretty hollow.

What about William Carlos Williams?

I like him very much. In fact in my early years I went through a period of being enchanted by his work. It always seemed to me much more lyrical and romantic and more closely knit than the people who surrounded him, such as the Beats or the Objectivists, had you believe.

Were you ever drawn to the experiments of the writers associated with Black Mountain College?

Not much, though I do like Robert Creeley – I didn't so much at first but in later years I've come really to admire him – his early minimalism has exfoliated naturally in the manner of John Adams's music. And Robert Duncan I've never really been able to fathom, though he intrigues me. His work strikes me the way my own work must appear to many people.

I assume you read Whitman in school. Did his work make an impact on you then?

I didn't enjoy Whitman until I was a consenting adult. In high school we read the sort of Whitman poems it was thought high school kids should read, but they struck me as too overblown and heart-on-sleeve. Then later on, the craft of his work, which I'd never noticed before, suddenly became evident to me. I find a tremendous technical excitement in the way he handles long lines. It's something very few people can manage.

"The Instruction Manual", which was written in 1955, has often been

seen as influenced by Whitman.

Yes, well, it came at a time when I was reading him a lot.

Critics also like to link you with Emily Dickinson. Your poetries both embody states of epistemological uncertainty, exploit the indeterminacies of language, etc., etc. Do you read her a lot?

Not very much, though when I do read her, I like her, and think I should read her more. I just came across an interview with the poet Dean Young, which expresses quite well my feelings about her. 'Emily Dickinson gives me a headache, but there's definitely a greatness there and something about the language is totally engaging; but finally it doesn't sustain me.'

Who do you feel were the most important influences on the poems collected in Some Trees?

Well, Marianne Moore and Elizabeth Bishop. I think the poem "Some Trees" was very influenced by Marianne Moore, and "The Painter" by Bishop's "Miracle for Breakfast". I probably discovered the sestina when I read her first book, *North & South*. Then there was Auden and Russian poetry, in particular Pasternak and Mandelstam. I had a J. M. Cohen translation of Pasternak, published in about 1945 in London. In fact in my new book, *Chinese Whispers*, I use a line of Mandelstam's as an epigraph for one of the poems: 'Golden fleece, where are you, golden fleece?' It's from his *Tristia*, which I first read years ago. I suddenly flashed on how much I liked it.

How did meeting Frank O'Hara and Kenneth Koch affect your work? Did their ways of writing push you in new directions?

We began, when we first knew each other, by copying each other's poetry; and then I think it became more a question of example: If this person can strike out in a new and interesting way, I'd think, maybe I can do so too, in some other way.

How much of Some Trees *was written while you were at Harvard?*

I think only "The Painter" and "Some Trees". I wrote quite a lot of poetry there, but I didn't include it in the book. The first year I lived in New York I wrote "The Picture of Little J.A. in a Prospect of Flowers" and quite a few others, such as "The Mythological Poet" and "Illustration". But then there was a period when I didn't write for about a year and a half. I had a writer's block that started in about June 1950, when the Korean War began. I thought I was probably going to end up going to the Pacific and having to be in it ... Then, as I remember it, it was when Frank and I went to hear a concert of John Cage on New Year's Day, 1952, a mere fifty years ago, that I suddenly saw a potential for writing in a new way.

Did you seriously doubt your vocation in that period, 1950-51?

I think I sort of did, yes. And I thought nobody's ever going to read it anyway, even if I do write it. In fact, I felt that for quite a long time after I *did* begin writing again. Anyway, I got revved up, and in the process wrote quite a lot of poetry that I've discarded since – well, not discarded, since it all ends up somewhere, namely the Harvard library.

You were doing an MA at this time?

Yes. I went to Columbia for two years, supposedly studying for an MA in English Literature. As at Harvard, I got by without doing a lot of work, by just sort of coasting. I wrote a quite undernourished thesis on Henry Green, which to my embarrassment Jeremy Treglown, Green's biographer, recently asked to see. I think he mentions it somewhere in his book.

How did your interest in English novelists of manners such as Green, Ronald Firbank, Ivy Compton-Burnett develop?

My first year in New York I discovered this wonderful bookshop of the kind we no longer have, called The Periscope, in the then civilised East Fifties. I became friendly with the owner, who was very Anglophile and imported a lot of books from England. I was also very Anglophile then – to the extent that even the English poetry I didn't like somehow seemed superior to its American equivalent. Later this bookstore merged with another and became The Periscope-Holliday bookstore, and Jimmy Schuyler worked there for a while. I think really it was because I so much wanted to go to Europe, but never thought I'd get the chance – so instead, *faute de mieux*, I'd read someone like Alec Waugh.

At the same time you were becoming interested in kinds of art that were rather more radical – I mean the experimental painters, sculptors and composers at work in New York in the Forties and Fifties. How involved were you in these various scenes?

A bit, mainly through friends such as Jane Freilicher, Larry Rivers, and of course Frank O'Hara – though he didn't arrive until 1951, a couple of years after I did. But almost immediately he started working at the Museum of Modern Art, and he was always very interested in de Kooning, and Joseph Cornell, Mark Rothko, Jackson Pollock, and then Robert Rauschenberg and Jasper Johns, whose work rather coincided for me with my discovery of John Cage's music.

Were you as enthusiastic as Frank about painting?

No. Well, I liked it but I never got to the point of wanting to hang out with those people to the extent that he did – and certainly not with the likes of Jackson Pollock.

Did you go to the Cedar Tavern often?

I did occasionally; but I was, I think, known as the person who was always tagging along after Frank O'Hara. More often we'd go to the San Remo, and Louis's, and then there were the gay bars on 8th Street: Mary's, Main Street, and the Old Colony, which I called the Lost Colony.

Why did you start writing plays in the Fifties?

I can't remember why I *started* writing them, but I can remember why I *stopped* writing them – which was that it didn't seem likely anybody would ever perform them. I'm sort of sorry that I did stop, because I think I had a certain facility I could have developed. Actually, the first one, *The Heroes*, has been done a few times, down the ages, and I quite like it. I was at Columbia that year, my first year at graduate school, and I took a course in Greek drama with Moses Hadas – whose daughter, by the way, is the poet Rachel Hadas. I was reading also a lot of Jean Cocteau, and I'd read André Gide's *Thésée*, which came out in *Partisan Review*. When I wrote *The Heroes*, however, I completely forgot that I'd read this work of Gide's, and so copied it outrageously. And then *The Compromise* was inspired by going to a film society that Edward Gorey belonged to, which was sort of semi-clandestine, as if they didn't really want people to come, and it moved around from one space to another. They showed very strange unknown films – it was run by William K. Everson, an English film scholar who lived in New York. *The Compromise* was inspired by a 1923 Rin Tin Tin movie I saw there, *Where the North Begins*. I took the plot of this movie, though I omitted the dog at the centre of it. This dog has been left to guard a baby in a trappers' cabin while the parents are out; they come back and find the baby missing and the whole place torn apart – in fact by the furious fight the dog had with the baby's kidnappers, but the parents wrongly conclude that the dog has eaten the baby, and cast the poor mutt out into the snow! There was something about this film which intrigued me – maybe because it was made just before I was born, around the time my parents got married, and I saw something of my parents in both of the leading actors, though I've no idea now who they were.

Didn't the Living Theatre stage The Heroes *in 1952?*

Yes, but it was closed down after only about three performances; the excuse given by the Fire Department was that the building was unsafe. This was the Cherry Lane Theatre, where plays are still being performed. It was obvious that the real reason the show was closed down was because my play, the curtain raiser, had a scene in which two men dance together, and Jarry's *Ubu*, the main event, begins with the word 'Shit!', which of course recurs frequently throughout. And then the third one I wrote after two years in France, when I was back in New York taking graduate courses in French at New York University, which was 1957-58. One of the writers I discovered then was the early nineteenth-century playwright Pixérécourt, the inventor of the spooky melodrama. I again went to the film society, and saw one of those Old Dark House movies, this one made by a German director in Hollywood, Paul Leni – I think it was called *The Cat and the Canary*. I also saw a few others in the genre on television – the plot was always the same: a bunch of heirs who didn't know each other were summoned to a creepy old mansion to hear the will of a recently deceased relative read out. There was even a Griffith film in this mode called *One Exciting Night*, one of his flops.

Your play, however, ends very abruptly, before the will is revealed?

Well, I was going to write a second act but then I sort of gave up. I didn't think anyone was going to stage this. And part of me felt these plays were probably just silly, and that I should attend to my poetry instead, where I might have a little more chance of achieving something worthwhile.

And it was in the summer of 1952, wasn't it, that you began collaborating with James Schuyler on A Nest of Ninnies?

Yes. That was Jimmy's idea. He suggested it in the car coming back from the Hamptons one day in the summer of 1952; he said, 'Why don't we write a novel?' I said, 'How do we do that?' He got out a pen and a pad of paper, and said, 'It's easy: you write the first line.'

Did you always write in each other's presence?

Yes.

And in alternate sentences?

At first, and then we thought if one of us had more sentences to write he should be allowed to continue.

In the early Fifties were you aware that you were all going to become famous?

No. Quite the opposite. We thought that no one would ever hear of us. I think we all thought that our poetry would never be known, and certainly never imagined that something like *A Nest of Ninnies* would be published or taken seriously.

It was much praised by Auden, wasn't it?

Yes, he said it was 'destined to become a minor classic'. He wrote a nice review in *The New York Times Book Review*. It began: 'My! What a pleasant surprise to read a novel in which there is not a single bedroom scene!' Which reminds me – I was reading Jimmy's letters the other day and found one that had some interesting information about Auden and the Yale Younger Poets Prize he awarded to *Some Trees*. It seems he hadn't liked either my book or Frank O'Hara's very much, but finally he chose mine by default. And apparently one reason he did so was because otherwise he wouldn't get paid for editing the series that year, and he was short of cash!

Yours and Frank's manuscripts were put forward by Chester Kallman.

Yes, Chester told us – or probably told Jimmy to tell us – to send our manuscripts directly to Wystan who was then at his summer place in Ischia; this was after they'd been returned by the first reader at Yale University Press.

What did you feel about his preface when you read it?

It seemed evasive. He didn't seem to like the poetry itself, but by that time I didn't like the poetry he was writing either. So there!

By the time Some Trees *was published you were living in Paris. Why were you so keen to leave America in the Fifties?*

I wanted to go to Europe the way everybody does. I wasn't sure that I wanted to live there, but I certainly wanted to travel.

But your first trip outside America was to Mexico in 1955?

Yes, except for Canada, which doesn't really count – my father used to take us on fishing trips just the other side of Lake Ontario.

And on your return from Mexico you found out you'd been awarded a Fulbright Scholarship?

I actually heard before leaving that I'd been rejected, but that I was on the waiting list, and then somebody didn't take theirs up. That year seemed to be a year of my just barely getting things ...

So you went to Montpellier?

Yes, but in fact I didn't really want to go there. You had to put down two choices of university, and of course everybody put the Sorbonne first. I didn't know what other universities there were in France, so I asked a friend of mine who'd lived in France, and he suggested Montpellier. It's in the south, he said, it's sunny, and so on. But when I got there I really hated the place. It was beautiful in a way but very depressing for some reason. It was very far from Paris then – it probably now only takes about two and a half hours by TGV – and it was also the worst winter for over a hundred years. I recently found a book of Janet Flanner's letters from France to *The New Yorker*, and was reading her pieces from that winter: she talks of two feet of snow in the middle of Nice, and the palm-trees all frozen. Everything, I remember, just froze solid. I only had a little butane heater in the room I had in a big roomy apartment building, and there was no bathroom, just a toilet. I had to go to the public baths, which froze during the big freeze, and were closed for about three weeks, and were probably what gave me scabies. But I immediately knew I loved Paris. We were there for a month before being shunted on to our respective universities, and as often as I could I would escape there. No one minded that much if you didn't go to class.

Was it on one of these trips that you met Pierre [Martory]?

Yes, that would have been about six months after I arrived. I arrived in late September and we met in March.

And where did you meet?

In a gay bar. Le Fiacre, rue du Cherche Midi.

I heard somewhere that your first question to him was: 'Do you like Roussel?' Is that true or not?

I think we did discuss Roussel, yes – we had a very long conversation that first evening. We went to another nearby gay bar in St Germain-des-Prés, La Reine Blanche, and continued there. Actually, he had read Roussel, but I don't remember what he said about him then.

Did he induct you into the mysteries of French culture?

Yes, but he was also very American oriented. I think he had spent his entire childhood at the movies. He also knew lots of American popular songs – he'd been in the war fighting with the American army in North Africa and had learnt all these songs like "Chattanooga Choo Choo" and "Kalamazoo".

It has seemed to some people a bit strange that an avant-gardiste such as yourself chose to exchange New York for Paris just at the time when New York was supplanting Paris as the city of the avant-garde ...

But that was all in the visual arts really, and I suppose in music, which was more experimental at that time than in Europe. But new American poetry wasn't terribly exciting, it didn't seem to me – and I don't really feel that I have to live in a place where there's a lot going on culturally. I didn't get much visual or audio stimulation from the contemporary art in Paris, but who needs it when you're living there?

You'd read Proust by the time you moved to Paris – did you view the city in Proustian terms?

Yes, very much. I was fascinated by the geography of Paris, and I used to make many long walks. I would set out to explore a particular *arrondissement*, often with some sort of *but de promenade*, such as going to see a Laurel and Hardy movie at some neighbourhood theatre. I was enchanted by their American accents when dubbed into French. 'Stanny, je crois que cette femme ne nous aime pas!' I also looked up all the places where I knew Proust had lived, and where his characters had lived, such as Odette in the rue La Pérouse. When Pierre and I first lived together we rented a *chambre de bonne* in the rue Spontini, a very elegant neighbourhood in the 16th *arrondissement*, which was near a lot of Proustian locations.

Did you miss America much?

I occasionally did, yeah. I would get certain cravings for things like Coca-Cola, which I'd never much fancied before and which was very popular with the French. There was also a place on the Place de l'Opéra called Pam Pam, the only place at that time that had American milk shakes and ice-cream sodas and hamburgers, and even hush puppies, which were a food before they became a shoe. I just read Victor Brombert's autobiography, *Trains of Thought*, in which he talks about frequenting a Pam Pam on the Champs-Elysées in the late Thirties. They served fruit juice, which was rare in those days – the name Pam Pam apparently comes from *pamplemousse*. I know that fruit juice was a novelty in 1930s France because Pierre won a national contest as a schoolboy for the best essay denouncing the evils of drinking wine and alcohol. He got to read it aloud in the presence of the President of France, and received a year's supply of bottled fruit juices. He always remained very anti-alcohol, though he of course drank wine and the occasional Scotch.

Did you teach while there?

Yes, my second year on the Fulbright I taught a couple of courses at the University of Rennes – one on American Literature, and another was a course they wanted on American Education, which it was assumed I could teach since I'd been educated in America. The number of students in that one kept dwindling, until it got to the point where only these two nuns kept coming back every week; they would meet me in my office, and felt very daring about this, but insisted I leave the door partly open. But Rennes was much more fun than Montpellier. It's quite a charming city and much closer to Paris. Actually, Montpellier now is no doubt completely different; there are places that in my lifetime have been totally transformed – have become either absolutely wonderful or absolutely horrible.

I was reading the other day about how baffled Elizabeth David found herself on her first trip to Paris by the difference between French and English manners: did you find yourself baffled by French manners?

I actually found English manners much more mysterious! I remember my first trip to England in March of 1956. I spent about two weeks in London, which I found tremendously exciting, but I was constantly making all kinds of faux pas which I wasn't aware of until afterwards, such as – I'd looked up someone I had met in New York, Patrick Trevor-Roper, who gave a little party for me, and afterwards took me to dinner with a few people at the Athenaeum; before dinner we had a sherry and then went down to the dining room; I was carrying a lighted cigarette and the waiter said as we went in to the dining room, 'Would you like an ashtray, sir?' 'Oh yeah,' I said, 'that'd be fine.' And then no ashtray was ever produced. Somebody told me afterwards, 'You idiot, what he meant was you were supposed to put your cigarette out!' I think, in that instance, the French would have told me to stop smoking!

Was it on that trip that you met Frank Prince?

Yes.

Had you read Prince's work before you met him?

Yes, I had read him while I was at Deerfield. On my first trip to New York I rushed to the Gotham Book Mart and bought all kinds of things, and one of them was a little Poet of the Month pamphlet of Prince's poems published by New Directions in 1939. I immediately fell in love with his poems, and after that would look out for them in magazines. Then I discovered we had a mutual friend, Richard Roud, a film buff who moved to London in the early Fifties and became critic for the *Guardian*. Anyway, Frank and I corresponded, and he and Elizabeth came up to London from Southampton, and we had tea together at Brown's Hotel.

What was your impression of mid-Fifties England? Did it seem very drab?

Well, a little, I suppose, but one sort of expected it to be – every place was drab after World War Two. It didn't seem so much so as Paris, which I found disappointingly seedy when I first got there. Of course this was before it cleaned itself up and got thoroughly modern. I think England looked more the way I expected it to look.

You spent about a year back in New York, and then returned to Paris in 1958, ostensibly to write a doctoral thesis on Raymond Roussel.

Yes, I persuaded my parents I had to go back and carry out research to get my graduate degree in French literature, not sure how long I'd stay. Initially I went just for the summer, but then I would postpone from one month to the next coming back, until after about a year or more of this I started making a little money; I translated a couple of French detective novels, then I wrote some articles for *ArtNews*, which I'd written for during that year back in New York, and finally I got the job of art critic for the *Herald Tribune*, but that wasn't until May 1960. That didn't pay anything but it did open the way to other things that did pay. Even after five years in that job I was making only about $30 an article; but they could pay slave wages because there were so many Americans in Paris who were dying for that kind of work. So I really just lived from hand to mouth. Actually, Pierre supported me for a while, although he wasn't making much money, either. My parents would always help me somewhat but they weren't rich either.

Did writing all these art reviews on such a regular basis help your poetry, do you think?

I think it finally did: having to be chained to a typewriter and turn out an article twice a week caused me, at one point, to wonder, 'Why can't I write poetry this way to meet my own deadlines instead of somebody else's?' That, plus the fact that I cultivated a quality of paying attention to the art I was supposed to write about so that I could remember when I got home what I had seen and could write about it, which might have been helpful in a more general way as well.

The collage poems in The Tennis Court Oath *such as "America" and "Idaho" and "Europe" have always seemed to me to have a kind of lyricism lacking in the cut-ups of, say, Burroughs, which are more purely destructive. Was this your intention?*

I didn't think what I was doing was destructive at all, at least I didn't want the end result to be. I've always been anti anti-art. The fact is that it doesn't work, as Dada has proved – once you've destroyed art you've actually created it. It just has to be changed and chopped up a bit to take on a new beauty – like an Alexander McQueen frock.

When I had dinner with Pierre in Paris in 1996, I asked him about your work habits; he said you worked all the time, were always typing away at some new poem.

Well, I was probably doing my translations and newspaper chores, rather than writing poetry. I wasn't that productive as a poet then.

Among my favourite poems from this period of your career are "How Much Longer Will I Be Able to Inhabit The Divine Sepulcher ...", and "They Dream Only of America". They also seem to me interestingly different from all your earlier poems – and from those that came after too.

Yes, I wrote those in the spring of 1957. At the time I was beginning to get all anxious about going back to New York, especially as I was living so happily – despite frequent fights – with Pierre and, as you say, I was trying to develop a different kind of writing than I'd done in *Some Trees*, and I think I succeeded in poems like those and a few others in *The Tennis Court Oath*.

Perhaps "A Last World" also?

Yeah, that was written in '57 too. I wrote that on a boat trip we took along the Adriatic coast as far as Piraeus from Trieste. And then the following winter, 1957-58, I had difficulty writing when I was back in New York; I wrote one called "Rain" which I quite like and, well, in those poems, I felt I had actually more or less figured out a new way to write that pleased me. Then I went back again to live in Paris, in the summer of '58, and a very difficult period set in, when I began doing extreme collage, a lot of which I didn't publish, and a lot of which I felt I shouldn't have put into *The Tennis Court Oath*. Those collage poems are actually later than the more successful ones that are in that book.

"Europe" was your first long poem. Keats once wrote that a long poem is 'a test of Invention which I take to be the Polar Star of Poetry'. Were those your sentiments?

I suppose they must have been. What gave me the idea, I wonder? First there was "Europe", then there was "The Skaters". Both Frank and Kenneth had written long experimental poems and I probably wanted to see what I could do in that genre. Indeed that phrase of Keats's may well have been in my mind.

When did you meet Harry Mathews?

About a month or two after I met Pierre, in the spring of 1956. We became very good friends quite quickly.

Do you think your Roussel research affected your own poetry? Were your experiments with words in this period a response to his procédé?

I don't know. I've often thought about that, and thought that there must be some influence – otherwise, why was I so passionately interested in him? But I don't see much evidence of it – except in the digressions of *Nouvelles Impressions d'Afrique,* which in a much less visible way I use regularly.

How about the relationship between the banality of the illustrations by Zo in that book, and the difficulties the cantos themselves present? I often feel your work spans exactly those sorts of polarity.

Yes, I think that was what attracted me to Roussel even before I knew how to read him. These illustrations were exactly like the ones I had in a French reader when I was at high school, and the elaborate punctuation was like an exercise in a textbook.

Whose idea was the magazine Locus Solus, *which was named after Roussel's novel of 1914?*

I think it was probably mostly Harry's, because he had the means to launch it. We probably talked about how nice it would be to have a magazine that would publish our work, and also the work of people we liked but who could never get published. For Harry it was also a way of getting his novel, *The Conversions,* into print in instalments. But once his novel was actually published as a book in 1962, I don't think he was that interested in the magazine any more.

I suppose a lot of The Tennis Court Oath *poems, which also appeared in*

Locus Solus, *would have been instantly rejected by most mainstream magazines of the period.*

Probably, but I did have some success at that time with poems I sent to places like *Evergreen Review*, and a magazine called *Big Table*.

Were you surprised when Wesleyan University Press agreed to publish The Tennis Court Oath?

Yes, I was. It never would have occurred to me to submit a manuscript to them; it was John Hollander who invited me to. I'd never met him at that time but he, it turned out, had read and liked *Some Trees*. He suggested I send in the book as soon as possible, before Richard Wilbur returned from a leave of absence.

Wilbur did once say he liked the poem "Some Trees".

Yes, just that one poem. And that was my farewell to poetry 'as we know it'.

Were you surprised by reactions to the book?

There were very few reviews. I didn't expect them to be very good, but I was surprised at some of the more vicious ones.

Did you enjoy feeling in opposition to the mainstream, somehow beyond the pale or unacceptable?

Oh, no. It would have been very nice to have received a little encouragement at that time. No, in fact I was very discouraged after I published *The Tennis Court Oath* and then really did think about quitting writing poetry.

The title is borrowed, isn't it, from the painting by Jacques-Louis David of the Fathers of the French Revolution, The Oath of the Tennis Court?

Yes, well, I was on a bus in Paris one day, going past the Jardins du Luxembourg, where there are tennis courts. It was a beautiful day and I saw these young people in their tennis whites playing – a lovely sight – and then I thought, 'Gee, and then there was the tennis court oath, which was such a serious violent event.' And this gave me the idea for writing the poem, and its title. Of course it wasn't actually a tennis court as we know it, but more like a handball court, the original *jeu de paume*. Then I found some wonderful David drawings for that painting; before he did paintings of clothed people he drew them naked, and then after he'd do them with clothes – so there are drawings of naked men waving their hats in the air, one of which I tried to get Wesleyan to use on the jacket, but they wouldn't.

The long poem that followed "Europe", "The Skaters", begun in the Autumn of 1963 is, I suppose, your most Whitmanesque poem – a sort of "Song of Myself".

Yes. It has very long lines and a general looseness – that's when I began writing my poems on a typewriter. I was writing such long lines I'd forget the end before I got to it. But I can type fast and I found if I composed on the typewriter I could remember the end of the line.

Did you travel around Europe much when you were living in Paris?

Unfortunately I had very little money and it was all I could do just to stay on in Paris – besides the fact I had to produce those articles weekly or biweekly. But I did manage to do some travelling. Pierre and I took that wonderful cruise in the Adriatic, a very low-budget affair, but it was wonderful – I think we only paid about $100 for the whole trip. Then I went to England several times with Rodrigo and Anne Moynihan. And I went to Holland.

How about Spain? I'm thinking of "Leaving the Atocha Station".

Oh, that was when I went with Frank, who was sent by the Museum of Modern Art to select material for the show they subsequently put on of contemporary Spanish painting. Let's see, I also went to Majorca with Harry, and stayed with him at Lans-en-Vercors in the French Alps. I quite often went to Italy – I had an Italian gent whom I used to go and see. In fact I met him in Amsterdam in a gay club. He had a car and for the next few days we went on a marvellous tour around Holland, to various places I wouldn't have gotten to on my own, such as Sneek, a lovely little eighteenth-century Baroque village and harbour. And I used to have to go to Switzerland when I was editing *Art and Literature* because it was printed there. I went there with Lee Harwood also, and I travelled in Italy and Morocco with Jane Freilicher and Larry Rivers in '64.

Frank O'Hara said that once an American has been to Europe he or she feels different. Did you feel so different?

Yes, you no longer feel that you have to get there. It's a sort of relief to have done it. As far as Frank goes, certainly after his first trip to Europe, which was, I think, the first year I was there – he came on some Museum of Modern Art business – there was a noticeable sense of relaxation of tension about him. The same was true for me too, probably. I remember running into Ned Rorem in Paris; I hadn't seen him since I first arrived and about two months later I met him in a bar, and he said, 'How are you liking it here?' I said, 'I think after one has lived in Paris for a while one doesn't want to live anywhere – including Paris.' Which eventually came out in his diaries, where he misquotes everyone, as: 'I think after one has lived in Paris for a while one doesn't want to live anywhere else,' completely puncturing the wit of my *mot*, intentionally no doubt.

And you were pursuing your Roussel researches as well? Did you go to Biarritz in search of the villa Madame Roussel had built there, with its special baths for her Chihuahuas?

Yes, I swung by Biarritz on my way back from Spain with Frank, and I managed to locate the villa, which is now a Thalasso-Therapy Institute where you can go and stay. But back then, nobody knew where Roussel's various residences were. There was no biographical information about him except what was in "Comment j'ai écrit certains de mes livres", and Michel Leiris's essays. Even his addresses weren't known.

How about your addresses in Paris? Where did you live?

Let's see. There were quite a few. The first few days I stayed at the *cité universitaire* in the Japanese Pavilion, which was unheated as far as I could tell, and seldom had hot water. And then I lived in various hotels around St Germain-des-Prés, which were about $2 a night for extended stays. There was the Hôtel Welcome on rue de Seine, which is still there, and charges a lot more these days, and another one called the Grand Hôtel de France, a real fleapit despite its pretentious name, which now I think is called Le Sénateur and has three stars, but actually had bedbugs when I was staying there. I was living there when I met Pierre, and then he got the place on the rue Spontini, which was nicer than the average *chambre de bonne*; it was a little bigger and had a usable fireplace and a private toilet next to it and a rather lovely terrace. Pierre stayed on there after I went back to New York in 1957; then the following year, on my return, Harry said we could stay at his place out near the Porte de Vanves in the 14th, on rue Alfred-Durand-Claye – who was apparently a renowned sanitation engineer, but certainly hadn't done much of his work in that neighbourhood. It was just off the rue Vercingétorix, where the Douanier Rousseau had lived. Then Harry bought an apartment in the rue de Varenne, and we stayed there while he was often away, and then I got the place at 16 rue d'Assas through a girl at the *Herald Tribune* who knew about it. It was three tiny rooms, in the back wing of a somewhat posh bourgeois building. It was like a servant's apartment. I never saw anything quite similar; the apartments at the front of the building were very grand, and we had at the back these three small rooms with one butane heater. It actually had a bathroom, unheated of course, a toilet and a small triangular kitchen – and it cost about $75 a month. It also had a telephone – it was very hard to get a telephone for many years in France. I moved there in January 1961, I think, and we left in about March of 1965. The *demoiselle* who owned the apartment claimed she needed it for a relative – but I think she just wanted us out, having discovered how unsavoury we were. It had a lovely courtyard with trees and backed up onto a beautiful little *faux François-1er hôtel,* which faced on to the boulevard Raspail. I learned recently from Mabel Dodge's correspondence that she and John Reed lived at 16 rue d'Assas in 1914.

And your first trip back to America was around 1963? I'm thinking of the reading you gave that is described so vividly by Richard Howard in Alone with America.

Yes, that was during my first trip back in five years, because I didn't have money to travel. My parents would probably have paid my fare back to the States, but not my return to France. I also went back in '64, and then my father died at the end of '64, and I had to fly back – I'd always taken the boat before. I went back also in the summer of '65 which was when Thomas Hess offered me a job as editor of *ArtNews.*

Which you accepted. Was it a difficult decision?

Yes, it was. I'd been offered a job as art critic of the *Washington Post* while I was back in America right after my father had died. I went down to Washington, but I've never liked Washington and I decided I couldn't live there, especially doing a job which I thought I'd probably screw up. So I decided to stay in Paris, but then my mother's health started deteriorating and she couldn't live alone. I had to arrange for people to come and live with her. Over a period of about twenty years, she just sort of continually slid downhill. She drank a lot, though she'd never drunk before in her life. She probably had Alzheimer's eventually, but you can only tell that by an autopsy.

Where was she living?

She sold our farm in the spring of '65; I should have come back for that but I didn't because I had a fear of planes. A lot of my papers got thrown out then, so there are lacunae in my archive up at Harvard. Then she moved to my grandparents' house in Pultneyville, and I used to visit every summer on my vacation, and other times.

Your third collection, Rivers and Mountains, *was published by Holt, Rinehart and Winston in 1966, and was rather better received than* The Tennis Court Oath.

It got some good reviews, yeah. It was favourably reviewed in the daily *New York Times* by a critic named Conrad Knickerbocker – not long before he committed suicide, in fact – and then it was nominated for the National Book Award.

When did you learn that Harold Bloom was interested in your work?

Well, he had apparently been interested in *Some Trees* when it came out, but I wasn't aware of this. Then when I published *Three Poems* in 1972 he was sent a copy of the galleys – I forget whether it was my idea or that of somebody at the publisher's – but he wrote an enthusiastic blurb, and ever since has supported my work.

And in no uncertain terms: 'No one now writing poems in the English language is likelier than Ashbery to survive the severe judgments of time ...' Did you feel in the period following your return to America that you'd been catapulted from obscurity to fame?

No! not at all. It felt *very* gradual and haphazard.

What was it like working in an office after your many years of drifting?

Well, it was nice to have a little security. I found a small apartment on East 95th Street in the brownstone home of the painter Giorgio Cavallon, that was convenient for the subway. It was sort of a hindrance to have to go to work every day, but on the other hand Tom Hess was a very enlightened boss, though he could also be very tyrannical. And I was able to take extended lunch-hours, pretending I was going to see art exhibitions. But it did become a drag after a while because I was really only writing poetry on weekends. I was a weekend poet.

How long did you work there?

Seven years. From December '65 to August '72, when the magazine was sold and everyone got fired.

Were you relieved to be fired?

Yes and no – because I didn't have anywhere to go. But then I heard of a teaching job at Brooklyn College, which I took in spite of the qualms I had about teaching. The same year, though, I got a Guggenheim, so I didn't have to start immediately. Actually I had about two years off but they weren't very productive because I was worried about money. Though I guess it was during that time that I wrote "Self-Portrait in a Convex Mirror", from February to about April '73.

To go back to The Double Dream of Spring – *that book ends with "Fragment", a long poem written in fifty ten-line stanzas, or dizains, à la Maurice Scève. Was that poem written in Paris?*

I began writing it at my parents' home when I went home for my father's funeral in 1964, and then I finished it in Paris, after I got back.

Do you think of that poem as an elegy?

I'm not sure. It's very likely there are elegiac aspects to it, since I started writing it soon after my father died, and I realized as I was writing it that these were the last days I'd ever live in our house, where I'd grown up.

How did you feel the American poetry scene had changed during the years you were in Paris?

Well, there seemed to have been a kind of poetry explosion provoked by the Beats, who made a lot of noise and attracted a great deal of attention, and this caused a trickle-down effect to other poets. When I came back to

New York in 1963, for the first time in five years, I was astonished to be invited to give a reading. I may have given a few before; I remember I did read once in the Fifties in a Young Poets Discovery Contest at the 92nd Street Y, which did host poetry readings, but it was normally the likes of Auden or Eliot or other elder statesmen. By the time I moved back in 1965 there were readings everywhere, and the New York School of Poetry thing was an entity, I mean the name itself had stuck, and then the St Mark's Poetry Project began in 1966, and still continues with readings and publications and so on.

I suppose the counter-culture was in full swing by then.

Yes, there was also drugs, and rock; these things all seemed to happen together and I always felt that the drug culture must have zeroed in on my poetry – at least I had visions of people sitting around and getting stoned, reading it aloud, and saying, 'Man, listen to this!'

Did you like rock and roll? I know you once went to a Velvet Underground concert.

That was just an accident – it was because they were playing at the same time as Andy Warhol's movie *Chelsea Girls* which I wanted to see. No, I've never had anything to do with rock and roll.

Well, what about that song by Peaches and Cream, which 'inspired' "The Songs We Know Best", in A Wave? *'Reunited, dum-de-dum-de-dum ...*

... and it feels so good' – and I'm afraid, dear, it was Peaches and Herb! They were more disco, I think.

Back in the Sixties, did you feel under pressure to be political, particularly as the Vietnam War escalated?

Yes, but the New York School managed largely to escape this phase. During the Vietnam War we all had to participate in anti-war poetry readings which I didn't very much enjoy, because I didn't think it could possibly have any effect on the War, and it seemed slightly hypocritical for me to declaim my arcane verses as if they were going to help end it. The peace marches I went on seemed to me much more – well, not *much* more, but *somewhat* more effective as a means of protest.

Did you have a greater sense of an audience when you came back?

Yes. I remember running into an editor named Arthur Cohen, I think at a show of Joe Brainard's, and he said 'Isn't it time you published another book of poetry?' At the time this greatly cheered me, since I'd got to feel that no one would ever want to publish another book of mine.

Did this affect your poetry? Did you feel you'd found a readership, and knew how to give them what they wanted?

That, never! It may have affected it. But also the fact I was once again living in the land of my own language probably made things easier, although I did succeed, after about a year of floundering around when I was living in France, in overcoming my need to hear American – American especially, but English would do in a pinch.

The Double Dream of Spring *includes references to Popeye and Happy Hooligan, and generally seems more attuned than your first three books to American popular culture.*

Yes, and maybe that was also the influence of Pop Art that was new then.

Which Pop artists did you like?

Lichtenstein and Jasper Johns very much. But Warhol never really interested me, though I seem to remember I wrote a couple of appropriately 'fascinated' articles on him.

The Double Dream of Spring *also includes a poem entitled "For John Clare", and its first poem, "The Task", borrows its title from William Cowper. It seems to me your fondness for British Romantic poetry is at its most apparent in this book.*

Yes, well, I've always read English poetry much more than American poetry, and I feel that English poetry is more important to my work than American, though the English themselves don't seem to think so.

Which English poets have meant most to you?

Shakespeare, Wyatt, Vaughan, Marvell, Donne. All the good ones. Pope not so much – the eighteenth century was a bit of a bore, though I always liked Collins and Cowper, and Johnson's "The Vanity of Human Wishes". I borrowed a line from it for a poem in *The Tennis Court Oath*: 'Where then shall hope and fear their objects find?'

The Double Dream of Spring contains a number of your most discussed and popular poems; "Soonest Mended", for instance – your 'one-size-fits-all' confessional poem – has attracted an enormous amount of critical attention, and features in most anthologies of twentieth-century American poetry. In comparison with The Tennis Court Oath, *this book is almost disconcertingly approachable.*

Well, in *The Tennis Court Oath* I was deliberately experimenting. I didn't necessarily think that these experiments would see the light of day, but I wanted to try doing different things – anything that would change my poetry – just to see what the result would be. My purpose was always to try eventually to fit it all back together so that it would be similar to the poetry I had started out writing, but also 'strangely different'. That was my agenda at the time, but of course one really can't control what or how one writes. I always felt that the first poem in which I began to fit things together again was the title poem of my third book, "Rivers and Mountains", which I wrote in '61; that I think was the beginning of my Sixties poetry.

On the subject of Rivers and Mountains – *I've always been fond of its opening poem, "These Lacustrine Cities", and was puzzled not to find it included in your 1985* Selected Poems.

You wouldn't believe how many people have scolded me for leaving that one out. I just forgot to include it. Of course up until my *Selected* appeared nobody had ever said a word about it.

Well, there's quite an interesting essay on it by David Rigsbee, in the first collection of critical essays on your work, Beyond Amazement, *which came out in 1981 – but I know you don't read academic criticism of your poetry.*

Oh. Didn't Veronica Forrest-Thomson also write something about it?

Well, she writes a bit about you in Poetic Artifice, *but mainly, as I remember, on a couple of poems from* The Tennis Court Oath. *Are you an admirer, by the way, of the work of Cambridge School Poets – with whom Forrest-Thomson was associated?*

Er, who are they?

Jeremy Prynne, Andrew Crozier, Denise Riley and co. Your work had quite a significant impact on theirs in the Sixties and early Seventies.

I've sometimes wondered how they found out about it; it was certainly a well-kept secret in America, around the time it was being discovered in England. As far as Prynne goes, I always feel that I like his work, but that there must be something I'm not getting. But I know many people feel exactly that way about me.

The back jacket of my copy of The Double Dream of Spring *features a quote from* Poetry *(Chicago): 'The chances are very good that John Ashbery will come to dominate the last third of the century as Yeats dominated the first.' Who made that farsighted prediction?*

It was written by someone named Howard Wamsley, whom I had known briefly, years before. He published a couple of poems in magazines, and that one review. That line has been quoted far and wide, but the source is always given as *Poetry* Chicago, since the review came out there, rather than attributed to a little-known writer.

In your 1967 lecture, "The Invisible Avant-Garde" ...

I'm so sorry I ever wrote that! People seem to take it so seriously. It was something I scribbled on the train going from New York to New Haven because I had to make some remarks to an art class taught by Jack Tworkov at Yale. Then Tom Hess used it to plug a hole in *ArtNews Annual*, and ever since it will not die.

Well, you talk in this hastily scribbled but undying lecture of the problems posed by what you call 'acceptance culture'. I just wanted to ask if you ever feared that your own creativity might be 'menaced' by acceptance?

No, not really, because I had learnt to get along without acceptance for so long that there was no possibility of my head being turned at that stage. I was about forty when I gave that lecture, and I'd long been used to the idea that if I was to go on writing poetry I'd have to write it basically for myself.

The Double Dream of Spring was followed by Three Poems, *published in 1972, which consists of three very long prose poems. In an early essay on Gertrude Stein you compare her* Stanzas in Meditation *to Henry James's* The Golden Bowl: *both create, you write, 'a texture of bewildering luxuriance – that of a tropical rainforest of ideas – [which] seems to obey some rhythmic impulse at the heart of all happening.' Was that the kind of 'texture' you were attempting to create in* Three Poems?

Yes, and another influence, although one that I didn't become aware of until after I'd finished writing them, as is so often the case, was Auden's parody of late James, "Caliban to the Audience", which concludes *The Sea and the Mirror*. David Herd has found a resemblance to Pascal's *Pensées*, which I read quite a long time before I wrote *Three Poems*, but that's the funny thing with influence – don't you agree? – it may well be something one read years ago that suddenly surfaces while one's writing, just as various memories will emerge in the course of composition and take over. Anyway, I remember I decided to write a long prose poem, because I realized that I hadn't done this before, and I was trying to think of something I hadn't done before. I started writing the first one, and then decided it would be a nice idea to have three of them. I thought of them as three oblong empty boxes to be filled with anything. I remember discussing it with my analyst, Carlos (a Chilean); I said, 'I'm writing these three long prose poems, but I can't think of anything to put in them,' and he said, 'Why don't you think about all the people who've meant most to you in your life, and then don't write about them, but write about what you think when you think about them?' I thought this a good idea, though I'm not sure I ever actually did it.

Was it in response to Three Poems *that someone called you the 'Doris Day of modern poetry'?*

You would drag that up! No, I think it was in a review of *The Double Dream of Spring*, by somebody I'd never heard of before – or since. His point was that I'd been around for an awfully long time and was still a virgin like Doris Day, because I'd never soiled my hands with political issues. Which puts me in mind of that remark by, I think, Oscar Levant – that he'd been around Hollywood so long he knew Doris Day before she was a virgin!

You began the long poem that's also the title poem of your next book, Self-Portrait in a Convex Mirror, *soon after you'd lost your job at* ArtNews. *Was Parmigianino a painter you'd long been interested in?*

Yes. When I was about twenty a monograph on him was published by Sydney Freedberg, and *The New York Times Book Review* reproduced the painting *Self-Portrait in a Convex Mirror* in a review I read of that book. Even then I had a feeling I would one day 'do' something with it.

You actually saw the painting in the Kunsthistorisches Museum in Vienna with Pierre in 1959, as you tell us in the poem. Have you any idea why it suddenly resurfaced when it did, about fifteen years later?

Yes. I'd seen the painting, as you say, in Vienna. Then in February 1973 I was in Provincetown, and was taking a walk, and I saw in a bookshop window a book on Parmigianino; it was one of those cheap books of reproductions of Italian masters, and *Self-Portrait* was on the cover. I bought it for $3 or $4 to take back to my room where I was staying for a month, supposedly to write, at the Provincetown Fine Arts Work Center. And I kept looking at the picture and started to write the poem but it didn't go very well. Then I wrote more when I went back to New York. It took an awfully long time to write. I kept changing it and tinkering with it. I think I worked on it for about four months at least. I could never get the lines right. I corrected it much more than I normally do, though they were all minor corrections. I'm still not sure I like the genre it seems to occupy – that of a poem about a work of art. I can't think of any examples of this genre I really like. Maybe Auden's "Musée des Beaux Arts".

Were you surprised at the response to the collection when it came out in 1975? It won the Pulitzer Prize for poetry, the National Book Award, and the National Book Critics Circle Award.

Yes. I was. I didn't really think it was going anywhere; it started out quite badly with a nasty review in *The New York Review of Books* by Irvin Ehrenpreis; David Kalstone mentioned this review to one of the paper's editors, Elizabeth Hardwick. He said, 'Well, it's too bad John got knocked off his pedestal before he was even on it!' She said, 'What do you mean? He's always winning prizes.' David said, 'No, he's not. He's never won anything.' And Elizabeth, who liked me, said, 'Well, we'll have to see about that.' And she was one of the founders that very year of the National Book Critics Circle Award. Through her efforts, I think, I was the first to get it. Meanwhile Richard Howard told me, even before the National Book Critics Circle Award was announced, which was at the end of January, I think, that I was going to get the Pulitzer Prize. 'They're going to announce it in June,' he told me, 'but you mustn't tell anybody.' So I didn't. Then all kinds of people I barely knew would come up and tell me: 'I hear you're getting the Pulitzer.' So I was truly surprised, as pictures of the event show, to get the National Book Award, because I'd already won the National Book Critics Circle Award and everyone seemed to know I was going to win the Pulitzer. I later asked Richard how come so many people seemed to know about the Pulitzer, since I hadn't told anyone, and he said: 'Well, dear, *I* told everyone so the rumour would get around, because, wonderful as it is that you're winning things, I really think these prizes should be spread around more equitably!'

Did you feel this kind of acclaim put pressure on you to, well, live up to your billing?

No, because as I said, it took so long in coming that, by the time it came, I was so resigned to being an unknown writer that I was inured to outside pressure.

I was wondering about a line in "Daffy Duck in Hollywood", which was collected in your next book, Houseboat Days: *'I scarce dare approach me mug's attenuated / Reflection in yon hubcap, so jaundiced, so déconfit are its lineaments'. Are you alluding here to "Self-Portrait" and the impact of its success on your sense of yourself?*

As a sort of *déconfit de canard*? Not consciously. There are lots of other kinds of reference, though, in that poem which have never been explicated, like the one to Aglavaine and Sélysette.

Maeterlinck?

Oh, well, maybe they have!

You've said that Daffy Duck's predicament somewhat resembles that of Satan in Paradise Lost.

Well, yes, in particular in relation to a Daffy Duck cartoon called *Duck Amuck*, in which you see the artist's pen being dipped in the inkwell and then drawing Daffy, and then sort of tormenting him by adding an extra beak or drawing a monster about to destroy him. All the time the artist is invisible. The same thing, it seems to me, happens to Satan and his fellow fallen angels in the first book of *Paradise Lost*, where God is almost comically absent, at least as far as the denizens of Hell are concerned.

Books such as The Vermont Notebook *and* Houseboat Days *seem to me to reflect a more deliberate attempt on your part to hear and record, as you put it in "Pyrography", 'America calling: / The mirroring of state to state, / Of voice to voice on the wires'.* The Vermont Notebook *creates a strong sense of the random clutter of the American landscape – 'Industrial parks, vacant lots, yards, enclosures, fields, arenas, slopes, siding, tarmac, blacktop, service roads, parking lots, drive-in deposits, libraries, roller rinks', etc., etc. Was this at all conscious?*

Maybe. By that time I had travelled a lot more in America. I didn't start taking planes regularly until '71, when I flew to London with David after Ann Lauterbach invited me to read at the ICA. And after that I was invited to give readings in places I wouldn't have gone to before because I didn't want to fly. So I got quite used to travelling. Whether that's reflected in the poetry or not, I don't know. Obviously I know quite a lot about parts of America where I haven't actually been, just as everybody does.

"Pyrography" is a poem that spans the geography and myths of America – what you call the 'whole incredible / Mass of everything happening simultaneously and pairing off, / Channelling itself into history'. It mentions boxcars, cities at the turn of the century, place names such as Warren, Ohio, and Bolinas, and 'the flat, sandpapered look the sky gets / Out in the middle west toward the end of summer'. This poem was actually written as a commission, wasn't it?

Yes. The Department of the Interior had assembled an exhibition of paintings of American landscapes, called "America 1976", which travelled around the country as part of the Bicentennial celebrations. Mark Strand was asked to write a poem for the catalogue, but then backed out. I was offered the commission; initially I thought, 'I can't do this,' and turned it down. Then I learned how much they were paying, and I decided I *could* do it. Incidentally a British reviewer once took me to task for mentioning Warren, Ohio, saying something like, how is an English reader supposed to know what Warren is like? But I've never been there either, and I think I have a pretty clear notion of what it's like.

You've talked of how a couple of poems in the book, such as "What Is Poetry" and "And Ut Pictura Poesis Is Her Name", came out of the process of beginning to teach poetry to students for the first time in your life. Literary theory was beginning to make its presence felt in the American academy around the time you began teaching in the mid-Seventies. Were you tempted to read it?

No.

Did you read philosophy ever?

I read philosophy that is close to poetry: Plato, Epictetus, Montaigne, Pascal, Kierkegaard, Nietzsche, William James. Wittgenstein a little. Not Spinoza, Hume or Kant. I took a basic philosophy course my first year at Harvard and did miserably on it. There was one philosopher, probably Hume, who based everything on the necessity of having a clear and distinct idea of something, in which case all systems are go. I could never figure out how you are supposed to know when you have a clear and distinct idea of something, and I still can't.

A number of theorists began to get interested in your work around this time. Do you think this was because your work mirrored their epistemological concerns?

I have no idea really. The whole question bores me – except it seems to create a lot of interest in my work, so I'm quite happy about it.

How did you get the idea of writing a long poem in two columns, i.e. "Litany"?

One thing that suggested it was going to the premiere of a work by Elliott Carter, a duo for violin and piano. It was performed at Cooper Union, on a very wide stage. The piano was at one end and the violin was at the other. And they were more or less doing different things, as is very often the case in Carter's work. Sometimes the instruments would be talking to – or at – each other, and sometimes just to themselves. It seemed to me a remarkably conversational, or non-conversational, kind of music. I thought it would be interesting to have to pay attention to two separate poems at the same time; it would be like eavesdropping on two different conversations at a cocktail party – something that happens to us all fairly often and therefore should have a poem written about it. We can't follow either one without neglecting the other one, at least briefly. Ann Lauterbach and I once made a taped recording of it under studio conditions for some experimental recording studio; it seemed that whenever there was a stanza break and one of us would be reading solo, whatever was being said at that particular moment had an overwhelming meaningfulness that disappeared as soon as the other person started again.

Why is it called "Litany"?

Let's see. I was going to church a lot at the time. Before I got the house in Hudson, which was in the late Seventies, I often used to go to a Sunday afternoon service at a chapel near here. I was thinking about the great litany, and then also about Messiaen's "Trois Petites Litanies de la Présence Divine", which I think is one of his most beautiful works. I'm not that acquainted with his music and haven't liked some of it that much, but that particular piece struck me very forcefully at around that time – it has the same forcefulness of utterance that I felt I wanted. And of course "Litany" is one of those words that mean many different things – it can be a list of complaints, a droning on and on, but it has a sacred sense too.

On the theme of complaining – the right hand column ends with a letter from a Disgusted of Terre Haute, Indiana, who receives an offer from a tape club offering him two tapes for the price of one: 'I accept- / Ed the deal, paid for one tape and / Chose a free one. But since I've been / Repeatedly billed for my free tape. / I've written them several times but / Can't straighten it out – would you / Try?' Where does this come from?

That was a found object, I think from one of the local newspapers that I used to collect on my travels while giving poetry readings, especially when I took buses to small places in the mid-West. I remember the school menu from "Grand Galop" that features sloppy joe on bun came from one of those, too.

When did you buy the house in Hudson?

I bought it in the autumn of '78, though I didn't actually go up there again until the spring of '79. David and I would go up there on weekends – we both had jobs in the city – and fix it up very slowly, because we didn't have enough money to do it all at once, or even a whole room at once. By the late Seventies I'd gotten myself into a terrible job bind; an editor at *New York Magazine* asked me if I would like to do art reviews for them. I found teaching stressful – although it was more having to go way out to Brooklyn that I didn't like – so I agreed, thinking if I could get to be a successful art journalist I could give up teaching. In fact, though, I ended up doing both jobs for two years, and really thought I'd go out of my mind at times. Then, in 1980, I was offered a job as art critic for *Newsweek,* which was much better paid, but in some ways worse, because *Newsweek* is a much bigger magazine; I'd have to produce an article on some subject I perhaps knew little about because there was an important exhibition opening. I'd take a crash course in whatever it was and then try to come up with something that sounded plausible on Chinese Bronzes or whatever. Then in 1985 I was awarded a MacArthur Fellowship. Actually, I heard about this while I was in London. I'd just given a reading at the Poetry Society, and came home quite sloshed to Danny Moynihan's, where I was staying. He said he'd had a call from my assistant at *Newsweek,* and I thought, 'Oh no, that means I'll have to completely rewrite my last article and have it in by 4 am,' which was the sort of thing that was not uncommon in my tenure at *Newsweek.* So I called my assistant, and found instead I'd got a MacArthur, which meant I could give everything up for five years, which then flew by in a trice. So from '85-'90 I didn't have to have a job, and that was when I wrote – what's the name of that poem that's so long?

Flow Chart.

Flow Chart. Unfortunately I also took on the Norton Lectures, because it seemed like Harvard were offering an awful lot of money. But it turned out that it was hardly any money because I had to pay the rent on an apartment there, which I thought they would pay for, and the toing and froing, and taxis ... And I was terrified by the whole business. I was worried I would be expected to talk about theory and Baudrillard and so on.

Well, I thought they were rather well received when finally published a couple of years ago, and got some people at least reading the likes of David Schubert and John Wheelwright and Thomas Lovell Beddoes – your 'other tradition'. To go back to the 1980s – it was in 1982, wasn't it, that you had an almost fatal illness?

Yes, it came on pretty suddenly. I had an excruciating pain in my neck, which started in my class at Brooklyn College (where one of the students was a major pain in the neck, but let it pass). It kept getting worse and worse over a period of several days. My doctor just kept giving me pain killers, which didn't work. My legs started to get paralysed and I was taken by ambulance to New York Hospital, where nobody could figure out what I had. My doctor offered David his condolences on my impending death, and left. They left me on a gurney in a deserted area far from the emergency room. David stayed with me, and when I was paralysed up to the neck and having difficulty breathing, he raised hell at the hospital and called everybody we knew, until finally the doctor of friends of ours came in and ordered an immediate operation. It lasted ten or eleven hours, at which point the surgeon told David and other friends who were waiting that I'd survived but would remain a vegetable, i.e. quadriplegic. I had an epidural abscess with a staph infection of the spinal fluid, which is supposedly sealed off. You're not supposed to be able to get infections there. So as soon as I was conscious the first thing the doctor asked was, 'How did you get it?' I had such a terror of going to the hospital – if I had gone earlier, when it first started, I might not have had to have such a severe operation, which has had a number of residual side effects. It's affected my walking and hip.

Did it affect the poems that went into A Wave, *which is a pretty death-haunted book?*

Well, "A Wave" begins, 'To pass through pain and not know it', which surely must have been a result of that experience, but I can't remember consciously thinking that when I wrote the poem, as is so often the case, like the poem about my brother, "The History of My Life". With hindsight it seems so straightforward, but I don't remember making the connection at the time. Obviously some other part of my mind – the part that makes these connections – is doing this work for me.

Was that your first brush with death?

I think so. It's the only serious illness I've ever had. But it didn't seem to make much of an impression on me. People would say, 'Did you have an out-of-body experience?' Well, not that I remember. I guess I have a way of ignoring the important things in life, such as death. I can't remember it affecting my poetry. After it was over I thought, 'Well, now that's out of the way, I can get on with things.'

In your Architectural Digest *piece on your house up in Hudson, you describe it as reminding you of your grandparents' house in Rochester. It's a very beautiful house, but also somewhat gloomy. Do you find gloom inspiring?*

A certain kind of gloom, yes – 'a gloom that one knows', I think is how I put it. The house has a sort of reassuring feel to it when I'm there, which does remind me of my grandparents' house, which also seemed to me gloomy and peaceful, I suppose because when I was there I wasn't always feeling nervous and wondering what mood my father was in. It doesn't look that much like my grandparents' house, which was on a more modest scale, but it was built in exactly the same period, the 1890s, and when I first looked at it, it immediately seemed somehow familiar. I guess it represented for me the happiest part of my childhood, when I felt secure and taken care of, and was living in a city and had other children to play with.

Memories of childhood surface in one way or another in many of your long poems, but Flow Chart *seems to me particularly saturated in a kind of nostalgia for some lost or vanished past; what were the origins of this, your longest poem?*

Well, Trevor Winkfield, the English painter (from Leeds) long resident in Manhattan, who did the book's cover, came to visit at Hudson some time in '87, and asked what I'd been writing. I said I'd been writing some very short poems, and he said, 'Why don't you write a hundred-page poem about your mother?', who had died earlier that year. I retained the idea of writing a hundred-page poem, as something to try to do, but I didn't really think about making it about my mother, since I don't write poems about subjects – but she does occasionally make a cameo appearance. I'm not sure the typescript is 100 pages long; I decided I would stop writing on a certain day, my sixtieth birthday, but think I in fact stopped shortly before, at the beginning of July. And then I put it aside, since I knew it would require a tremendous amount of revising which would take a lot of time that I would rather devote to writing more poetry. Also I wasn't pleased with the way it ended. I think I've found this true on a number of occasions when you've been writing for so long and at such a high energy level, it's very difficult to put on the brakes when you get to the end. So I think I ended it around the required date or stage, but I knew I would have to do more work on it. It wasn't actually until my year of giving the Norton Lectures, which was 1989-90 – that is almost two years later – that I went back to it. It was curing for quite a long time. So I went back to Harvard, to give the lectures, and this awoke many long slumbering memories. I was in one of the Harvard houses – actually a building that hadn't been built when I was there, but which had a view of Memorial Drive and of the Charles River similar to that I'd had from my room in Dunster House – and I'd watch the evening traffic, which was very loud ...

'By evening the traffic has begun / again in earnest, color-coded ...' Do you think of this poem as an apologia pro vita tua – *along the lines of Wordsworth's* The Prelude?

I would never have the temerity to compare it to *The Prelude*.

Since Flow Chart *your poems seem to have got funnier, and sometimes your readings are like some stand-up comic's performance.*

Yes, I've noticed that, but I can't account for it. Maybe it's that over the last fifteen years I've been more influenced by James Tate than I used to be. He, on the other hand, seems to be going in the opposite direction. His most recent book consists of prose poems, and although they're still very funny, they're not as disjointed and indirect as his earlier poems were. A lot of them tell a small story very quietly.

You've written quite a few prose poems yourself recently as well.

Me and everybody else. They are tremendously popular these days. There are magazines devoted to prose poems and anthologies of them.

Most Language Poetry seems to be written in prose – have you followed their experiments with interest?

Yes, but from a distance – like the English lady in Firbank's *Prancing Nigger*: 'I always follow the fashions, my dear, at a distance.' Probably like Surrealism it will become more fascinating as it disintegrates – or like Minimalism in music: it's like there's a certain hard kernel that can stand the pressure only for so long, and then it starts to decay, giving off beneficial fumes.

I know Elizabeth Bishop is one of your favourite poets, and in fact you were instrumental in getting her awarded the Books Abroad / Neustadt International Prize for Literature in 1976. There's a phrase from her late poem, "Crusoe in England", that seems to express what your very different ways of writing have in common: 'Home-made, home-made! But aren't we all?' There's an improvisational aspect to both your poetries. I often feel that you're putting together a poem with bits and pieces that happen to be lying around, building, to borrow a title from one of my favourite poems in Hotel Lautréamont, *'a driftwood altar'.*

Was it Lévi-Strauss who said the world could be divided into 'ingénieurs et bricoleurs'? It's in *Tristes Tropiques,* I think. According to this definition, I'm certainly one of the *bricoleurs,* someone who patches things together any old way rather than starting out with a concept and developing it. But on the subject of Elizabeth Bishop, I was in fact responsible for the epigraph used in her last book, *Geography III.* I was visiting my mother sometime in the mid-Seventies; there was never much to do there except go out and visit antique shops, in one of which I found a little textbook. I don't know if the title of it was *Geography III,* but in any case it had belonged to a student at a school in Sodus, New York in 1880-something. It had questions and answers about geography. Apparently Elizabeth had been upset because *Geography III* was so short, so I sent her the geography book, and she included extracts from a couple of the lessons in the front of her book.

Your latest long poem, Girls on the Run, *is based on the eccentric, often quite disturbing pictures of Henry Darger. He's another artist whose works are very much 'home-made'.*

The pure products of America go crazy!

What appealed to you about his peculiar saga of the Vivian Girls?

I don't know exactly. I first saw his work in a museum in Lausanne, when I went to the university there to give a reading. I suppose it rang some distant chime because the little girls looked like the little girls I had crushes on when I was six or seven years old. The illustrations he used are all from that era. And it reminded me of the illustrated children's books I had when I was very young. I don't really like to think about the more gruesome aspects of his work.

I guess that should be left to the Chapman brothers.

Absolutely. Also, I was always fascinated by girls' and women's dresses; I liked them to have lots of pattern and ornament. When I was growing up, it was the era of Shirley Temple, and little girls tried to dress like her;

66

they always had a row of smocking going across the top of the dress, which I found very attractive. I remember not liking women wearing solid-coloured dresses. My grandfather took me to his university once and introduced me to a secretary, who was wearing a rather ordinary frock. I complained to her, 'You're wearing a plain dress,' meaning all one colour. 'Well, yes, I suppose I am, laddie,' she said, 'now, run along.'

Wakefulness, which came out in 1998, includes a cento, "The Dong with the Luminous Nose". Most of the lines come from nineteenth-century British poets – Hopkins, Tennyson, Coleridge, Edward Lear, Wordsworth, Arnold, Kipling, Keats, Housman, Blake, etc.

I keep forgetting where they all come from. I guess that poem's a sort of tribute to the period when I used to read nineteenth-century poetry with a sense of awe that great poets could write great poems.

I seem to remember you once told an interviewer that you think of yourself as 'John' and of the voice of your poems as 'Ashbery'. Could you explain the difference?

I don't remember ever telling an interviewer that, though I don't doubt that I said it, since it's exactly the sort of stupid thing one says in interviews, this one being no exception.

How does a poem begin, and end, for you these days? I mean, is there anything in particular that prompts you to start – or urges you to stop?

How does a poem begin, and end, for me these days? Well, very much as it always has. A few words will filter in over the transom, as they say in publishing, and I'll grab them and start trying to put them together. This causes something to happen to some other words that I hadn't been thinking of which may well take over the poem to the point of excluding the original ones. What prompts me to start is a vague feeling that I ought to write a poem, and what 'urges' (rather too strong a word) me to stop is a sudden feeling that it would be pointless to continue. I've often described this as a kind of timer that goes off to tell me the poem is done and I must remove it from the oven. If I try to go on and write some more, it turns out to be a fiasco – 'flatter than a bride's soufflé', as I insensitively put it many years ago in my play, *The Compromise*.

Your recent books in particular are extremely diverse in terms of the

forms they use: the pantoum of "Hotel Lautréamont", the rhyming quat-
rains of "Tuesday Evening", the Robert Walser-style prose poems. Is there
a form you'd like to try your hand at, but haven't so far?

Well, you know I tried recently to write several villanelles, but I don't
think any of them worked out. There was one I was maybe going to use
in a collection, but then I finally axed it. I was rereading William Emp-
son's poetry, which I like a lot, and of course he wrote several very successful villanelles. 'They bled an old dog dry ...'

Is that any kind of hint? A last question: your new book is called Chinese
Whispers, *which suggests to me Roussel's* procédé, *and his penchant for*
parlour games, such as the one played in "Parmi les noirs". It also re-
minds me of some lines in "Self-Portrait in a Convex Mirror" where you
allude to the game in which

> *A whispered phrase passed around the room*
> *Ends up as something completely different.*
> *It is the principle that makes works of art so unlike*
> *What the artist intended.*

When you look back on your poetic career, does it seem very different
from what you 'intended'?

Well, I'm not sure I ever 'intended' anything I could define. As far as the
new book goes, I did think of using the definition of Chinese Whispers in
the *Oxford Dictionary of Word Games* for its jacket copy. But then I
thought that if somebody picks it up and sees the phrase 'word games'
next to my name, they'll think, 'Oh it's just Ashbery trying to pull the
wool over our eyes again.'

Well, that depends on who picks it up: they might think, 'Magister ludi!'

After So Strident a Riposte

Silly, it's a tea-ball,
and those opaque squares are ridges.
If you touch the moth the pollen will rub off
on your hand, and it will fly no more.
Your hands, on the other hand,
will perform amazing tasks,
serving needs as yet undreamed of.

That is what I wanted to talk of today
'cause we don't have too much time.
Soon you're hungry again, the more fleet
projects take on a sinister allusiveness.
Beware of that, but also of churning
your hunger into inappropriate mist
from which one falls temporarily always, as from a cloud.

So, as always, doff the weird getup.
Do you recall a puncture wound?
Are you nuts?
I don't know anything about it.
Came stamping down the region made pliable with unknowing.
Badger sympathy from those who hurriedly pass you by.
The remains of some czar float down the river
to an underground rendezvous with the unsalvageable
and these moth-wings know just what to do.

Keep it bright for the time being,
which is all anybody can really ask of anything.
The mambo-like shudders bearing kisses
in your direction should be adjourned to a more exclusive occasion.
That's it. Evening sparkles bright, like spite
given in to; the glass river is a toccata
to the salving of many early unwormed-out ambitions.

Just because he couldn't stay around too much longer
is no reason to execrate him. In a complete universe
the love-handles would be competing with love,
and rosy strife (or stripes) be all our itinerary.

Just because somebody decided to do something and it lasts forever
is no reason to throw out the old menagerie.
Some cats and lepers are waiting to be found,
looking for a friend. It never darkens sans champagne.

Mother. She follows you around
and makes you change your *slip* and shoes when they are dirty.
You may have to admit her half-right.
The dust coils in cool closets.

Half the public found it amateurishly dull.
And oh I think so, go for the rest of it.
But they were like sex humans, low on accomplishment,
tall on the phantom poet's intricate thermometer.

We think we read "diseased chickens found,"
and are happy for once in the embarrassed pause that follows.
If this is the mummy's tomb it's not too unpleasant,
only exciting. He must have had many followers

to end up here, alone and upside down.

John Ashbery

With his mother, Rochester, New York, 1927

With his father, Rochester, New York, 1927

By Lake Ontario, Pultneyville, New York, ca. 1930

With his brother Richard, and grandfather Henry Lawrence,
Pultneyville, New York, ca. 1931

Pultneyville, New York, ca. 1933

With Richard, Sodus, New York, ca. 1934

With Richard and Mary Wellington, Pultneyville, New York, ca. 1934

With his parents and Richard, Pultneyville, New York, ca. 1934

Upper step, left to right: JA's maternal aunt, Janet Taft, his mother, his maternal grandmother, Adelaide Lawrence (holding Janet's son, Lawrence Taft); lower step,
left to right: JA, Richard, his grandfather, Henry Lawrence;
Pultneyville, New York, 1937

The house at Sodus, New York ("Ashbery Farm"), ca. 1940

Sodus, New York, ca. 1944

Harvard University (under the boathouse), 1949

Washington Square, New York, ca. 1950

With Jane Freilicher, Acapulco, 1955

With Kenneth Koch, New York, 1956

New York, 1957
© Harry Redl

With Pierre Martory, Paris, ca. 1958

With James Schuyler, Southampton, Long Island,
New York, ca. 1964

25 rue Charles V, Paris, 1965
© Shunk Kender

25 rue Charles V, Paris, 1965
© Shunk Kender

25 rue Charles V, Paris, 1965
© Shunk Kender

At Bob Dash's house, Sagaponack, New York, ca. 1971
© Gustavo Hoffman

With David Kermani at the Gotham Book Mart party for *Three Poems*,
New York, 1972

Richard Thomas, Alma Thomas, JA, David Kermani, Daniel Levans,
Disneyland, California, 1978

Pierre Martory, JA and Harry Mathews,
Saint-Maurice, near Paris, 1993

Being presented with the medal of the Chevalier des Arts et Lettres
by Jack Lang, the French Minister for Culture,
at a small gathering at Harry Mathews's apartment in Paris, 1993

With David Kermani and Mary de Rachewiltz,
Schloss Brunnenberg, Merano, Italy, 1999

Les trois Rousellâtres
JA, Mark Ford and François Caradec (Roussel's first biographer), Paris, 1999

Bibliography

Compiled by Danny Gillane and Philip Hoy
with the assistance of Ryan Roberts

Restrictions on space and time have made it impossible for us to include everything that a truly comprehensive Ashbery bibliography would incorporate. Thus the reader will find no reference to works by Ashbery not written in English, or to translations of his work, or to poems published but not collected in books of which he is the author, or to letters to the press, or to book endorsements, or to art works ... However, as well as these deliberate omissions, there are bound to be many other omissions which are due to oversight. There are also bound to be errors of various kinds – inaccurate citations, misplaced items, unnecessary duplications, etc. The editors would be very pleased to hear from anyone who can help us to identify such omissions and errors, which it would be their hope to repair in future editions.

Primary Works

Poetry

Books

Some Trees. With a foreword by W.H. Auden. New Haven, Connecticut: Yale University Press, 1956; London: Geoffrey Cumberlege, Oxford University Press, 1956; New York: Corinth Books, 1970; New York: Ecco Press, 1978.

The Poems. With prints by Joan Mitchell. New York: Tiber Press, 1960.

The Tennis Court Oath. Middletown, Connecticut: Wesleyan University Press, 1962; New York: Columbia University Press, 1980; Lebanon, New Hampshire: University Press of New England, 1997.

Rivers and Mountains. New York: Holt, Rinehart and Winston, 1966; New York: Ecco Press, 1977, 1989.

Selected Poems. London: Jonathan Cape, 1967.

Fragment. Los Angeles: Black Sparrow Press, 1969.

The Double Dream of Spring. New York: E.P. Dutton & Co., 1970; New York: Ecco Press, 1976; New York: Norton, 1977.

Penguin Modern Poets, 19: John Ashbery, Lee Harwood, Tom Raworth. Middlesex: Penguin Books, 1971.

Three Poems. New York: Viking Press, 1972; Middlesex and New York: Penguin Books, 1977; New York: Ecco Press, 1989.

The Vermont Notebook. Los Angeles: Black Sparrow Press, 1975; New York: Granary Books / Calais, Vermont: Z Press, 2001.

Self-Portrait in a Convex Mirror. New York: Viking Press, 1975; New York: Penguin, 1976; Middlesex, Penguin, 1977; Manchester: Carcanet New Press, 1977; San Francisco: Arion Press, 1984 [special edition including original prints by Richard Avedon, Jim Dine, Jane, Alex Katz, R.B. Kitaj, Elaine and Willem de Kooning, and Larry Rivers; together with a foreword by the poet, a recording of his reading of the poem and, on the album, an essay by Helen Vendler].

Houseboat Days. New York: Penguin, 1976; New York: Viking Press, 1977; Manchester: Carcanet, 1977; Middlesex: Penguin, 1979; New York: Farrar, Straus and Giroux, 1999.

As We Know. New York: Viking Press, 1979; Manchester: Carcanet, 1981; New York: Farrar, Straus and Giroux, 1999.

Shadow Train. New York, Viking Press, 1981; New York: Penguin, 1981; Manchester: Carcanet, 1982.

A Wave. New York, Viking Press, 1984; New York: Penguin, 1984; Manchester: Carcanet, 1984; New York: Farrar, Straus and Giroux, 1998.

Selected Poems. New York: Viking, 1985; New York: Penguin, 1986; Manchester: Carcanet, 1986; London: Paladin, 1987 [expanded edition]; Helsinki: Eurographica, 1991.

April Galleons. New York: Elisabeth Sifton Books, Viking, 1987; New York: Penguin, 1988; Manchester: Carcanet, 1988; London: Paladin, 1990; New York: Farrar, Straus and Giroux, 1999.

Flow Chart. New York: Knopf, 1991; Manchester: Carcanet, 1991; New York: Random House, 1992; New York: Farrar, Straus and Giroux, 1998.

Hotel Lautréamont [This volume contains the title poem only]. New York: Nadja, 1991.

Hotel Lautréamont. New York: Alfred A. Knopf, 1992; Manchester: Carcanet, 1992; New York: Random House, 1994; New York: Farrar, Straus and Giroux, 2000.

Three Books: Poems [*Houseboat Days, Shadow Train, A Wave*]. New York: Penguin Books, 1993.

And the Stars Were Shining. New York: Farrar, Straus and Giroux, 1994; Manchester: Carcanet, 1994.

Can You Hear, Bird. New York: Farrar, Straus, and Giroux, 1995.

The Mooring of Starting Out: the First Five Books of Poetry [*Some Trees, The Tennis Court Oath, Rivers and Mountains, The Double Dream of Spring, Three Poems*]. Hopewell, New Jersey: Ecco Press, 1997; Manchester: Carcanet, 1997.

Wakefulness: Poems. New York: Farrar, Straus and Giroux, 1998; Manchester: Carcanet, 1998.

Girls on the Run: a Poem. New York: Farrar, Straus and Giroux, 1999; Manchester: Carcanet, 1999.

Your Name Here. New York: Farrar, Straus, and Giroux, 2000; Manchester: Carcanet, 2000.

As Umbrellas Follow Rain. Lenox, Massachusetts: Qua Books, 2001.

Chinese Whispers. New York: Farrar, Straus and Giroux, 2002; Manchester: Carcanet, 2002.

CHAPBOOKS, PAMPHLETS, BROADSIDES, EPHEMERA

Turandot and Other Poems. With four drawings by Jane Freilicher. New York: Editions of the Tibor de Nagy Gallery, 1953.

Sunrise in Suburbia. New York: The Phoenix Bookshop, 1968.

Three Madrigals. New York: The Poets Press, 1968.

Evening in the Country. Broadside. San Francisco: Spanish Main Press, 1970.

The New Spirit. New York: Adventures in Poetry, 1970.

A White Paper. Broadside, 1971.

I Open My Eyes to the Strange Unhappiness of Autumn. Broadside. Kent, Ohio: Kent State University Libraries, 1971.

From The New Spirit. Brockport, New York: State University College at Brockport, 1972.

Fear of Death. Broadside. With "Happy End" by Charles Simic. Washington, D.C.: Library of Congress, Poetry Office, 1975.

The Serious Doll. Broadside. Syracuse, New York: The Kermani Press, 1975.

L'Heure Exquise: Collage. Postcard. Artists' Postcards, 1977.

Two Scenes. Broadside. Washington, D.C., 1979.

Spring Day. Broadside. Winston-Salem, North Carolina: Palaemon Press Limited, 1984.

In the Keyhole. Broadside. North Bennington, Vermont: Inkspot Press, 1986.

Not a First. With drawings by Jonathan Lasker. New York: Printed in the Tower of Poestenkill, 1987.

Offshore Breeze. Card. 1987.

Poems. New York: Dia Art Foundation, 1987.

The Ice Storm. New York: Hanuman Books, 1987.

Coventry. Broadside. New York: Nadja, 1993.

Jane Hammond: the John Ashbery Collaboration. New York: Jose Freire Fine Art, 1994.

Poem and Portrait. With Larry Rivers. Charleston, West Virginia: Humanities Division, the University of Charleston, 1997.

The Chateau Hardware. Bookmark. New York: Academy of American Poets, 1997.

The Kaiser's Children. With images by Eric Stotik. Portland, Oregon: C. Seluzicki, 1997.

Description of a Masque. With watercolour woodblock prints by Jane Freilicher. New York: The Limited Editions Club, 1998.

Novel. With drawings by Trevor Winkfield. New York: Grenfell Press, 1998.

Who Knows What Constitutes a Life. Illustration by Elizabeth Murray. Calais, Vermont: Z Press, 1999.

100 Multiple-Choice Questions. New York: Adventures in Poetry, 2000.

Mephisto Waltz No. 3. Broadside. William Corbett, 2000.

If I Don't Hear from You Again I Shall Wonder. Broadside. New York: Poetry Project, Granary Books, 2002.

INDEX OF POEMS APPEARING IN ASHBERY'S ENGLISH-LANGUAGE COLLECTIONS

"Alborada". HL.
"Album Leaf". ST; MSO.
"Alive at Every Passage". W.
"All and Some". SPCM.
"All Kinds of Caresses". HBD; TB.
"All That Now". CW.
"Allotted Spree". CYHB.
"Alone in the Lumber Business". AG.
"Alone, I". AUFR; CW.
"America". TCO; MSO.
"American Bar". HL.
"Amid Mounting Evidence". AG.
"Amnesia Goes to the Ball". YNH.
"An Additional Poem". TCO; SP2; SP3; MSO.
"An Outing". DDS; MSO.
"And Again, March Is Almost Here". YNH.
"And Forgetting". HL.
"And I'd Love You to Be in It". AWK; SP2; SP3.
"And Others, Vaguer Presences". HBD; SP2; SP3; TB.
"And Socializing". HL.
"And Some Were Playing Cards, and Some Were Playing Dice". AG.
"And the Stars Were Shining". ASWS.
"And *Ut Pictura Poesis* Is Her Name". HBD; SP2; SP3; TB.
"And You Know". ST; SP1; SP2; SP3; MSO.
"Angels You". CYHB.
"Animals of All Countries". P.
"Animals of All Countries, II". P.
"Animals of All Countries, III". P.
"Another Aardvark". YNH.
"Another Chain Letter". ShT; SP2; SP3; TB.
"Another Example". HL.
"Another Kind of Afternoon". W.
"Answering a Question in the Mountains". ST; MSO.
"Anxiety and Hardwood Floors". CYHB.
"Any Other Time". W.
"April Galleons". AG.
"Around the Rough and Rugged Rocks the Ragged Rascal Rudely Ran". AW; TB.
"As Oft It Chanceth". HL.
"As One Put Drunk into the Packet-Boat". SPCM; SP2; SP3.
"As Umbrellas Follow Rain". AUFR; CW.
"As We Know". AWK; SP2; SP3.
"As You Came from the Holy Land". SPCM; SP2; SP3.
"Assertiveness Training". ASWS.
"At First I Thought I Wouldn't Say Anything About It". CYHB.
"At Liberty and Cranberry". CYHB.
"At Lotus Lodge". ShT; TB.
"At North Farm". AW; SP2; SP3; TB.
"At the Inn". ShT; SP2; SP3; TB.
"At the Station". W.
"Atonal Music". CYHB.
"Autumn Basement". YNH.
"Autumn in the Long Avenue". W.
"Autumn on the Thruway". HL.
"Autumn Telegram". HL.
"Avant de Quitter Ces Lieux". HL.
"Avenue Mozart". YNH.
"Awful Effects of Two Comets". CYHB.
"Baked Alaska". HL.
"Baltimore". W.
"Becalmed on Strange Waters". AG.
"Beverly of Graustark". YNH.
"Bilking the Statues". AG.

"Bird's-Eye View of the Tool and Die Co". HBD; SP2; SP3; TB.
"Birds of Paradise and Hummingbirds". P.
"Bloodfits". YNH.
"Blue Sonata". HBD; SP2; SP3; TB.
"Bogus Inspections". W.
"Brand Loyalty". YNH.
"Breezy Stories". ShT; TB.
"Bromeliads". ASWS.
"Brute Image". HL.
"Business Personals". HBD; SP2; SP3; TB.
"But Not That One". ShT; TB.
"But These Are Merely Quibbles". AUFR.
"But What Is the Reader to Make of This?". AW; TB.
"By an Earthquake". CYHB.
"By Forced Marches". HL.
"By Guess and By Gosh". CYHB.
"By the Flooded Canal". AG.
"Caesura". ShT; TB.
"Can You Hear, Bird". CYHB.
"Cantilever". CYHB.
"Canzone". ST; MSO.
"Caravaggio and His Followers". YNH.
"Catalpas". ShT; TB.
"Central Air". HL.
"Chaos". ST; MSO.
"Chapter II, Book 35". CYHB.
"Chinese Whispers". AUFR; CW.
"Chronic Symbiosis". CYHB.
"Cinéma Vérité". YNH.
"City Afternoon". SPCM.
"Civilization and Its Discontents". RM; SP1; MSO.
"Clepsydra". RM; SP2; SP3; MSO.
"Clouds". DDS; MSO.
"Collected Places". CYHB.
"Collective Dawns". HBD; TB.
"Come On, Dear". W.
"Coming Down From New York". CYHB.
"Commercial Break". ASWS.
"Conventional Wisdom". YNH.
"Cop and Sweater". HL.
"Corky's Car Keys". ShT; TB.
"Cousin Sarah's Knitting". W.
"Coventry". ASWS.
"Crazy Weather". HBD; SP2; SP3; TB.
"Crossroads in the Past". YNH.
"Crowd Conditions". YNH.
"Cups with Broken Handles". AW; TB.
"Daffy Duck in Hollywood". HBD; SP2; SP3; TB.
"Dangerous Moonlight". CYHB.
"Darlene's Hospital". AW; SP2; SB3; TB.
"De Imagine Mundi". SPCM.
"De Senectute". YNH.
"Dear Sir or Madam". W.
"Debit Night". CYHB.
"Decoy". DDS; SP2; SP3; MSO.
"Deeply Incised". W.
"Definition of Blue". DDS; MSO.
"Description of a Masque". AW; TB.
"Destiny Waltz". AW; TB.
"Dinosaur Country". ASWS.
"Disagreeable Glimpses". AUFR; CW.
"Disclaimer". CW.

"Discordant Data". W:.
"Disguised Zenith". AG.
"Distant Relatives". AWK.
"Ditto, Kiddo". AW; TB.
"Do Husbands Matter?". CYHB.
"Don't Ask". AUFR.
"Down By the Station, Early in the Morning". AW; TB.
"Drame Bourgeois". HBD; TB.
"Dream Sequence (Untitled)". YNH.
"Dreams of Adulthood". AG.
"Drunken Americans". ShT; TB.
"Dull Mauve". CYHB.
"Echolalia Rag". AUFR; CW.
"Eclogue". ST; MSO.
"Edition Peters, Leipzig". AW; TB.
"Elephant Visitors". HL.
"Enjoys Watching Foreign Films". YNH.
"Erebus". HL.
"Errors". ST; SP2; SP3; MSO.
"Eternity Sings the Blues". CYHB.
"Europe". TCO; MSO.
"Evening in the Country". DDS; MSO.
"Evening Quatrains". P.
"Every Evening When the Sun Goes Down". ShT; TB.
"Everyman's Library". ShT; TB.
"Fade In". YNH.
"Fall Pageant". AG.
"Fallen Tree". AWK.
"Falls to the Floor, Comes to the Door". ASWS.
"Fantasia on 'The Nut-Brown Maid'". HBD; excerpt published in SP2; excerpt published in SP3; TB.
"Farm Film". ShT; TB.
"Farm II". SPCM.
"Farm III". SPCM.
"Farm Implements and Rutabagas in a Landscape". DDS; SP2; SP3; MSO.
"Farm". SPCM.
"Fascicle". CYHB.
"Faust". TCO; SP2; SP3; MSO.
"Fear of Death". SPCM.
"Figures in a Landscape". AWK.
"Film Noir". HL.
"Finnish Rhapsody". AG.
"Five O'clock Shadow". CYHB.
"Five Pedantic Pieces". AWK.
"Floatingly". W.
"Flow Blue". ShT; TB.
"Flow Chart". *Flow Chart*.
"Flowering Death". AWK; SP2; SP3.
"Flowers on Your Way". P.
"Footfalls". ASWS.
"For John Clare". DDS; SP2; SP3; MSO.
"Foreboding". SPCM.
"Forgotten Sex". AG.
"Forgotten Song". AG.
"Forties Flick". SPCM; SP2; SP3.
"Fortune". P.
"Fourth Prize". AG.
"Fragment". DDS; MSO.
"Fragment". *Fragment*.
"Free Nail Polish". ASWS.
"French Opera". HL.
"French Poems". DDS; MSO.
"Friends". HBD; SP2; SP3; TB.

94

"Frogs and Gospels". YNH.
"From Estuaies, from Casinos". HL.
"From Old Notebooks". W.
"From Palookaville". HL.
"From Such Commotion". W.
"From the Diary of a Mole". AUFR; CW.
"From the Observatory". CYHB.
"Frontispiece". ShT; SP2; SP3; TB.
"Frost". AG.
"Fuckin' Sarcophagi". CYHB.
"Full Tilt". YNH.
"Gentle Reader". W.
"Get Me Rewrite". YNH.
"Getting Back In". CYHB.
"Ghost Riders of the Moon". ASWS.
"Girls on the Run". Girls on the Run.
"Gladys Palmer". CYHB.
"Glazunoviana". ST; SP2; SP3; MSO.
"Going Away Any Time Soon". W.
"Gorboduc". AG.
"Grand Abacus". ST; MSO.
"Grand Galop". SPCM; SP2; SP3.
"Gummed Reinforcements". ASWS.
"Haibun". AW; TB.
"Haibun 2". AW; TB.
"Haibun 3". AW; TB.
"Haibun 4". AW; TB.
"Haibun 5". AW; TB.
"Haibun 6". AW; TB.
"Hang-Up Call". YNH.
"Harbor Activities". HL.
"Hard Times". ShT; TB.
"Has to Be Somewhere". YNH.
"Haunted Landscape". AWK; SP2; SP3.
"Haunted Stanzas". HL.
"Haven't Heard Anything". CW.
"He". ST; SP2; SP3; MSO.
"Heartache". YNH.
"Heavenly Days". CW.
"Hegel". CYHB.
"Heidi". P.
"Heidi, II". P.
"Her Cardhoard Lover". CW.
"Here Everything Is Still Floating". ShT; SP2; SP3; TB.
"Here We Go Looby". YNH.
"Hints and Fragments". CW.
"Histoire Universelle". AWK.
"Hittite Lullaby". AWK.
"Homecoming". W.
"Homesickness". AWK.
"Honored Guest". YNH.
"Hop o' My Thumb". SPCM; SP2; SP3.
"Hotel Dauphin". MSO.
"Hotel Lautréamont". HL.
"Houseboat Days". HBD; SP2; SP3; TB.
"How Dangerous". YNH.
"How Much Longer Will I Be Able to Inhabit the Divine Sepulcher . . .". TCO; MSO; SP2; SP3; TB.
"How to Continue". HL.
"Humble Pie". YNH.
"I Asked Mr. Dithers Whether It Was Time Yet He Said No to Wait". CW.
"I Found Their Advice". HL.
"I Had Thought Things Were Going Along Well". AWK.

"I Might Have Seen It". AWK.
"I Saw No Need". CYHB.
"I See, Said the Blind Man, As He Put Down His Hammer and Saw". AW; TB.
"I, Too". CYHB.
"Ice Cream in America". ASWS.
"Idaho". TCO; MSO.
"If the Birds Knew". RM; MSO; SP2; SP3.
"If You Ask Me". CW.
"If You Said You Would Come with Me". YNH.
"Illustration". ST; SPO; MSO.
"Implicit Fog". YNH.
"In a Boat". AWK.
"In an Inchoate Place". CYHB.
"In Another Time". HL.
"In My Head". W.
"In My Way / On My Way". HL.
"In Old Oklahoma". CYHB.
"In the Meantime, Darling". ASWS.
"In the Time of Pussy Willows". AUFR; CW.
"In Vain, Therefore". HL.
"In Whatever Mode". CW.
"Indelible, Inedible". ShT; TB.
"Industrial Collage". YNH.
"Insane Decisions". AG.
"Into the Dusk-Charged Air". RM; SP2; SP3; MSO.
"Intricate Fasting". AUFR; CW.
"Introduction". AW; TB.
"Invasive Procedures". YNH.
"Irresolutions on a Theme of La Rochefoucauld". HL.
"It Must Be Sophisticated". HL.
"It Was Raining in the Capital". DDS; SP2; SP3; MSO.
"Joe Leviathan". ShT; TB.
"Joy". HL.
"Just For Starters". ASWS.
"Just Someone You Say Hi To". AW; TB.
"Just Walking Around". AW; SP2; SP3; TB.
"Just Wednesday". HL.
"Just What's There". ASWS.
"Kamarinskaya". HL.
"Knocking Around". AWK.
"Korean Soap Opera". HL.
"Landscape (After Baudelaire)". AW; SP2; SP3; TB.
"Landscape". TCO; SP1; MSO.
"Landscapeople". AWK.
"Last Legs". YNH.
"Last Month". RM; SP2; SP3; MSO.
"Last Night I Dreamed I Was in Bucharest". W.
"Late Echo". AWK; SP2; SP3.
"Laughing Gravy". W.
"Le Livre est sur la table". ST; SP2; SP3; MSO.
"Le Mensonge de Nine Petrovna". HL.
"Leaving the Atocha Station". TCO; MSO.
"Leeward". ASWS.
"Lemurs and Pharisees". YNH.
"Letters I Did or Did Not Get". AG.
"Life As a Book That Has Been Put Down". AG.
"Life Is a Dream". YNH.
"Light Turnouts". HL.
"Like a Sentence". ASWS; CYHB.
"Like Air, Almost". CW.
"Like America". W.
"Limited Liability". CYHB.

"Litany". AWK; an extract published in SP2; an extract published in SP3.
"Lithuanian Dance Band". SPCM.
"Little Sick Poem". CW.
"Livelong Days". HL.
"Local Legend". AUFR; CW.
"Local Time". ASWS.
"Lost and Found and Lost Again". HBD; TB.
"Lost Profile". YNH.
"Love in Boots". CYHB.
"Love's Old Sweet Song". HL.
"Love's Stratagem". CYHB.
"Loving Mad Tom". HBD; TB.
"Man in Lurex". ASWS.
"Many Are Dissatisfied". CYHB.
"Many Colors". W.
"Many Wagons Ago". AWK; SP2; SP3.
"Märchenbilder". SPCM; SP2; SP3.
"Measles". TCO; MSO.
"Meditations of a Parrot". ST; MSO.
"Meet Me Tonight in Dreamland". AUFR; CW.
"Melodic Trains". HBD; TB.
"Memories of Imperialism". YNH.
"Merrily, We Live". YNH.
"Metamorphosis". AWK.
"Military Pastoral". CYHB.
"Mixed Feelings". SPCM; SP2; SP3.
"Moderately". W.
"Moi, je suis la tulipe. . .". ShT; TB.
"Moon, Moon". AUFR; CW.
"Mordred". CW.
"More Hocketing". YNH.
"More Pleasant Adventures". AW; SP2; SP3; TB.
"Morning Jitters". AG.
"Mountain Flowers". P.
"Musica Reservata". HL.
"Mutt and Jeff". ASWS.
"My Erotic Double". AWK; SP2; SP3.
"My Gold Chain". ASWS.
"My Name Is Dimitri". CYHB.
"My Philosophy of Life". CYHB.
"Myrtle". ASWS.
"Never Seek to Tell Thy Love". AW; TB.
"Never to Get It Really Right". AG.
"New Constructions". W.
"Nice Morning Blues". CYHB.
"Night Life". ShT; TB.
"Night". TCO; MSO.
"No Earthly Reason". CYHB.
"No Good at Names". HL.
"No I Don't". AG.
"No Longer Very Clear". CYHB.
"No Two Alike". AG.
"No Way of Knowing". SPCM.
"No, but I Seen One You Know You Don't Own". AWK.
"Nobody Is Going Anywhere". YNH.
"Not a First". AG.
"Not Now but in Forty-five Minutes". HL.
"Not only / but also". AWK.
"Not Planning a Trip Back". ASWS.
"Not You Again". YNH.
"Notes from the Air". HL.
"Obedience School". CYHB.

"Obsidian House". CW.
"October at the Window". AG.
"Ode to Bill". SPCM.
"Ode to John Keats". CYHB.
"Oeuvres Complétes". HL.
"Of a Particular Stranger". CYHB.
"Of Dreams and Dreaming". HL.
"Of Linnets and Dull Time". HL.
"Of the Islands". ShT; TB.
"Of the Light". YNH.
"Offshore Breeze". AG.
"Oh Evenings". CW.
"Oh, Nothing". ShT; TB.
"Oleum Misericordiae". SPCM; SP2; SP3.
"On Autumn Lake". SPCM.
"On First Listening to Schreker's *Der Schatzgräber*". ASWS.
"On His Reluctance to Take Down the Christmas Ornaments". CW.
"On the Empress's Mind". HL.
"On the Terrace of Ingots". ShT; TB.
"On the Towpath". HBD; SP2; SP3; TB.
"One Coat of Paint". AG.
"One Man's Poem". W.
"One of the Most Extraordinary Things in Life". AW; TB.
"Onion Skin". YNH.
"Operators Are Standing By". CYHB.
"Or in My Throat". ShT; SP2; SP3; TB.
"Orchids". P.
"Ornery Fish". AUFR; CW.
"Ostensibly". AG.
"Others Shied Away". CYHB.
"Otherwise". AWK; SP2; SP3.
"Our Leader Is Dreaming". YNH.
"Our Youth". P; TCO; SP1; SP2; SP3; MSO.
"Out over the Bay the Rattle of Firecrackers". AWK.
"Outside My Window the Japanese ...". W.
"Over at the Mjtts'". YNH.
"Pale Siblings". YNH.
"Palindrome of Evening". W.
"Palindrome". CYHB.
"Pantoum". ST; MSO.
"Paperwork". YNH.
"Paradoxes and Oxymorons". ShT; SP2; SP3; TB.
"Paraph". ASWS.
"Parergon". DDS; MSO; SP2; SP3.
"Part of the Superstition". HL.
"Pastilles for the Voyage". YNH.
"Pathless Wanderings". ASWS.
"Penny Parker's Mistake". ShT; TB.
"Penthesilea". CYHB.
"Plain As Day". CYHB.
"Plainness in Diversity". DDS; DDS; MSO; SP2; SP3.
"Pleasure Boats". ASWS.
"Poem at the New Year". HL.
"Poem in Three Parts". SPCM.
"Poem on Several Occasions". YNH.
"Poem". ST; MSO.
"Point Lookout". CYHB.
"Polite Distortions". AG.
"Poor Knights of Windsor". CYHB.
"Popular Songs". ST; SP1; SP2; SP3; MSO.
"Portrait with a Goat". CW.
"Postilion of Autumn". CW.

"Posture of Unease". AG.
"Pot Luck". YNH.
"Pretty Questions". ASWS.
"Prisoner's Base". CW.
"Private Syntax". HL.
"Probably Based on a Dream". W.
"Problems". AW; TB.
"Proust's Questionnaire". AW; TB.
"Proximity". W.
"Punishing the Myth". ShT; SP2; SP3; TB.
"Purists Will Object". AW; SP2; SP3; TB.
"Pyrography". HBD; SP2; SP3; TB.
"Qualm". ShT; SP2; SP3; TB.
"Quarry". W.
"Quartet". HL.
"Quick Question". CYHB.
"Railroad Bridge". AG.
"Railroaded". YNH.
"Rain". TCO; MSO.
"Rain in the Soup". YNH.
"Rain Moving In". AW; TB.
"Random Jottings of an Old Man". AUFR; CW.
"Real Time". CW.
"Redeemed Area". YNH.
"Reminiscences of Norma". CW.
"Retablo". HL.
"Reverie and Caprice". CYHB.
"Revisionist Horn Concerto". HL.
"Riddle Me". AG.
"River". SPCM.
"Rivers and Mountains". RM; SP1; SP2; SP3; MSO.
"Robin Hood's Barn". SPCM.
"Robinson Crusoe". P.
"Runway". AUFR; CW.
"Rural Objects". DDS; MSO.
"Sacred and Profane Dances". YNH.
"Safe Conduct". CYHB.
"Salon de The". CYHB.
"Sand Pail". SPCM.
"Savage Menace". AG.
"Saying It to Keep It from Happening". HBD; SP2; SP3; TB.
"Scheherazade". SPCM; SP2; SB3.
"School of Velocity". ShT; TB.
"Seasonal". HL.
"See How You Like My Shoes". CYHB.
"Self-Portrait in a Convex Mirror". SPCM; SP2; SP3.
"Shadow Train". ShT; TB.
"Shadows in the Street". W.
"Short-Term Memory". YNH.
"Sicilian Bird". ASWS.
"Sighs and Inhibitions". AG.
"Sight to Behold". CW.
"Signs". AUFR.
"Silhouette". AWK; SP2; SP3.
"Sir Gammer Vans". CW.
"Sleepers Awake". CYHB.
"Sleeping in the Corners of Our Lives". AWK.
"Slumberer". YNH.
"Small City". YNH.
"Snow". W.
"So Many Lives". AW; TB.
"Some Money". AG.

"Some Old Tires". ShT; SP2; SP3; TB.
"Some Trees". ST; SP2; SP3; MSO.
"Some Words". DDS; SP2; SP3; MSO.
"Someone You Have Seen Before". AG.
"Something Similar". ShT; SP2; SP3; TB.
"Something Too Chinese". CYHB.
"Sometimes in Places". ASWS.
"Sonatine Mélancolique". YNH.
"Song of the Windshield Wipers". AG.
"Song". DDS; SP2; SP3; MSO.
"Song: 'Mostly Places ... '". AG.
"Songs Without Words". ShT; TB.
"Sonnet". ST; SP1; SP2; SP3; MSO.
"Soonest Mended". DDS; SP2; SP3; MSO.
"Sortes Vergilianae". DDS; SP2; SP3; MSO.
"Spotlight on America". ASWS.
"Spring Cries". ASWS.
"Spring Day". DDS; SP2; SP3; MSO.
"Spring Light". HBD; TB.
"Staffage". AW; TB.
"Stanzas Before Time". YNH.
"Statuary". AWK.
"Still Life with Stranger". HL.
"Strange Cinema". YNH.
"Strange Occupations". YNH.
"Strange Things Happen At Night". ASWS.
"Street Musicians". HBD; SP2; SP3; TB.
"Stung by Something". W.
"Suite". SPCM.
"Summer". DDS; SP2; SP3; MSO.
"Sunrise in Suburbia". DDS; MSO.
"Susan". HL.
"Swaying, the Apt Traveler Exited My House". CYHB.
"Syllabus". CW.
"Syringa". HBD; SP2; SP3; TB.
"Tangled Star". W.
"Tapestry". AWK; SP2; SP3.
"Tarpaulin". SPCM.
"Taxi in the Glen". CYHB.
"Tenebrae". W.
"Tenth Symphony". SPCM.
"Terminal". YNH.
"Thank You for Not Cooperating". AW; SP2; SP3; TB.
"That You Tell". HL.
"The Absence of a Noble Presence". ShT; SP2; SP3; TB.
"The American". AUFR; CW.
"The Archipelago". ASWS.
"The Art of Speeding". HL.
"The Ascetic Sensualists". TCO; MSO.
"The Beer Drinkers". HL.
"The Big Cloud". AG.
"The Big Idea". CW.
"The Blessed Way Out". CW.
"The Blot People". CYHB.
"The Bobinski Brothers". YNH.
"The Bungalows". DDS; SP2; SP3; MSO.
"The Burden of the Park". W.
"The Business of Falling Asleep". CW.
"The Business of Falling Asleep (2)". CW.
"The Captive Sense". CYHB.
"The Cathedral Is". AWK.
"The Chateau Hardware". DDS; SP2; SP3; MSO.

"The Circus". P.
"The Confronters". CYHB.
"The Conquest of the Sky". P.
"The Corrupt Text". AUFR.
"The Couple in the Next Room". HBD; SP2; SP3; TB.
"The Decals in the Hallway". AUFR; CW.
"The Decline of the West". ASWS.
"The Departed Lustre". HL.
"The Desolate Beauty Parlor on Beach Avenue". CYHB.
"The Desperado". ShT; TB.
"The Desperate Hours". ASWS.
"The Don's Bequest". YNH.
"The Dong with the Luminous Nose". W.
"The Double Dream of Spring". DDS; MSO.
"The Earth-Tone Madonna". W.
"The Ecclesiast". RM; SP2; SP3; MSO.
"The Evening of Greuze". AUFR; CW.
"The Explanation". HBD; TB.
"The Faint of Heart". CYHB.
"The Favor of a Reply". ASWS.
"The File on Thelma Jordan". YNH.
"The Fortune Cookie Crumbles". YNH.
"The Freedom of the House". ShT; TB.
"The Friend at Midnight". W.
"The Friendly City". ASWS.
"The Garden of False Civility". HL.
"The Gazing Grain". HBD; SP2; SP3; TB.
"The Gods of Fairness". YNH.
"The Grapevine". ST; SP2; SP3; MSO.
"The Great Bridge Game of Life". HL.
"The Green Mummies". CYHB.
"The Haves". CW.
"The Hero". ST; MSO.
"The Hills and Shadows of a New Adventure". AWK.
"The History of My Life". YNH.
"The Hod Carrier". DDS; MSO.
"The Ice Storm". AG.
"The Ice-Cream Wars". HBD; SP2; SP3; TB.
"The Image of the Shark Confronts the Image of the Little Match Girl". ShT; TB.
"The Improvement". ASWS.
"The Impure". YNH.
"The Instruction Manual". ST; SP2; SP3; MSO.
"The Ivory Tower". ShT; SP2; SP3; TB.
"The King". HL.
"The Lament upon the Waters". HBD; SP2; SP3; TB.
"The Large Studio". HL.
"The Last Romantic". W.
"The Latvian". CYHB.
"The Laughter of Dead Men". W.
"The Leasing of September". ShT; SP2; SP3; TB.
"The Leopard and the Lemur". AG.
"The Lightning Conductor". CW.
"The Little Black Dress". HL.
"The Lonedale Operator". AW; SP2; SP3; TB.
"The Lounge". ASWS.
"The Love Scenes". ASWS.
"The Lozenges". TCO; MSO.
"The Mandrill on The Turnpike". ASWS.
"The Military Base". CYHB.
"The Mouse". AG.
"The Mythological Poet". ST; MSO.
"The New Realism". TCO; extract published in SP2; extract published in SP3; MSO.

"The New Spirit". TP; MSO.
"The Night Cry". P.
"The Old Complex". HL.
"The Old House in the Country". YNH.
"The One Thing That Can Save America". SPCM.
"The Ongoing Story". AW; SP2; SP3; TB.
"The Orioles". ST; MSO.
"The Other Cindy". AWK; SP2; SP3.
"The Other Tradition". HBD; SP2; SP3; TB.
"The Painter". ST; SP2; SP3; MSO.
"The Passive Preacher". TCO; MSO.
"The Path to the White Moon". AW; TB.
"The Pathetic Fallacy". W.
"The Peace Plan". CYHB.
"The Pearl Fishers". YNH.
"The Penitent". CYHB.
"The Phantom Agents". HL.
"The Picnic Grounds". AWK.
"The Picture of Little J.A. in a Prospect of Flowers". ST; SP2; SP3; MSO.
"The Pied Piper". ST; SP2; SP3; MSO.
"The Plural of 'Jack-in-the-Box'". AWK; SP2; SP3.
"The Preludes". AWK.
"The Poems" [(1) "Animals of All Countries", (2) "Heidi", (3) "The Conquest of the Sky", (4) "The Circus", (5) "Mountain Flowers", (6) "Tropical Butterflies", (7) "Flowers on Your Way", (8) "Animals of All Countries, II", (9) "Robinson Crusoe", (10) "Heidi, II", (11) "Orchids", (12) "Animals of All Countries, III", (13) "Birds of Paradise and Hummingbirds"]. P.
"The Problem of Anxiety". CYHB.
"The Prophet Bird". ShT; TB.
"The Pursuit of Happiness". ShT; SP2; SP3; TB.
"The Recent Past". RM; SP2; SP3; MSO.
"The Recital". TP; MSO.
"The Ridiculous Translator's Hopes". ASWS.
"The Romantic Entanglement". AG.
"The Sea". CYHB.
"The Serious Doll". HBD; TB.
"The Seventies". CW.
"The Shocker". CYHB.
"The Shower". TCO; AWK; MSO.
"The Skaters". RM; SP1; extract published in SP2; extract published in SP3; MSO.
"The Sleeping Animals". CW.
"The Songs We Know Best". AW; SP2; SP3; TB.
"The Spacious Firmament". W; TB.
"The Story of Next Week". ASWS.
"The Sun". AWK.
"The Suspended Life". TCO; MSO.
"The System". TP; SP2; SP3; MSO.
"The Taken". AUFR.
"The Task". DDS; SP2; SP3; MSO.
"The Tennis Court Oath". TCO; MSO.
"The Thief of Poetry". HBD; TB.
"The Thinnest Shadow". ST; MSO.
"The Thousand Islands". RM; MSO.
"The Ticket". TCO; MSO.
"The Tomb of Stuart Merrill". SPCM.
"The Underwriters". YNH.
"The Unknown Travelers". TCO; MSO.
"The Variorum Edition". CW.
"The Vegetarians". ShT; SP2; SP3; TB.
"The Village of Sleep". W.
"The Waiting Ceremony". CYHB.
"The Walkways". CYHB.
"The Water Carrier". CYHB.

"The Water Inspector". YNH.
"The Way They Took". ST; MSO.
"The White Shirt". HL.
"The Whole Is Admirably Composed". HL.
"The Wind Talking". HL.
"The Wine". AWK.
"The Woman the Lion Was Supposed to Defend". HL.
"The Wrong Kind of Insurance". HBD; SP2; SP3; TB.
"The Young Son". ST; SP2; SP3; MSO.
"The Youth's Magic Horn". HL.
"Their Day". AWK; SP2; SP3.
"Theme Park Days". CW.
"Theme". CYHB.
"There's No Difference". AWK.
"These Lacustrine Cities". RM; SP3; MSO.
"They Don't Just Go Away, Either". YNH.
"They Dream Only of America". P; TCO; SP1; MSO.
"They Like". AW; TB.
"37 Haiku". AW; SP2; SP3; TB.
"This Configuration". AWK; SP2; SP3.
"This Deuced Cleverness". CW.
"This Room". YNH.
"Thoughts of a Young Girl". TCO; SP2; SP3; MSO.
"Three Dusks". CYHB.
"Three Philosophers". AUFR.
"Tide Music". ShT; TB.
"Till the Bus Starts". ASWS.
"Title Search". ASWS.
"To Good People Who Should Be Going Somewhere Else". YNH.
"To Redouté". TCO; MSO.
"To the Same Degree". TCO; MSO.
"Today's Academicians". CYHB.
"Token Resistance". ASWS.
"Too Happy, Happy Tree". AG.
"Too Much Sleep Is Bad". CW.
"Touching, the Similarities". CYHB.
"Tower of Darkness". CYHB.
"Toy Symphony". YNH.
"Train Rising out of the Sea". AWK; SP2; SP3.
"Trefoil". AW; TB.
"Tremendous Outpouring". CYHB.
"Tropical Butterflies". P.
"Tropical Sex". W.
"Truth Gleams". AUFR; CW.
"Try Me! I'm Different!" AW; TB.
"Tuesday Evening". CYHB.
"Twilight Park". CYHB.
"Two Deaths". HBD.
"Two for the Road". YNH.
"Two Pieces". ASWS.
"Two Scenes". ST; SP2; SP3; MSO.
"Two Sonnets". TCO; MSO.
"Umpteen". CYHB.
"Unctuous Platitudes". HBD; SP2; SP3; TB.
"Under Cellophane". AUFR; CW.
"Unpolished Segment". CW.
"Unreleased Movie". AG.
"Untilted". ShT: 26; SP2; SP3; TB.
(Untitled). HL.
"Unusual Precautions". ShT; SP2; SP3; TB.
"Valentine". HBD; TB.
"Variant". HBD; SP2; SP3; TB.

"Variation on a Noel". AW; TB.
"Variations on 'La Folia'". YNH.
"Variations on an Original Theme". AWK.
"Variations, Calypso and Fugue on a Theme of Ella Wheeler Wilcox". DDS; SP2; SP3; MSO.
"Vaucanson". AG.
"Vendanges". YNH.
"Vetiver". AG.
"View of Delft". CW.
"Villanelle". HL.
"Vintage Masquerade". YNH.
"Vocalise". P.
"Vowels". YNH.
"Voyage in the Blue". SPCM.
"Wakefulness". W.
"We Hesitate". ShT; SP2; SP3; TB.
"We Were on the Terrace Drinking Gin and Tonics". AWK.
"Weather and Turtles". ASWS.
"Weekend". YNH.
"Well, Yes, Actually". ASWS.
"Wet Are the Boards". AG.
"Wet Casements". HBD; SP2; SP3; TB.
"What Do You Call It When". ASWS.
"What Is Poetry". HBD; SP2; SP3; TB.
"What Is Written". YNH.
"What the Plants Say". CYHB.
"What To Do with Milk". AUFR.
"Whatever It Is, Wherever You Are". AW; SP2; SP3; TB.
"When All Her Neighbors Came". CYHB.
"When Half the Time They Don't Know Themselves ...". AG.
"When Pressed". YNH.
"When the Sun Went Down". AW; TB.
"Where It Was Decided We Should Be Taken". CYHB.
"Where We Went for Lunch". HL.
"Whether It Exists". HBD; TB.
"White Roses". TCO; SP2; SP3; MSO.
"White-Collar Crime". ShT; TB.
"Whiteout". W.
"Who Knows What Constitutes a Life". YNH.
"Why Not Sneeze?". CW.
"Wild Boys of the Road". HL.
"William Byrd". ASWS.
"Winter Daydreams". CW.
"Winter Weather Advisory". AG.
"Withered Compliments". HL.
"Within the Hour". W.
"Woman Leaning". CYHB.
"Wooden Buildings". HBD; SP2; SP3; TB.
"Works on Paper I". ASWS.
"World's End". ASWS.
"Worsening Situation". SPCM; SP2; SP3.
"Written in the Dark". ShT; TB.
"Years of Indiscretion". DDS; MSO.
"Yes, Dr. Grenzmer. How May I Be of Assistance to You?". CYHB.
"Yesterday, For Instance". CYHB.
"You Dropped Something". CYHB.
"You, My Academy". CYHB.
"You Who". AUFR.
"You Would Have Thought". CYHB.
"Young Man with Letter". DDS; MSO.
"Young People". CYHB.
"Your Name Here". YNH.

TRANSLATIONS OF BOOKS BY OTHERS

The Dice Cup: Selected Prose Poems. Max Jacob. Edited and with an introduction by Michael Brownstein. New York: SUN, 1979.
Every Question but One. Pierre Martory. New York: Groundwater Press / InterFlo Editions, 1990.
Selected Poems. Pierre Reverdy. Translated by John Ashbery, Mary Ann Caws and Patricia Terry. Edited by Timothy Bent and Germaine Brée. Winston-Salem, North Carolina: Wake Forest University Press, 1991; Newcastle upon Tyne: Bloodaxe, 1991.
The Landscape Is Behind the Door. Pierre Martory. Riverdale-on-Hudson, New York: Sheep Meadow Press, 1994.

EDITED AND CO-EDITED WORKS

The American Literary Anthology/1. With others. New York: Farrar, Straus and Giroux, 1968.
Penguin Modern Poets 24: Kenward Elmslie, Kenneth Koch, James Schuyler. Middlesex and New York: Penguin, 1974.
Marcus, Bruce. *Muck Arbour*. Chicago: O'Hara, 1975.
Snow, Richard F. *The Funny Place*. Chicago: O'Hara, 1975.
The Best American Poetry, 1988. With David Lehman. New York: Scribner, 1989.
Children's Haiku (108 haiku selected by Ashbery). London: Candy Hall, 1995.

PROSE

BOOKS

FICTION

A Nest of Ninnies. With James Schuyler. New York: E.P. Dutton & Co., 1969; Manchester: Carcanet, 1987; Calais, Vermont: Z Press, 1976; Manchester: Carcanet, 1987; London: Paladin, 1990; New York: Ecco Press, 1997.

PLAYS

Three Plays (*The Compromise, The Heroes, The Philosopher*). Calais, Vermont: Z Press, 1978; Manchester: Carcanet, 1988.

ART CRITICISM

Reported Sightings: Art Chronicles 1957-1987, edited by David E. Bergman. New York: Knopf, 1989; Manchester: Carcanet, 1989; Cambridge, Massachusetts: Harvard University Press, 1991.

LITERARY CRITICISM

Other Traditions (The Charles Eliot Norton Lectures). Cambridge, Massachusetts: Harvard University Press, 2000.

INDEX OF CRITICAL PIECES, COLLECTED AND UNCOLLECTED

RS = *Reported Sightings*
OT = *Other Traditions*

AI(Z) = *Art International* (Zurich)
AN = *ArtNews*
ANA = *ArtNews Annual*
NYHT(IE) = *New York Herald Tribune* (International Editional)

"The Impossible" (Review of Gertrude Stein's *Stanzas in Meditation*). *Poetry* 90.4 (Jul, 1957): 250-254; portions reprinted in the entry for Stein in *A Library of Literary Criticism: Modern American Literature*, compiled and edited by Dorothy Nyren. New York: Frederick Ungar, 1960.

"Bradley Walker Tomlin". AN 56.6 (Oct, 1957): 28-[29], 54; reprinted in RS: 191-194.

"Reviews and Previews". AN 56.7 (Nov, 1957).

"Reviews and Previews". AN 56.8 (Dec, 1957).

"Reviews and Previews". AN 56.9 (Jan, 1958).

"Reviews and Previews". AN 56.10 (Feb, 1958).

"Reviews and Previews". AN 57.1 (Mar, 1958).

"Robert Rauschenberg". AN 57.1 (Mar, 1958); 40, 56-57.

"Reviews and Previews". AN 57.2 (Apr, 1958).

"Reviews and Previews". AN 57.3 (May, 1958).

"Reviews and Previews". AN 57.4 (Summer, 1958).

"Jean Hélion Paints a Picture". AN (Feb, 1960); reprinted in RS: 58-66.

"The Century of Flemish Primitives" (American-Belgian exhibition at Bruges). NYHT(IE) (Jun 29, 1960): 6.

"Last-Minute Flare-Up of Gallery Activity" (Art and artists in Paris). NYHT(IE) (Jul 6, 1960): 6.

"Georges Braque". NYHT(IE) (Jul 13, 1960); reprinted in RS: 149-150.

"No Xenophobia Showing in Paris Galleries". NYHT(IE) (Jul 20, 1960): 6.

"19th Century Revisited at the Louvre" (19th century French painting). NYHT(IE) (27 Jul, 1960): 7.

"'Accrochages' Convenient for Hurried Tourists in Paris". NYHT(IE) (Aug 3, 1960): 4.

"A Good Time to Visit Small Museums" (The art scene in Paris). NYHT(IE) (Aug 10, 1960): 5.

"Rouault at Marseilles, Matisse at Aix". NYHT(IE) (Aug 17, 1960): 5.

"Werner Bischof Photos Being Exhibited". NYHT(IE) (Aug 24, 1960): 7.

"Tour of Paris Churches Now is Rewarding". NYHT(IE) (Aug 31, 1960): 6.

"Paris Modern Art Museum Full of Surprises" (Musée National d'Art Moderne). NYHT(IE) (Sep 8, 1960): 8.

"Modern Brazilian Painting and Sculpture". NYHT(IE) (Sep 14, 1960): 5.

"Impressionists' Work Dealt with Art, Spririt; Highly Personal Vision of the School Becomes Reality to Many Visitors". NYHT(IE) (Sep 17-18, 1960): 9.

"Georges Mathieu". NYHT(IE) (Sep 21, 1960); reprinted in RS: 142-144.

"Summer Lingers in Painting Galleries". NYHT(IE) (Sep 28, 1960): 5.

"Gustave Moreau and His Museum". NYHT(IE) (Oct 5, 1960); reprinted in RS: 174-176.

"American Sculpture, Painting in Paris". NYHT(IE) (Oct 12, 1960): 6.

"Derain Show in Paris – a Pleasant Surprise". NYHT(IE) (Oct 19, 1960): 8.

"Vuillard and Bonnard, Albert André, Audubon and 'Women of Yesterday and Today'". NYHT(IE) (Oct 26, 1960): 4.

"Drawings Shown by Dubuffet and Masson". NYHT(IE) (Nov 2, 1960): 8.

"Giant Art Show Reveals 'Sources of 20th Century'". NYHT(IE) (Nov 5-6, 1960): 2.

"Abstractionist Inroads at Fall Salon". NYHT(IE) (Nov 9, 1960): 4.

"Gulbenkian Show Extended; 'Ecole de Paris' Abstract". NYHT(IE) (Nov 12-13, 1960): 4.

"18th-Century Italian Art Shown in Paris". NYHT(IE) (Nov 16, 1960): 5.

"Colours and Lines". NYHT(IE) (Nov 19-20, 1960): 10.

"Pre-Impressionist Revival". NYHT(IE) (Nov 23, 1960): 4.

"'Landscapes of East, West' at Louvre". NYHT(IE) (Nov 26-27, 1960): 5.

"Something Rare: Ine-Man Sculpture Shows". NYHT(IE) (Nov 30, 1960): 4.

"A Rush of Offbeat and Familiar Painting". NYHT(IE) (Dec 7, 1960): 5.

"Picasso Drawings, Leger Lithos". NYHT(IE) (Dec 14, 1960): 4.

"Dubuffet Enters the Louvre". NYHT(IE) (Dec 21, 1960): 5.

"Hartung's Long Road into Abstraction". NYHT(IE) (Dec 28, 1960): 5.

"Goya Etchings Shown at Galerie Gaveau". NYHT(IE) (Jan 4, 1961): 13.

"Big 'Sources' Show in Paris". NYHT(IE) (Jan 8, 1961): 13.

"Hokusai's Fuji and French Impressionism". NYHT(IE) (Jan 11, 1961): 4.

"Delaney, Downing, Lee: Study in Contrasts". NYHT(IE) (Jan 18, 1961): 5.

"Gargallo Sculpture at Galerie de Varenne". NYHT(IE) (Jan 25, 1961): 4.

"Gouaches, Elastic Sculpture, Geometrical Forms, Collages". NYHT(IE) (Feb 1, 1961): 5.

"'Comparisons' at Musée National d'Art Moderne; Schools Meet – from Middle-of-Road to Neo-Dada". NYHT(IE) (Feb 8, 1961): 5.

"80 Doanier Rousseau Paintings in Paris; U.S., Europe Collections Assembled". NYHT(IE) (Feb 11-12, 1961): 5.

"Left Bank Offers Two Kandinsky Shows". NYHT(IE) (Feb 15, 1961): 7.

"Miro in a Different Mood at Paris Gallery". NYHT(IE) (Feb 22, 1961): 5.

"Ilse Getz". *Aujourd'hui* 5 (Feb, 1961): 32-33.

"Berthe Morisot's Paintings Shown in Paris". NYHT(IE) (Mar 1, 1961): 5.

"Christian Bérard". NYHT(IE) (Mar 1, 1961); reprinted in RS: 147-148.

"Americans Infiltrate Paris Galleries". NYHT(IE) (Mar 8, 1961): 9.
"Picasso Potpourri at the Galerie Mott". NYHT(IE) (Mar 15, 1961): 6.
"André Lhote Gets a Retrospective Show". NYHT(IE) (Mar 22, 1961): 5.
"Paris Exhibitions of Matisse Collages". NYHT(IE) (Mar 25-26, 1961): 5.
"Art Galleries Busy in Paris; Sculptors Star; 'Interior Space', Nudes Are Getting Attention". NYHT(IE) (Mar 29, 1961): 6.
"An Interview with Henri Michaux". AN (Mar, 1961); reprinted in RS: 396-400.
"Musée National d'Art Moderne". NYHT(IE) (Apr 5, 1961): 5.
"Paris Notes". AI(Z) 3 (Apr 5, 1961): 51-53.
"Revival of Montparnasse Indicated at Students' Center". NYHT(IE) (Apr 12, 1961): 6.
"Exhibit of Whistler's Works To Be Opened Today in Paris". NYHT(IE) (Apr 15-16, 1961): 5.
"Daumier's Biting Satire on View". NYHT(IE) (Apr 19, 1961): 5.
"Paintings of Berlin from 1750 to 1950". NYHT(IE) (Apr 26, 1961): 7.
"Paris Notes". AI(Z) 5.4 (May 1, 1961): 63-65.
"Ruth Francken". AI(Z) 5.4 (May 1, 1961): 66-67.
"Kandinsky's Road to Abstraction: 1902-1912". NYHT(IE) (May 3, 1961): 7.
"Jacques Villon Retrospective Shows Shift in Last Decade". NYHT(IE) (May 10, 1961): 10.
"Contemporary Painting, Sculpture in Paris". NYHT(IE) (May 17, 1961): 5.
"German Drawings, Florentine Engravings". NYHT(IE) (May 24, 1961): 5.
"Works by Klee, Dufy Go on View at Paris Galleries". NYHT(IE) (May 31, 1961): 7.
"Giacometti, Mathieu in Paris Shows; Figurative-Abstract Rivalry Held Pointless". NYHT(IE) (Jun 7, 1961): 7.
"Louvre Showing Works of Gustave Moreau". NYHT(IE) (Jun 10-11, 1961): 5.
"Avant-Gardist Jean Hélion at Galerie Cahiers d'Art". NYHT(IE) (Jun 14, 1961): 7.
"Chagall's Latest Techniques in Stained Glass". NYHT(IE) (Jun 21, 1961): 7.
"Spain's Miro, Tapies, Cuixart Exhibit at Galleries in Paris". NYHT(IE) (Jun 28, 1961): 7.
"Paris Notes". AI(Z) 5.5-6 (Jun-Aug, 1961): 42, 92-94.
"Niki de Saint-Phalle". NYHT(IE) (Jul 2, 1961); reprinted in RS: 145-146.
"Chinese Tachism, More of Moreau, and a Cluster of Sculpture". NYHT(IE) (Jul 5, 1961): 9.
"Early Paintings of Hartung Are Shown in Paris Gallery". NYHT(IE) (Jul 12, 1961): 7.
"Landscapes Good Start for Vacation in France". NYHT(IE) (Jul 19, 1961): 5.
"Midsummer Madness Fills Void in Paris Art Calendar". NYHT(IE) (Jul 26, 1961): 4.
"Rarely Seen Paintings on View Now in Paris". NYHT(IE) (Aug 2, 1961): 4.
"Parisians See Russians of School of Paris". NYHT(IE) (Aug 9, 1961): 6.
"Cézanne and Desportes at Home in Their Own Landscapes". NYHT(IE) (Aug 16, 1961): 4.
"Paris Pays Honor to Maillol and Bourdelle". NYHT(IE) (Aug 23, 1961): 4.
"Paris Adds Still Another Museum". NYHT(IE) (Aug 30, 1961): 7.
"Vuillard". NYHT(IE) (Sep 6, 1961); reprinted in RS: 52-53.
"Soviet Exhibit Art: Cow Is a Cow Is a Cow; Socialist Realism in Full Bloom in Paris". NYHT(IE) (Sep 13, 1961): 13.
"History of Malta Recalled in Art Exhibit at Versailles". NYHT(IE) (Sep 20, 1961): 5.
"Plenty of Art Works for $50 in Paris". NYHT(IE) (Sep 27, 1961): 6.
"French Dominate Paris Biennale (Avant-Garde Bazaar)". NYHT(IE) (Oct 11, 1961): 11.
"Savage Splendor in Paris Persian Show". NYHT(IE) (Oct 18, 1961): 6.
"Paris Summer Letter". AI(Z) 5.8 (Oct 20, 1961): 89-92.
"Mark Tobey". NYHT(IE) (Oct 25, 1961); reprinted in RS: 188-190.
"Ecole de Paris Show Reveals Fresh Works". NYHT(IE) (Nov 1, 1961): 5.
"Can Art Be Excellent If Anybody Could Do It?". NYHT(IE) (Nov 8, 1961): 11.
"Galleries Vie with Paris Autumn Salon". NYHT(IE) (Nov 14, 1961): 5.
"Paris Notes". AI(Z) 5.9 (Nov 20, 1961): 48-50.
"Modern Old Masters on View in Paris; Galleries Show Ernst, Delaunay, Picabia". NYHT(IE) (Nov 22, 1961): 5.
"Ancients and Moderns in Paris Galleries". NYHT(IE) (Nov 29, 1961): 5.
"Louise Nevelson". Ring des Arts (Zurich) 2 (Autumn, 1961): 26.
"Paris Museums Show Work of Goya, Braque and Méryon". NYHT(IE) (Dec 6, 1961): 9.
"Korean Opulence at Paris Museums". NYHT(IE) (Dec 13, 1961): 5.
"Rube Goldberg Art That Makes the Fur Fly". NYHT(IE) (Dec 20, 1961): 5.
"Minor 18th-Century Masters Show Un-Pompadour Trend". NYHT(IE) (Dec 27, 1961): 5.
"Yugoslavs Enter Abstract Commonwealth". NYHT(IE) (Jan 3, 1962): 6.
"January Bonus at Paris Galleries". NYHT(IE) (Jan 10, 1962): 13.
"New Show of Carracci Drawings at the Louvre". NYHT(IE) (Jan 17, 1962): 5.
"Photos Rival Paintings in Paris Shows; Brassai, Forel Do Avant-Garde Work". NYHT(IE) (Jan 24, 1962): 6.
"Picasso's Latest on View in Paris". NYHT(IE) (Jan 31, 1962): 5.
"From Degas to Bicat, by Way of Lapoujade". NYHT(IE) (Feb 7, 1962): 9.

"Paris Galleries Show Bérard, Survey of Experimental Art". NYHT(IE) (Feb 14, 1962): 8.
"Surrealistic Off-Season Resorts". NYHT(IE) (Feb 21, 1962): 4.
"In Paris: Arp's Objective Lyricism". NYHT(IE) (Feb 28, 1962): 6.
"Paris Notes". AI(Z) 6.1 (Feb, 1962): 74-75.
"Paris Galleries Show a Bit of Everything". NYHT(IE) (Mar 7, 1962): 11.
"3 Shows of Italian Drawings Being Presented in Paris". NYHT(IE) (Mar 14, 1962): 5.
"Kline Show Gives Paris Taste of New York Painting". NYHT(IE) (Mar 21, 1962): 7.
"Practical 'Antagonismes', Chad Art Shown in Paris". NYHT(IE) (Mar 28, 1962): 5.
"Uncultured Bourgeoisie's Buying Called Peril For Art". NYHT(IE) (Apr 3, 1962): 3.
"3,500 Years of Mexican Art, and Brancusi". NYHT(IE) (Apr 4, 1962): 6.
"Cathedral Art Shown at Louvre; Collection of Drawings Also Put on Display". NYHT(IE) (Apr 11, 1962): 4.
"Paris Art Season Starts with 'Way-Out' Clarity". NYHT(IE) (Apr 18, 1962): 5.
"20th-Century French Watercolors". NYHT(IE) (Apr 25, 1962): 5.
"Paris Letter". AI(Z) 6.3 (Apr, 1962): 59-63.
"Henie-Onstad Collection on Display in Paris". NYHT(IE) (May 2, 1962): 5.
"Painters Return to Using Brushes". NYHT(IE) (May 9, 1962): 5.
"From Zen to Illusions to Abstracts". NYHT(IE) (May 16, 1962): 5.
"Avant-Garde Sculpture on View in Paris". NYHT(IE) (May 23, 1962): 5.
"Chamber Music Composed by IBM Computer Played" (Music of Iannis Xenakis). NYHT(IE) (May 30, 1962): 3.
"Surrealist Revival May Be on the Way". NYHT(IE) (May 30, 1962): 5.
"Art in Paris: Hélion, Daphnos, Tal Coat, Downing and Levee". NYHT(IE) (Jun 6, 1962): 7.
"Venice Biennale Starts the Cocktails – and Deals – Flowing". NYHT(IE) (Jun 13, 1962): 7.
"Venice Biennial: Art and Vacuum". NYHT(IE) (Jun 17, 1962): 4, 6A.
"Pissarro Show in Paris Has Late Works". NYHT(IE) (Jul 18, 1962): 5.
"Corot Figure Paintings in Show at Louvre". NYHT(IE) (Jun 27, 1962): 5.
"Miro Retrospective Is Major Paris Event". NYHT(IE) (Jul 4, 1962): 5.
"One Paris Art Show by Non-Master: Emile Bernard Was Associate of Gauguin". NYHT(IE) (Jul 11, 1962): 5.
"Few Oases in Summer Art Desert; Cycladic Sculpture, Dufy Shown in Paris". NYHT(IE) (Jul 25, 1962): 5.
"Tapestries of Lebrun at Gobelins; His Designs Called Highest Point of Art". NYHT(IE) (Aug 1, 1962): 6.
"New Style Evident in Recent Pignon Paintings". NYHT(IE) (Aug 15, 1962): 5.
"Works of Old Masters Lent for Art Display Near Paris". NYHT(IE) (Aug 22, 1962): 6.
"Moreau Show in Marseilles Covers Pupils; Influence on Matisse, Rouault Demonstrated". NYHT(IE) (Aug 29, 1962): 5.
"Provence's Aix Popular with Artists; Intellectual Life Is Always Lively". NYHT(IE) (Sep 5, 1962): 5.
"Inflation Nothing New in Art Mart; New Book Reviews Speculation in Painting". NYHT(IE) (Sep 12, 1962): 5.
"Hals Show in Haarlem; Moderns Have Fun". NYHT(IE) (Sep 19, 1962): 5.
"Paris Letter: May-June 1962". AI(Z) 6.7 (Sep 25, 1962): 58-65.
"Isolated Dutch Museum Has 270 Works by Van Gogh". NYHT(IE) (Sep 26, 1962): 5.
"Lautrec Drawings in Paris Show; 'New Forces' Exhibit Also Opens". NYHT(IE) (Sep 26, 1962): 5.
"19th-Century Landscapists on Show in Paris". NYHT(IE) (Oct 10, 1962): 9.
"Cubists on View in Paris". NYHT(IE) (Oct 17, 1962): 7.
"Astrological Automobiles". NYHT(IE) (Oct 19, 1962): 12; reprinted in RS: 361-362.
"Brianchon's Traditionalist Painting". NYHT(IE) (Oct 24, 1962): 5.
"'Blue Rider' Show in Paris Includes 6 Kandinsky Works". NYHT(IE) (Oct 31, 1962): 5.
"Francis Bacon". NYHT(IE) (Nov 7, 1962): 6; reprinted in RS: 160-162.
"Reply to the Cult of the Object". NYHT(IE) (Nov 14, 1962): 6.
"American Art Shows Flood Paris; Grandma Moses Among Exhibitions". NYHT(IE) (Nov 21, 1962): 6.
"Paris Notes". AI(Z) 6.9 (Nov 25, 1962): 57-60.
"Paintings of La Fresnaye Displayed at Paris Gallery". NYHT(IE) (Nov 28, 1962): 5.
"Re-Establishing Raymond Roussel". Portfolio and ArtNews Annual 6 (Autumn, 1962); reprinted as "On Raymond Roussel" in Raymond Roussel, How I Wrote Certain of My Books, translated by Trevor Winkfield. New York: Sun, 1977; reprinted in Michel Foucault, Death and the Labyrinth: the World of Raymond Roussel, translated by Charles Ruas; Garden City, New York: Doubleday, 1986; London: The Athlone Press, 1987; reprinted as "Introduction" in Raymond Roussel, How I Wrote Certain of My Books and Other Writings, edited by Trevor Winkfield. Boston: Exact Change, 1995.
"Proof That, Nowadays, a Painter Really Need Not Starve in a Garret". NYHT(IE) (Dec 4, 1962): 7.
"Grandma Moses". NYHT(IE) (Dec 5, 1962); RS: 179-180.
"Four Shows of Oriental Art in Paris; 2 Devoted to Chinese, 2 to Japanese Painting". NYHT(IE) (Dec 12, 1962): 5.
"Paintings at Holiday Prices for Art-Minded Gift-Givers". NYHT(IE) (Dec 19, 1962): 5.
"Paris Notes". AI(Z) 6.10 (Dec 20, 1962): 48-52.
"Rothko at Paris Musée d'Art Moderne". NYHT(IE) (Dec 26, 1962): 5.

"'Unknown' Rodin revealed in Show at Louvre". NYHT(IE) (Jan 9, 1963): 5.
"Paris Show Reveals New Side of Arp; Goldberg Eskimo Art Also Exhibited". NYHT(IE) (Jan 16, 1963): 5.
"Sculpture Respectable Again, Paris Galleries Demonstrate". NYHT(IE) (Jan 23, 1963): 5.
"Paris Notes". AI(Z) 7.1 (Jan 25, 1963): 79-80.
"Paris' Biggest Exhibition of Spanish Painting Since 1848". NYHT(IE) (Jan 30, 1963): 5.
"Bulgarian, Buffet Shows on in Paris". NYHT(IE) (Feb 6, 1963): 5.
"Villon Engravings at Paris Gallery". NYHT(IE) (Feb 13, 1963): 5.
"Sargent Canvases and Indian Miniatures". NYHT(IE) (Feb 20, 1963): 5.
"Kramer's Motor-Driven Sculptures Shown in Paris". NYHT(IE) (Feb 27, 1963): 5.
"Paris Notes". AI(Z) 7.2 (Feb 25, 1963): 72-76.
"Raoul Dufy". NYHT(IE) (Mar 6, 1963): 9; reprinted in RS: 140-141.
"Galleries Sprout Like Mushrooms in Milan". NYHT(IE) (Mar 13, 1963): 5.
"Shockers for a Shockproof Art Public". NYHT(IE) (Mar 13, 1963): 5.
"Fantasies of Bresdin in Paris Show; Selection of Etchings on View Till April 15". NYHT(IE) (Mar 20, 1963): 5.
"Braque Jewelry on Display in Paris". NYHT(IE) (Mar 27, 1963): 5.
"Kierkegaard Subject of Paris Show". NYHT(IE) (Mar 30-31, 1963): 5.
"Paris Pays Homage to Delacroix". NYHT(IE) (Apr 3, 1963): 5.
"Mathieu Retrospective in Paris". NYHT(IE) (Apr 10, 1963): 11.
"Boldoni Show Is New Sign of Fin-de-Siècle Revival". NYHT(IE) (Apr 17, 1963): 6.
"Paris 'Boutique Culturelle' Encourages Young Collectors". NYHT(IE) (Apr 24, 1963): 5.
"Paris Notes". AI(Z) 7.4 (Apr 25, 1963): 73-75.
"American Gallery in Paris Sells US Art to Europeans". NYHT(IE) (May 2, 1963): 7.
"Photos Show Vuillard Deft with Camera; Candid Shots Included in Paris Exhibition". NYHT(IE) (May 8, 1963): 9.
"Delacroix, Watteau, Chardin, Boucher, Lancret and American Pop Art". NYHT(IE) (May 15, 1963): 7.
"From Greek Classicism to Modern Fantasy Via Blowtorch 'Painting'". NYHT(IE) (May 15, 1963): 7.
"Odilon Redon and Maurice Denis". NYHT(IE) (May 22, 1963); reprinted in RS: 133-134.
"Range of Styles Includes Organized Debris". NYHT(IE) (May 22, 1963): 5.
"Appel's 8-Foot Book; Motor-Driven Mobiles". NYHT(IE) (May 29, 1963): 5.
"Commerce Teams with Art in Foire de Paris Exhibition". NYHT(IE) (May 29, 1963): 5.
"Anthology of Swedish Art at Louvre; Oldest Work Show Is Neolithic Ax". NYHT(IE) (Jun 5, 1963): 5.
"'Cobra School' of Painting, 'School of Paris' Russians". NYHT(IE) (Jun 5, 1963): 5.
"From Pop to Metaphysical Landscapes". NYHT(IE) (Jun 12, 1963): 7.
"Kandinsky Retrospective and Kubin, Tanguy Shows". NYHT(IE) (Jun 12, 1963): 7.
"Anne Harvey, Derain in Paris Shows; Zao Wou-Ki, Laurencin Also Seen". NYHT(IE) (Jun 19, 1963): 5.
"Range in Paris Galleries: Surrealist to All Black". NYHT(IE) (Jun 19, 1963): 5.
"Paris Notes". AI(Z) 7.6 (Jun 25, 1963): 76-78.
"Expressionism, Abstraction, Hot Dogs in Paris Shows". NYHT(IE) (Jun 26, 1963): 5.
"New Interest in 20th-Century Sculpture". NYHT(IE) (Jun 26, 1963): 5.
"Delacroix's Drawings". NYHT(IE) (Jul 3, 1963); reprinted in RS: 41-43.
"Turin Provides Appropriate Setting for Show of Baroque Art". NYHT(IE) (Jul 10, 1963): 5.
"Carpaccio Works Shown in Venice". NYHT(IE) (Jul 17, 1963): 5.
"Popular Arts Museum to Get New Paris Home Next Year". NYHT(IE) (Jul 24, 1963): 5.
"Constantin Guys". NYHT(IE) (Jul 30, 1963); reprinted in RS: 44-45.
"That Painter as 'a Prince Traveling Incognito'". NYHT(IE) (Jul 31, 1963): 5.
"Art in the Roman Occident at Louvre". NYHT(IE) (Aug 14, 1963): 6.
"Delacroix Exhibit Held in Bordeaux; Shows His Position in History of Painting". NYHT(IE) (Aug 14, 1963): 6.
"Montauban Is Magnet to Art Lovers; Southwest French City Boasts Ingres Museum". NYHT(IE) (Aug 21, 1963): 5.
"Beats, Fat Cats Rubbing Elbows". NYHT(IE) (Aug 28, 1963): 5.
"New Havre Museum Held Success – Inside and Outside". NYHT(IE) (Sep 4, 1963): 5.
"Nice Now Has Matisse Museum". NYHT(IE) (Sep 11, 1963): 5.
"200 Years of German, Swiss Art; Winterthur Boasts Reinhart Collection". NYHT(IE) (Sep 18, 1963): 5.
"A Place Where Artists Can Work". NYHT(IE) (Sep 25, 1963): 5.
"The Odyssey of Britain's Moynihan; Painter Now Has One-Man Show in London". NYHT(IE) (Oct 9, 1963): 11.
"Current Paris Biennale Bigger and Most Exciting to Date". NYHT(IE) (Oct 16, 1963): 5.
"'After-Life in Japanese Art' at Petit Palais". NYHT(IE) (Oct 23, 1963): 5.
"Ecole de Paris Show Belies Ideas of Stodginess". NYHT(IE) (Oct 30, 1963): 5.
"The New Realism". C (New York) 1.5 (Oct - Nov, 1963): 2-3.
"'Figurative', 'Abstract' Seem Inadequate". NYHT(IE) (Nov 6, 1963): 11.
"American Painters Have French Touch". NYHT(IE) (Nov 13, 1963): 5.
"Paris is Full of Art Shows From Now Till Yule; All the Important Ones Are Packed into 2 or 3 Months". NYHT(IE)

(Nov 13, 1963): 5.
"Catlin's Paintings of Indians on Show at US Paris Center". NYHT(IE) (Nov 20, 1963): 5.
"Calder Depicts 'Poetry of Flight' in Paris Show of Stabiles". NYHT(IE) (Nov 27, 1963): 5.
"If Aillaud Likes It, He Paints It; Work Said to Offset Too Much Tachism". NYHT(IE) (Nov 27, 1963): 5.
"Messagier Retrospective Show Among Modern Displays". NYHT(IE) (Nov 27, 1963): 5.
"Brauner, Canogar, Ciry, Cascella and Others in Paris". NYHT(IE) (Dec 4, 1963): 5.
"Shows Feature Drawings, Pastels, Watercolors". NYHT(IE) (Dec 4, 1963): 5.
"Byronic Atmosphere Found in Marie-Laure's Paintings". NYHT(IE) (Dec 11, 1963): 9.
"Léon Lehman, Show Ends His Obscurity". NYHT(IE) (Dec 11, 1963): 9.
"Original Works of Art Now Popular As Christmas Gifts". NYHT(IE) (Dec 18, 1963): 5.
"What's Happened to Chauvinism?". NYHT(IE) (Dec 18, 1963): 5.
"Italians Who Made the French Renaissance". NYHT(IE) (Dec 25, 1963): 5.
"Louvre Retrospective Devoted to Signac". NYHT(IE) (Jan 1, 1964): 5.
"Icon Show at Russian Cathedral of Paris". NYHT(IE) (Jan 8, 1964): 5.
"Pop Artist's Horror Pictures Silence Snickers". NYHT(IE) (Jan 15, 1964): 5.
"Picasso Show Proves He Has Lost Nothing". NYHT(IE) (Jan 22, 1964): 5.
"Bérard's Sketches of Colette Subjects on Show". NYHT(IE) (Jan 29, 1964): 6.
"Lurçat's Tapestries Featured". NYHT(IE) (Feb 5, 1964): 5.
"Fantasy at Art Galleries". NYHT(IE) (Feb 12, 1964): 5.
"US Center's Last Show". NYHT(IE) (Feb 12, 1964): 5.
"Lifting the Shroud of Mystery from the Hittite Empire". NYHT(IE) (Feb 18, 1964): 5.
"The 1964 Models Come Off the Buffet Assembly Line". NYHT(IE) (Feb 18, 1964): 5.
"Matta Returns to Painters' Fold". NYHT(IE) (Feb 25, 1964): 5.
"Michelangelo Pistoletto". NYHT(IE) (Mar 3, 1964); reprinted in RS: 158-159.
"Musée d'Art Moderne Shows Little-Known Works by Picasso, Léger, Gris." NYHT(IE) (Mar 10, 1964): 5.
"Emblems and Totems". NYHT(IE) (Mar 17, 1964): 5.
"It's Been a Good Year for Sculptors". "Emblems and Totems". NYHT(IE) (Mar 24, 1964): 5.
"Dufy: Only the Sunny Hours". NYHT(IE) (Mar 31, 1964): 5.
"Surrealist Dado Paints Disgusting Subjects". NYHT(IE) (Apr 7, 1964): 5.
"Jean Fautrier". NYHT(IE) (Apr 14, 1964); reprinted in RS: 135-137.
"In the Surrealist Tradition". NYHT(IE) (Apr 21, 1964); reprinted in RS: 3-4.
"Staechelin Collection at Musée d'Art Moderne; from Corot to the Cubists". NYHT(IE) (Apr 28, 1964): 5.
"'The New Tendency': Mechanical Marvels". NYHT(IE) (May 5, 1964): 5.
"US Takeover in Paris". NYHT(IE) (May 26, 1964): 5.
"Two Shows of French Drawings". NYHT(IE) (Jun 2, 1964): 5.
"Louis XV's Boucher Back in 'Court's' Favor at Last?". NYHT(IE) (Jun 9, 1964): 5.
"Cunningham Ballet in Paris (First Leg of World Tour). NYHT(IE) (Jun 13-14, 1964): 5.
"The Venice Biennale Begins to Show Its Changing Face". NYHT(IE) (Jun 16, 1964): 5.
"Venice Biennale Center of Controversy". NYHT(IE) (Jun 23, 1964): 5.
"Rouault – 'Unfinished' but Best; 200 Paintings on Show in Paris". NYHT(IE) (Jun 30, 1964): 5.
"American Developments Worry French". NYHT(IE) (Jul 7, 1964): 5.
"Marcoussis Retrospective in Paris". NYHT(IE) (Jul 14, 1964): 5.
"A Tribute to Derain". NYHT(IE) (Jul 21, 1964): 5.
"New Modern Art Museum on the Riviera". NYHT(IE) (Jul 28, 1964): 5.
"Austrian Treasures at Versailles". NYHT(IE) (Aug 11, 1964): 5.
"Biot Museum Shows Léger to Sunstruck". NYHT(IE) (Aug 18, 1964): 5.
"Want a Loudspeaker for Water Music?". NYHT(IE) (Aug 25, 1964): 5.
"Two Careers Combined at Saint Paul; Hotelier-Painter Roux at Colombe d'Or". NYHT(IE) (Sep 1, 1964): 5.
"Sculpture Outdoors in Paris". NYHT(IE) (Sep 8, 1964): 5.
"Art News from Paris". AN 63.5 (Sep, 1964): 50-51.
"Segui Shows Horrors in Double Paris Show". NYHT(IE) (Oct 6, 1964): 5.
"Galleries in Paris Shake Off Lethargy". NYHT(IE) (Oct 13, 1964): 5.
"Toulouse-Lautrec". NYHT(IE) (Oct 13, 1964); reprinted in RS: 130-132.
"Parmigianino". NYHT(IE) (Oct 20, 1964); reprinted in RS: 31-33.
"Naive Painting to the Fore". NYHT(IE) (Oct 27, 1964): 5.
"Nine Unknown Works by Degas". NYHT(IE) (Nov 3, 1964): 5.
"Around the Paris Galleries". NYHT(IE) (Nov 10, 1964): 5.
"In Paris, Rare Chance to Study the Work of Géricault". NYHT(IE) (Nov 10, 1964): 5.
"Current Surrealist Shows in Paris". NYHT(IE) (Nov 17, 1964): 5.
"Millet Rehabilitated by Paris Retrospective". NYHT(IE) (Nov 17, 1964): 5.
"Op's Copping Pop's Top Spot". NYHT(IE) (Nov 24, 1964): 5.
"Art News from Paris". AN 63.7 (Nov, 1964): 48.

"Fantastic Architecture". NYHT(IE) (Dec 1, 1964); reprinted in RS: 324-326.
"Three Fantastic Architects in Paris Show". NYHT(IE) (Dec 1, 1964): 5.
"Trip Around the Paris Galleries". NYHT(IE) (Dec 1, 1964): 5.
"Paris Accent on Pop – Little Snap or Crackle". NYHT(IE) (Jan 19, 1965): 5.
"Pop Painters Hold Mirror Up". NYHT(IE) (Jan 26, 1965): 5.
"Art News from Paris". AN 63.9 (Jan, 1965): 50-51.
"Art Exhibition in Paris Focused on Dutch Life in 17th Century". NYHT(IE) (Feb 2, 1965): 5.
"French Religious Art Assembled in Paris". NYHT(IE) (Feb 9, 1965): 5.
"Poet-Painter Reflects Self in Paris Show; Michaux Exhibition at Art Moderne". NYHT(IE) (Feb 16, 1965): 5.
"Soviet Avant-Garde Painter Zverev Has His First Exhibition in Paris". NYHT(IE) (Feb 23, 1965): 5.
"Louvre Caravaggio Exhibit". NYHT(IE) (Mar 2, 1965): 5.
"Rouault's Craftsmanship on View in Paris". NYHT(IE) (Mar 9, 1965): 5.
"Seldom Seen Painters Given Paris Showing". NYHT(IE) (Mar 9, 1965): 5.
"'Jean Cocteau and His Time' Revives the Paris of the Lost Generation". NYHT(IE) (Mar 16, 1965): 5.
"Suggestion, Machines in Paris Shows; Jean Dupuy Found Dynamic, Ascetic". NYHT(IE) (Mar 16, 1965): 5.
"Abstractionism, Mystic Anti-Cubism". NYHT(IE) (Mar 23, 1965): 5.
"Paris Exhibit Reflects Many Facets of Nadar". NYHT(IE) (Mar 23, 1965): 5.
"Greek Artist Ghika Shows Oils, Gouaches in Paris". NYHT(IE) (Mar 30, 1965): 5.
"Pastels and Miniatures on Display at Louvre". NYHT(IE) (Mar 30, 1965): 5.
"Sculpture Like Instruments of Torture – in Gay Colors". NYHT(IE) (Apr 5, 1965): 5.
"Malraux's Dynamic Policy Brightens Some State Museums". NYHT(IE) (Apr 6, 1965): 5.
"Danish Art Treasures Show Flawless Design". NYHT(IE) (Apr 13, 1965): 5.
"Tobey, an Unknown and Jacquet in Paris". NYHT(IE) (Apr 13, 1965): 5.
"Yves Klein". NYHT(IE) (Apr 20, 1965); reprinted in RS: 138-139.
"Paintings, Sculpture of Gonzalez in Paris". NYHT(IE) (Apr 27, 1965): 5.
"Joan Mitchell". AN (Apr, 1965): 44-45, 63-64; reprinted in RS: 98-101.
"Nothing Trite at Paris Salon of Jeune Sculpture". NYHT(IE) (May 4, 1965): 5.
"Exuberance Flares at Salon de Mai; Picasso, As Usual, and Younger Artists". NYHT(IE) (May 11, 1965): 5.
"Moretti Makes Splash at Opening". NYHT(IE) (May 11, 1965): 5.
"Andy Warhol in Paris". NYHT(IE) (May 18, 1965); reprinted in RS: 120-122.
"German Expressionists in France". NYHT(IE) (May 25, 1965): 5.
"Paris Galleries Play Trumps in June". NYHT(IE) (Jun 1, 1965): 5.
"Paris Shows: Arp, Miro and Unknown Braques". NYHT(IE) (Jun 1, 1965): 5.
"Proust and His Times in Paris Exhibition". NYHT(IE) (Jun 8, 1965): 5.
"Pop Artists Switches to Aggressive Neutral Banality". NYHT(IE) (Jun 15, 1965): 5.
"Europe's Largest Show of US Sculpture Opens". NYHT(IE) (Jun 22, 1965): 5.
"Composer Gian Carlo Menotti – the Busiest Man in Italy Now". NYHT(IE) (Jul 3-4, 1965): 10.
"Avant-Garde at Spoleto: Landscape Painting Is In". NYHT(IE) (Jul 6, 1965): 5.
"Calder Retrospective Is Climax of Paris Shows". NYHT(IE) (Jul 13, 1965): 5.
"Emigré's Return to Paris." NYHT(IE) (Jul 20, 1965): 5.
"Boudin's Love of the Sea and the Sky". NYHT(IE) (Aug 3, 1965): 5.
"New Versailles Rooms Open". NYHT(IE) (Aug 10, 1965): 5.
"Little-Known Monument in France; Ledoux's Salt Works 18th-Century Gem". NYHT(IE) (Aug 17, 1965): 5.
"Six Stages in the Gestation of Painting". Réalités (Paris) 177 (Aug, 1965): 34-35.
"The Seicento; When Italian Painting Came Down to Earth". Réalités (Paris) 177 (Aug, 1965): 60-67.
"Paris: From Pre-History to Outer Space" (Musée de L'Homme). AN 64.4 (Summer, 1965): 45-47.
"Paris Lithographer Draws World's Greats". NYHT(IE) (Sep 21, 1965): 5.
"Russia's French Treasures at Louvre". NYHT(IE) (Sep 28, 1965): 5.
"Young Artists of Paris Biennale Suffer in Comparison with 1963's". NYHT(IE) (Oct 5, 1965): 5.
"What's New in Paris Art? Murder, That's What". NYHT(IE) (Oct 12, 1965): 5.
"Art News from Paris". AN 64.6 (Oct, 1965): 52-53, 58-59.
"Art News from Paris". AN 64.8 (Dec, 1965): [37], 54.
"Paris Sculptors: New Generations Create Striking New Forms". ANA 30 (1965):143-157, 175-176, 179-180.
"Reviews and Previews". AN 64.9 (Jan, 1966).
"Reviews and Previews". AN 64.10 (Feb, 1966).
"Brooms and Prisms". AN 65.1 (Mar, 1966): 58-59, 82-84.
"Reviews and Previews". AN 65.1 (Mar, 1966).
"French Painting, 1820-1879". AN 65.2 (Apr, 1966): [28]-30, 56; reprinted in RS: 34-36.
"Reviews and Previews". AN 65.2 (Apr, 1966).
"Benefit Bonanza". AN 65.3 (May, 1966): [32]-33, 65.
"Fin-de-Siècle Freshness". AN 65.3 (May, 1966): 43, 57-58.
"Introducing Rodrigo Moynihan". AN 65.3 (May, 1966): [40], 68.

"Reviews and Previews". AN 65.3 (May, 1966).

"Young Masters of Understatement". AN 65.3 (May, 1966), 42, 62.

"Gauguin: the Hidden Tradition". AN 64.4 (Summer, 1966): 26-29.

"Talking of Michelangelo". AN 65.4 (Summer, 1966): 42-43, 64-65.

"Tradition and Talent" (Review of Philip Booth's *Weathers and Edges*, Adrienne Rich's *Necessities of Life: Poems 1962-65*, and Stanley Moss's *The Wrong Angel*). *Book Week* 3.52 (Sep 4, 1966): 2, 14-15.

"Frank O'Hara's Question". *Book Week* 4.3 (Sep 25, 1966): 6.

"Frank O'Hara". AN 66.5 (Sep, 1966): 45, 62.

"Jerboas, Pelicans, and Peewee Reese" (Review of Marianne Moore's *Tell Me, Tell Me: Granite, Steel and Other Topics*). *Book Week* 4.8 (Oct 30, 1966): 1, 8.

"Max Klinger". ANA 32 (Oct, 1966): 46-53; reprinted in RS: 125-129.

"School of Paris Dropouts". AN 65.7 (Nov, 1966): 56-57, 71-72.

"The Unknown Sisley". AN 65.7 (Nov, 1966): 44-45, 82-84.

"The Decline of the Verbs" (Review of Giogio di Chirico's *Hebdomeros*). *Book Week* 4.15 (Dec 18, 1966): 5.

"Post-Painterly Quattrocento". AN 65.8 (Dec, 1966): 40-[41], 61-62.

"Reviews and Previews". AN 65.8 (Dec, 1966).

"American Sanctuary in Paris". ANA 31 (1966): 84-95, 144-146, 163-165; reprinted in RS: 87-97.

"Up from the Underground" (Review of *The Collected Works of Jane Bowles*). *New York Times Book Review* (Jan 29, 1967): 5, 28, 30.

"Reviews and Previews". AN 65.9 (Jan, 1967).

"Williamstown-sur-Seine". AN 65.10 (Feb, 1967): [44]-47, 62.

"Chester's Sweet Freaks" (Review of Alfred Chester's *The Exquisite Corpse*). *Book Week* 4.27 (Mar 12, 1967): 3, 13.

"A Game with Shifting Mirrors" (Review of Jorge Luis Borges's *A Personal Anthology*). *New York Times Book Review* (Apr 16, 1967): 4.

"At Mrs Kelso's" (With James Schuyler, a chapter from their novel in progress, *A Nest of Ninnies*). *Art and Literature* 12 (Spring, 1967): 73-85.

"Gallery Companions" (Omnibus Review). *New York Times Book Review* (Jun 4, 1967): 10, 12, 14.

"Ecrivain Maudit" (Review of Witold Gombowicz's *Ferdyduke* and *Pornografia*). *New York Times Book Review* (Jul 9, 1967): 4-5, 51.

"Joseph Cornell". AN 66.4 (Summer, 1967): 56-59, 63-[64]; reprinted in RS: 13-18.

"In Darkest Language" (Review of Raymond Roussel's *Impressions of Africa* and Rayner Heppenstall's *Raymond Roussel: a Critical Study*). *New York Times Book Review* (Oct 29, 1967): 58, 60, 62.

"Straight Lines over Rough Terrain" (Review of *The Complete Poems of Marianne Moore*). *New York Times Book Review* (Nov 26, 1967): 1, 42.

"Reviews and Previews". AN 66.7 (Nov, 1967).

"Drawn from Dublin". AN 66.8 (Dec, 1967): 46.

"Reviews and Previews". AN 66.8 (Dec, 1967).

"Space and Dream". AN 66.8 (Dec, 1967): 48-[49]; reprinted in RS: 9-12.

"In Memory of My Feelings". AN 66.9 (Jan, 1968): 50-51, 67-68.

"Reviews and Previews". AN 66.9 (Jan, 1968).

"Reviews and Previews". AN 66.10 (Feb, 1968).

"Homage to France" (Painting in France 1900-1967, at the National Gallery in Washington). *New Republic* 158.13 (Mar 30, 1968): 32-34.

"Reviews and Previews". AN 67.1 (Mar, 1968).

"Four American Exhibits of 1968". *New Republic* 158.16 (Apr 20, 1968): 40, 42-43; reprinted in RS: 252-256.

"Paris in April: Three Major Modern French Shows Open in New York". AN 67.2 (Apr, 1968): 32-37, 75.

"Growing up Surreal: a Mammoth Show at the Museum of Modern Art". AN 67.3 (May, 1968): [40]-44, 65.

"The Heritage of Dada and Surrealism". *New Republic* 158.22 (Jun 1, 1968): 35-36, 38; reprinted in RS: 5-8.

"Italians Bearing Gifts" (Show at the Jewish Museum). *New Republic* 159.5 (Aug 3, 1968): 32-34.

"Further Adventures" (With James Schuyler, an extract from their novel in progress, *A Nest of Ninnies*). *Paris Review* 11.43 (Summer, 1968): 32-54.

"Reviews and Previews". AN 67.4 (Summer, 1968).

"The Invisible Avant-Garde". ANA 34(1968): 124-[133]; reprinted in RS: 389-395.

"Black Pollock". AN 68.1 (Mar, 1969): 28, 66, 68.

"Reviews and Previews". AN 68.1 (Mar, 1969).

"Reviews and Previews". AN 68.2 (Apr, 1969).

"Reviews and Previews". AN 68.3 (May, 1969).

"Further Adventures of Qfwfq" (Review of Italo Calvino's *T Zero*). *New York Times Book Review* (Oct 12, 1969): 5, 36.

"Before the Deluge". AN 68.7 (Nov, 1969): 54-55, 80-81.

"Reviews and Previews". AN 68.7 (Nov, 1969).

"Saul Steinberg". AN 68.7 (Nov, 1969): 45, 72, 74; reprinted in RS: 285-286.

"Reviews and Previews". AN 68.9 (Jan, 1970).

"Leland Bell". AN 68.10 (Feb, 1970): [44-45], 64-68; reprinted in RS: 195-202.

"Reviews and Previews". AN 68.10 (Feb, 1970).

"A Place for Everything". AN 69.1 (Mar, 1970): 32-33, 73-75.

"The Johnson Collection at Cranbrook". *Craft Horizons* 30.2 (Mar-Apr, 1970): 34-38, 57-58.

"Miro's Bronze Age". AN 69.3 (May, 1970): 34-36.

"Reviews and Previews". AN 69.6 (Oct, 1970).

"Saul Steinberg". ANA 36 (Oct, 1970): 52-59; reprinted in RS: 279-284.

"Reviews and Previews". AN 69.7 (Oct, 1970).

"Reviews and Previews". AN 69.8 (Nov, 1970).

"Reviews and Previews". AN 69.9 (Jan, 1971).

"G.M.P. (The Collections of Gertrude, Leo, Michael and Sarah Stein Are Reunited in a Magnificent Show at the Museum of Modern Art)". AN 69.10 (Feb, 1971): 44-47, 73-74.

"All the Birds and the Beasts Were There". AN 70.1 (Mar, 1971): 36-37, 62-63.

"Reviews and Previews". AN 70.1 (Mar, 1971).

"Reviews and Previews". AN 70.2 (Apr, 1971).

"English Subtitles; 'Information' Dominated the British Avant-Garde Show". *Herald* (New York) 1.7 (week of May 30, 1971): "The Now Section", 12.

"Gertrude Stein". AN 70.3 (May, 1971); reprinted in RS: 106-111.

"Picasso at 90". AN 70.6 (Oct, 1971): 29, 68-69.

"Reviews and Previews". AN 70.6 (Oct, 1971).

"Willem de Kooning". ANA 37 (Oct, 1971): 117-128; reprinted in RS: 181-187.

"Reviews and Previews". AN 70.7 (Nov, 1971).

"Underneath the Archness" (Editorial about the SoHo art community). AN 70.7 (Nov, 1971): 29.

"Where Have All the Eggplants Gone?, by Raymond Mason". AN 70.7 (Nov, 1971): 72.

"Reviews and Previews". AN 70.8 (Dec, 1971).

"Reviews and Previews". AN 70.9 (Jan, 1972).

"North Light". AN 70.10 (Feb, 1972): 44-45, 71-72.

"Reviews and Previews". AN 70.10 (Feb, 1972).

"Brice Marden". AN 71.1 (Mar, 1972): 26-27, 64-66; reprinted in RS: 212-216.

"Indian Summer of Frank Duveneck". AN 71.2 (Apr, 1972): 27-29, 69-71.

"Absence and Illusion" (Work of Esteban Vicente). AN 71 (May, 1972): 32-33, 60-62.

"Taking Care of the Luxuries" (With David Kermani, a discussion of the Shiraz Festival of arts). *Saturday Review* 55 (Nov 4, 1972): 60-63.

"In the American Grain" (Review of *The Collected Poems of John Wheelwright,* and A.R. Ammons's *Collected Poems, 1951-1971* and *Tape for the Turn of the Year*). *New York Review of Books* (Feb 22, 1973): 3-6.

"Dash, Dodd and Rose at FAR, Green Mountain and Landmark". *Art in America* 62.2 (Mar-Apr, 1974): 108-110.

"Esteban Vicente". AN (May, 1974); reprinted in RS: 203-208.

"R.B. Kitaj at Marlborough". *Art in America* 62.3 (May-June, 1974): [103].

"The New Old Masters". *New York* 7.29 (Jul 22, 1974): 52-53.

"Cultured Pearls". *New York* 7.31 (Aug 5, 1974): 62.

"Rivette Masterpiece(s?)" (Review of Jacques Rivette's *Out One/Spectre*). *SoHo Weekly News* (New York) 2.3 (Oct 24, 1974): 24-26.

"Yves Tanguy". *Art in America* 62.6 (Nov-Dec, 1974): 71-75; reprinted in RS: 19-27.

"Bottoms Up". *New York* 8.4 (Jan 27, 1975): 66-67.

"What a Life!" (From the Introduction to E.V. Lucas and George Morrow's *What a Life!*). *Horizon* (New York) 17.1 (Jan, 1975): 107-[112].

"Jess". *Art in America* 63.2 (Mar-Apr, 1975): 89-90; reprinted in RS: 294-296.

"Jane Freilicher at Fischbach". *Art in America* 63.3 (May-Jun, 1975): 92-93.

"What a Life!" (Satirical novel composed of engravings from an illustrated catalog). *Horizon* 17 (Winter, 1975): 107-112.

"Fairfield Porter". *Art in America* (Jan, 1976); reprinted in RS: 312-313.

"Anne Dunn". *Arts Magazine* (Mar, 1977); reprinted in RS: 166-168.

"1976 and All That" ("America 1976 at the Brooklyn Museum"). *New York* 11 (Apr 3, 1978): 63-64.

"John Cage and Jules Olitski". *New York* (Apr 10, 1978); reprinted in RS: 221-224.

"Rome Away from Home" (Artists in Rome in the Eighteenth Century at the Metropolitan). *New York* 11 (Apr 17, 1978): 86-88.

"Lucian Freud: Beyond the Pleasure Principle" (Show at Davis & Long Gallery). *New York* 11 (Apr 24, 1978): 96-97.

"New Dine in Old Bottles" (Exhibition at New York's Pace Gallery). *New York* 11 (May 22, 1978): 107-109.

"Trashing the Sixties" (Young American Artists at the Guggenheim). *New York* 11 (May 29, 1978): 64-65.

"Joyful Noise" (Solo show at the Tibor de Nagy Gallery). *New York* 11 (Jun 5, 1978): 91-92.
"Emblazoned Shields" (Paintings, prints, and constructions at the Paula Cooper Gallery). *New York* 11 (Jun 12, 1978): 97-99.
"Fabergé of Funk" (Exhibition at the Whitney). *New York* 11 (Jun 19, 1978): 63-64.
"Pleasures and Palaces" (Screens at Japan House Gallery in New York City). *New York* 11 (Jun 26, 1978): 64+.
"Forging Ahead" (Spanish Forger exhibition at the Morgan Library). *New York* 11 (Jul 3, 1978): 63-64.
"Out of the Ashes: Pompeii A.D. 79". *New York* 11 (Jul 17, 1978): 65-66+.
"Everything's Coming up Poses" (Imperial China: Photography 1846-1912). *New York* 11 (Jul 24, 1978): 62-63.
"Great Kahn" (Show at the Drawing Center). *New York* 11 (Jul 31, 1978): 58-59.
"Art About Art". *New York* (Aug 7, 1978); reprinted in RS: 249-251.
"Birds on the Wing Again". *New York* 11 (Sep 11, 1978): 90-91.
"Art" (Show at the Holly Solomon Gallery in New York City). *New York* 11 (Sep 18, 1978): 88-89.
"Piranesi and Michaux". *New York* (Sep 25, 1978); reprinted in RS: 327-330.
"Gift from the Nile" (Temple of Dendur). *New York* 11 (Oct 9, 1978): 157-159.
"Anxious Architecture". *New York* 11 (Oct 16, 1978): 161-163.
"Environmental Art". *New York* (Oct 16, 1978); reprinted in RS: 342-345.
"Frank Lloyd Wright". *New York* (Oct 23, 1978); reprinted in RS: 321-323.
"MOMA's Matisse" (Museum of Modern Art's collection exhibition). *New York* 11 (Nov 13, 1978): 148-150.
"Second Chance for the Second Empire" (Philadelphia Museum Exhibit). *New York* 11 (Nov 20, 1978): 100-101.
"Living Legend". *New York* 11 (Dec 4, 1978): 149-150.
"Abstract Expressionism: the Formative Years". *New York* (Dec 11, 1978); reprinted in RS: 257-260.
"Japanese Folk Art". *New York* (Jan 8, 1979); reprinted in RS: 370-372.
"Ut Pictura Poesis" (Exhibition at New York's Fischbach Gallery). *New York* 12 (Jan 22, 1979): 58-59.
"Climbing the Wallpaper" (New Image Painting at the Whitney). *New York* 12 (Jan 29, 1979): 103-104.
"Sweet Arshile, Bless Your Dear Heart" (Exhibition at the Newark Museum). *New York* 12 (Feb 5, 1979): 52-53.
"Visionary Drawings of Architecture and Planning". *New York* (Feb 12, 1979); reprinted in RS: 331-333.
"Victorian High Renaissance". *New York* (Feb 26, 1979); reprinted in RS: 67-70.
"Neil Welliver and Alex Katz". *New York* (Mar 12, 1979); reprinted in RS: 231-232.
"Perennial Biennial" (Whitney Biennial). *New York* 12 (Mar 19, 1979): 70+.
"Make Mine Munch" (Exhibit at the Museum of Modern Art). *New York* 12 (Apr 9, 1979): 68-69.
"R.B. Kitaj". *New York* (Apr 16, 1979); reprinted in RS: 299-301.
"Fantastic British Illustration and Design". *New York* (Apr 23, 1979); reprinted in RS: 379-381.
"Country Idyll: a Rustic Complex in New York's Hudson Valley". *Architectural Digest* 36.3 (Apr, 1979): 133-139.
"Icing on the Divine Cake" (Fragonard's drawings at the Frick Collection). *New York* 12 (May 7, 1979): 90+.
"From Russia with Golubov" (Show at Tibor de Nagy Gallery, New York City). *New York* 12 (May 14, 1979): 72-73.
"James Bishop". *New York* (May 21, 1979); reprinted in RS: 102-105.
"High Tea" (Tea ceremony and other arts at Japan House). *New York* 12 (May 28, 1979): 92-94.
"The Japanese Tea Ceremony". *New York* (May 28, 1979); reprinted in RS: 366-369.
"Resurrection of Elihu" (Brooklyn Museum exhibition). *New York* 12 (Jun 18, 1979): 62+.
"Alien Porn" (Exhibition of erotic Japanese prints at the Ronin Gallery). *New York* 12 (Jun 25, 1979): 61-62.
"Textiles and Pattern Art". *New York* (Jul 2, 1979); reprinted in RS: 373-375.
"Sculpture in Gardens". *New York* (Jul 23, 1979); reprinted in RS: 355-357.
"Art" (Marion Wolcott and David Plowden show at the Witkin Gallery). *New York* 12 (Jul 30, 1979): 55-56.
"Fabrics of Life" (Indonesian textiles at Asia House). *New York* 12 (Jul 30, 1979): 55-56.
"Old Folks at Home" (Seven Artists in Israel, 1948-78). *New York* 12 (Aug 13, 1979): 66-67.
"Telling It on the Mountain" (Prospect Mountain Sculpture Show in New York State). *New York* 12 (Aug 27, 1979): 83-84.
"Capital Gains" (Art of Russia, 1800-1850 at the Renwick Gallery, Washington, D.C.). *New York* 12 (Sep 3, 1979): 56-57.
"Patrick Henry Bruce". *New York* 12 (Sep 10, 1979); reprinted in RS: 112-115.
"Art" (Fall preview). *New York* 12 (Sep 17, 1979): 46-47.
"Two Worlds and Their Ways" (Shows at Grey Gallery and Artists' Choice Museum). *New York* 12 (Sep 24, 1979): 88+.
"From Italy, via Russia, con Amore" (From Leonardo to Titian: Italian Renaissance Paintings from the Hermitage). *New York* 12 (Oct 1, 1979): 106+.
"Blake and the Fuseli Circle". *New York* 12 (Oct 8, 1979); reprinted in RS: 71-73.
"Aldo Rossi". *New York* (Oct 15, 1979); reprinted in RS: 334-336.
"Larry Rivers". *New York* 12 (Oct 29, 1979); reprinted in RS: 217-220.
"Gewgaws a Go-Go" (American Renaissance at the Brooklyn Museum). *New York* 12 (Nov 5, 1979): 80-81.
"Chardin". *New York* 12 (Nov 12, 1979); reprinted in RS: 46-48.

"American Socialist and Symbolist Painting". *New York* 12 (Nov 19, 1979); reprinted in RS: 261-263.
"Socialists and Symbolists" (Realist Exhibitions: the Working American and American Imagination and Symbolist Painting). *New York* 12 (Nov 19, 1979): 92+.
"Last of the Red-Hot MOMAs" (Show called "Art of the Twenties"). *New York* 12 (Dec 10, 1979): 140+.
"Still Lives". *New York* 12 (Dec 3, 1979): 94+.
"Crowd Teasers". *New York* 12 (Dec 17, 1979): 106-107.
"Fly with the Baron" (Collection of Baron Thyssen-Bornemisza of the National Gallery). *New York* 12 (Dec 24, 1979): 70+.
"Japanning of Japan" (Show at Japan House). *New York* 13 (Jan 14, 1980): 61-62.
"Case of the Reluctant Polymath" (Show of R. Burckhardt's work at Gotham Book Mart Gallery). *New York* 13 (Jan 28, 1980): 64-65.
"Puttin' on the Brits" (British Art Now at the Guggenheim). *New York* 13 (Feb 4, 1980): 50+.
"Metaphysical Overtones". *New York* 13 (Feb 11, 1980): 72-73.
"Punch Lines" (Domenico Tiepolo's Punchinello series at the Frick). *New York* 13 (Feb 18, 1980): 80.
"Charles Gleyre". *New York* 13 (Feb 25, 1980): 56+.
"Gourmet Goulash" (Tibor de Nagy's personal collection at Lubin House). *New York* 13 (Feb 25, 1980): 56.
"Marvin Torffield" (Central Park). *New York* 13 (Mar 3, 1980): 99.
"Pleasures of Paperwork" (New work on paper at the Museum of Modern Art). *Newsweek* 97 (Mar 16, 1981): 93-94.
"American Ceramics". *New York* 13 (Mar 17, 1980); reprinted in RS: 376-378.
"On Winter's Traces" (Six New York art exhibitions). *New York* 13 (Mar 24, 1980): 58+.
"Marsden Hartley". *New York* 13 (Mar 31, 1980); reprinted in RS: 116-119.
"Joys in the Attic" (Opening of the André Meyer Galleries at the Metropolitan Museum). *New York* 13 (Apr 7, 1980): 74-75.
"Carl Andre". *New York* 13 (Apr 14, 1980); reprinted in RS: 229-230.
"Major Andre". *New York* 13 (Apr 14, 1980): 97-98.
"David Hockney" (Grey Gallery). *New York* 13 (Apr 28, 1980): 53.
"From the Bronze Age to the Age of Anxiety" (Metropolitan Museum of Art). *New York* 13 (Apr 28, 1980): 52-53.
"The Camden Town Painters". *New York* 13 (May 5, 1980); reprinted in RS: 74-77.
"Vanessa Bell". *New York* 13 (May 5, 1980): 49.
"Picasso: the Art" (Museum of Modern Art). *New York* 13 (May 12, 1980): 28+.
"Brussels Sprouts". *New York* 13 (May 19, 1980): 68+.
"Georges Vantongerloo" (Corcoran Gallery). *New York* 13 (May 19, 1980): 70.
"Joseph Shannon". *New York* 13 (Jun 2, 1980); reprinted in RS: 287-293.
"Lives of Our Time". *New York* 13 (Jun 2, 1980): 54.
"The Metropolitan Museum of Art's American Wing". *New York* 13 (Jun 16, 1980); reprinted in RS: 264-267.
"Horace Vernet" (Ecole des Beaux-Arts). *New York* 13 (Jun 23, 1980): 52+.
"Jean Hélion" (Galerie Karl Flinker). *New York* 13 (Jun 23, 1980): 52.
"Paris: Looking Backward". *New York* 13 (Jun 23, 1980): 52+.
"Looking Good on Paper". *New York* 13 (Jun 30, 1980): 58-59.
"The Drawing Center" (New York). *New York* 13 (Jun 30, 1980): 59.
"William Sommer" (Robert Miller Gallery, New York). *New York* 13 (Jun 30, 1980): 58+.
"Owen Morrel". *New York* 13 (Jul 18, 1980); reprinted in RS: 351-354.
"Robert Wilson's Drawings". *New York* 13 (Jul 18, 1980); reprinted in RS: 349-350.
"Léon Spilliaert". *New York* 13 (Aug 4, 1980); reprinted in RS: 155-157.
"Tal Streeter" (Japan House, New York). *New York* 13 (Aug 4, 1980): 51.
"Baroque Is Back". *New York* 13 (Aug 11, 1980): 54+.
"Wallpaper". *New York* 13 (Sep 8, 1980); reprinted in RS: 382-385.
"Edward Hopper's Full Range of Styles Is Coming to the Whitney". *New York* 13 (Sep 22, 1980): 38+.
"Ramshackle Kennels Glimpsed by Moonlight". *New York* 13 (Oct 6, 1980): 61.
"Edwin Dickinson". *New York* 13 (Oct 13, 1980); reprinted in RS: 209-211.
"Rodrigo Moynihan". *Newsweek* (Oct 27, 1980); reprinted in RS: 163-165.
"Art of Future Shock" ("Futurism and the International Avant-Garde"). *Newsweek* (Nov 10, 1980): 118-119.
"The Realist Tradition". *Newsweek* (Nov 17, 1980); reprinted in RS: 37-40.
"Time Machines" (The Clockwork Universe at the Smithsonian's National Museum of American History). *Newsweek* (Nov 24, 1980): 100.
"Fine Art of German Angst" (Guggenheim Museum's show). *Newsweek* (Dec 1, 1980): 114-115.
"Cornell's Sublime Junk". *Newsweek* (Dec 8, 1980): 110-111.
"Spaced-out Rosenquist". *Newsweek* (Feb 9, 1981)· 84.
"Flat Becomes Beautiful" (Exhibition at Toronto's Art Gallery of Ontario called Vincent van Gogh and the Birth of Cloisonism). *Newsweek* (Feb 16, 1981): 93+.
"Exhilarating Mess" (Directions 1981 at the Hirshhorn, the Whitney Biennial and 19 artists – emergent Americans

at the Guggenheim). *Newsweek* (Feb 23, 1981): 82-83.
"Artists' Valentines: an Atlantic Portfolio" (Illustration). *Atlantic* 247 (Feb, 1981): 65+.
"The Sculpture of Space" (Whitney Museum of American Art). *New York* 13 (Mar 3, 1980): 98+.
"God and Man at Yale" (Alumni show at Yale Art Gallery). *Newsweek* (Mar 30, 1981): 88-89.
"Back to the Drawing Board". *Newsweek* (Apr 6, 1981): 92-93.
"André Derain". *Newsweek* (Apr 20, 1981); reprinted in RS: 151-154.
"Red Grooms". *Newsweek* (Apr 20, 1981); reprinted in RS: 225-228.
"R.B. Kitaj". *Art in America* (Jan, 1982): 130-135; reprinted in RS: 301-308.
"Don't Look Down" (O. Morrel's Boomerang). *Newsweek* (Feb 1, 1982): 77.
"Lords of the Three Rings". *Newsweek* (Feb 1, 1982): 76.
"Master of Land and Sky". *Newsweek* (Feb 15, 1982): 94-95.
"A Brilliant New Alice" ("B. Moser's illustrations for *Alice in Wonderland*"). *Newsweek* (Mar 1, 1982): 74-75.
"The Storm over the Fogg". *Newsweek* (Mar 15, 1982): 81.
"The Look of Music" (Exhibit of John Cage's musical notation engravings). *Newsweek* (Mar 22, 1982): 80.
"Portraits and Puzzles". *Newsweek* (Apr 5, 1982): 79-80.
"A de Chirico Retrospective". *Newsweek* (Apr 12, 1982); reprinted in RS: 401-404.
"Jess". *Newsweek* (Apr 24, 1982); reprinted in RS: 296-298.
"Painting Becomes Theatre". *Newsweek* (Apr 24, 1982): 63.
"Fairfield Porter". *Newsweek* (Jan 24, 1983): 309-312.
"Things As They Are" (Fairfield Porter). *New York Review of Books* (Feb 3, 1983): 30-32.
"John F. Peto". *Newsweek* (Mar 14, 1983): reprinted in RS: 78-80.
"Siah Armajani". *Newsweek* (Apr 4, 1983); reprinted in RS: 346-348.
"A Prisoner of His Own Fame?" (Metropolitan Museum of Art, New York). *Newsweek* (May 23, 1983): 71+.
"An Artist's Daring Dream House". *House and Garden* (May, 1983): 98-109.
"Chinese Firecrackers" (Asian Art Musuem, San Francisco). *Newsweek* (Jun 13, 1983): 75+.
"Beyond 'American Gothic'". *Newsweek* (Jul 4, 1983): 80+.
"Fantin-Latour". *Newsweek* (Jul 18, 1983); reprinted in RS: 49-51.
"Jasper John" (Castelli Gallery, New York). *Newsweek* (Feb 27, 1984): 81.
"Balthus". *Newsweek* (Mar 5, 1984): 88+.
"Reflections of Nature: Flowers in American Art". *Newsweek* (Mar 19, 1984): 95.
"Houston Comes to Paris: the Amazing Menil Collection Is Unveiled Not at Home But Abroad". With Tessa Namuth. *Newsweek* (Apr 23, 1984): 60+.
"The Eyes of Texas" (Dominique de Menil's art collection). With Tessa Namuth. *Newsweek* (Apr 23, 1984): 62.
"An International Survey of Recent Painting and Sculpture". *Newsweek* (May 21, 1984): 90.
"Gallé's Vases". *Newsweek* (May 28, 1984); reprinted in RS: 363-365.
"Bonnard". *Newsweek* (Jul 16, 1984); reprinted in RS: 54-57.
"Abstract Art in America 1927-44". *Newsweek* (Jul 30, 1984); reprinted in RS: 268-270.
"Two Serious Ladies". *New York Times Book Review* (Sep 30, 1984): 46.
"Poets and Art". *Artforum International* 23 (Nov, 1984): 86.
"The Prinzhorn Collection". *Newsweek* (Feb 11, 1985); reprinted in RS: 271-273.
"The Parisian Primitive: a New Exhibition Celebrates Rousseau's Naive Genius" (Henri Rousseau, Museum of Modern Art, New York). *Newsweek* (Feb 25, 1985): 83+.
"Dark-Horse Painter: a Major New Show Reveals the Many Facets of Stubbs" (George Stubbs; Yale University. Center for British Art, New Jersey). *Newsweek* (Mar 11, 1985): 79+.
"Rediscovering the Landscape" (Jane Freilicher, Neil Welliver, Fischbach Gallery, New York). *Newsweek* (Apr 1, 1985): 77.
"A Spotlight on Class: Tissot Is That Rarity: a Society Painter Back in Vogue". *Newsweek* (May 27, 1985): 76+.
"Banality Made Beautiful" (Jean Dubuffet). Obituary. *Newsweek* (May 27, 1985): 75.
"Jennifer Bartlett". *Newsweek* (Jun 10, 1985); reprinted in RS: 233-235.
"Fragments of Celestial Trash" (Kurt Schwitters retrospective, Museum of Modern Art). *Newsweek* (Jul 1, 1985): 59.
"Representation Abroad". *Newsweek* (Jul 22, 1985); reprinted in RS: 274-276.
"Trevor Winkfield". *Art in America* (Jun, 1986); reprinted in RS: 169-173.
"Sarah Winchester's Llanda Villa". *House & Garden* (Mar, 1987): 148-153; reprinted in RS: 337-341.
"Darragh Park at Tibor de Nagy". *Art in America* 75 (May, 1987): 186.
"Robin Utterback at Tibor de Nagy". *Art in America* 75 (Jun, 1987): 152.
"Fantastic Voyages: Joe Shannon's Paintings Are Crowded with Nearly Inexplicable References, Gestures and Events: the 'Unconscious Made Real'". *Art in America* 75.12 (Dec, 1987): 148+.
"Under the Volcano" (Francesco Clemente). *Interview* 18.3 (Mar, 1988): 62+.
"On Inspiration" (Authors writings about their sources of inspiration: John Ashbery, John Barth, Saul Bellow, John Berryman, Guillermo Cabrera Infante, Erskine Caldwell, Truman Capote, Joyce Cary John Cheever, James Dickey, Joan Didion, E.L. Doctorow, J.P. Donleavy, William Faulkner and Joseph Heller). *Paris Review*

116

30.107 (Summer, 1988): 233+.

"Tales of the Hudson River Valley: Local Landmarks Embody Centuries of Life in a Patrician Preserve". *House & Garden* 164.4 (Apr, 1992): 158-167.

"By Indirection" (Mark Ford's *Landlocked*). *PN Review* 19.3 (Jan-Feb, 1993): 63-64.

"Guest Speaker: John Ashbery: the Poet's Hudson River Restoration". *Architectural Digest* 51 (Jun, 1994): 36+.

"Frederic Church at Olana: an Artist's Fantasy on the Hudson River". *Architectural Digest* 54.6 (Jun, 1997): 60+.

"Moderately". *New Yorker* 74.4 (Mar 16, 1998): 68+.

"Thomas Lovell Beddoes". *Brick* 61 (Winter, 1998): 50-51.

"Images" (Time capsule image selection). Mark Crispin Miller, John Szarkowski, John Waters, Arthur C. Danto, Andrew Ross, Ingrid Sischy, Luc Sante, Peter Arnell and John Ashbery. *New York Times Magazine* (Dec 5, 1999): 184.

"The Enabler" (Rudy Burckhardt). *New York Times Magazine* (Jan 2, 2000): 20.

"The Book That No One Knows". *New York Review of Books* 47.15 (Oct 5, 2000): 38-41.

"More Hocketing". *Iowa Review* 30.2 (Fall, 2000): 87+.

"Le Nouvel Esprit". *L'Oeil de Boeuf* 22 (a special issue devoted to John Ashbery) (Paris) (Dec, 2000): 63.

"John Clare: 'Grey Openings Where the Light Looks Through'". OT (2000): 1-22.

"Olives and Anchovies. The Poetry of Thomas Lovell Beddoes". OT (2000): 23-44.

"The Bachelor Machines of Raymond Roussel". OT (2000): 45-68.

"'Why Must You Know?' The Poetry of John Wheelwright". OT (2000): 69-94.

"'The Unthronged Oracle'. Laura Riding". OT (2000): 95-120.

"David Schubert. 'This Is the Book That No One Knows'". OT (2000): 121-146.

"F.T. Prince". *PN Review* 29.1 (147) (Sep-Oct, 2002): 33-34.

CONTRIBUTIONS

The Coconut Milk. Play; scenes 1 and 2. *Semi-Colon*, 2.3 (1956?): 4.

The Coconut Milk. Play; scenes 3 and 4. *Semi-Colon*, 2.5-6 (1956?): 5-6.

Artists' Theatre: Four Plays, edited by Herbert Machiz. Contains John Ashbery's *The Heroes*, Lionel Abel's *Absalom*, Frank O'Hara's *Try! Try!*, and James Merrill's *The Bait*. New York: Grove Press, 1960.

The Hasty Papers, edited by Alfred Leslie. Contains the plays, *To the Mill* and *The Compromise*. New York: Alfred Leslie, 1960.

Dunn, Anne. *Catalogue of an Exhibition of Recent Paintings by Anne Dunn*. Preface. London: The Leicester Galleries, 1962.

Niki de Sainte-Phalle. 48-line statement for exhibition catalogue. Paris: Galerie Rive Droite, 1962.

Richard Lucas. Contains "Richard Lucas". Musée des Arts Décoratifs, Gand, April 7-22, 1962. Brussels: Guiaux, 1962.

Rivers, Larry. *Larry Rivers – Paris*. 32-line statement. Paris: Galerie Rive Droite, 1962.

Rivers, Larry. *Rivers*. Statement (a revised version of the referred to in the entry above). London: Gimpel Fils Gallery, 1962.

Sidney Janis Presents an Exhibition of Factual Paintings and Sculpture from France, England, Italy, Sweden and the United States. Preface. New York: Sidney Janis Gallery, 1962.

The New Realists. Preface to exhibition catalogue. New York: Sidney Janis Gallery, 1962; reprinted in RS: 81-83.

Alain Jacquet. 34-line statement for exhibition catalogue. London: Robert Fraser Gallery, 1963.

Beryl Barr-Sharrar. 14-line statement for exhibition catalogue. Kauserlautern, Germany: The Gallery, [1963].

Alice Baber. 32-line statement for exhibition catalogue. Paris: Galerie de la Librairie Anglaise, 1963; reprinted in *Alice Baber*. New York: Fine Arts Museum of the Women's Interart Center, 1975: 17.

James Bishop. 23-line statement for exhibition catalogue. Brussels: Galerie Smith, 1963.

Dictionary of Modern Painting, edited by Carlton Lake and Robert Maillard. Entries by Ashbery for Stuart Davis, Charles Demuth, Arthur G. Dove, Marsden Hartley, Morris Hirshfield, Hans, Hofmann, Stanton Macdonald-Wright, Grandma Moses, Joseph Pickett, Maurice Prendergast, Man Ray, Morgan Russell, Société Anonyme, Niles Spencer, Joseph Stella, Bradley Walker Tomlin, Max Weber. London: Methuen, 1964; New York: Tudor, 1964; Toronto: Bonellie, 1964.

Hervé Télémaque, Paintings, Klaus Geissler, Space Chambers: 10 March-11 April 1964. Hanover Gallery. Statement for exhibition catalogue. London: Hanover Gallery, 1964.

Ipousteguy: 14 July-29 August, 1964. Introduction for exhibition catalogue. London: Hanover Gallery, 1964.

Jacquet. Statement for exhibition catalogue. New York, Alexander Iolas Gallery, 1964.

Martial Raysse. 31-line statement for exhibition catalogue. New York: Alexander Iolas, 1964.

Munford (Robert W. Munford). Foreword for exhibition catalogue. Hanover: Galerie Dieter Brusberg, 1964.

Bertholo. 39-line statement for exhibition catalogue. Paris: Galerie Mathias Fels & CIE, 1965.

Francis Salles. 16-line statement for exhibition catalogue. Paris: Galerie Eirope, 1965.

Joe Brainard. Statement for exhibition catalogue. New York: The Alan Gallery, 1965.

Perreault, John. *Camouflage*. Introduction. New York: Lines Books, 1966.

What's Happening: the Arts 1966, Princeton University, April 22-23, 1966. Princeton, New Jersey: Nassau Lit, 1966.

American Masters: Art Students League. Notes on Edwin Dickinson and Roy Lichtenstein. New York: Art Students League, 1967.

Anne Dunn. 13-line statement for exhibition catalogue. New York: Fischbach Gallery, 1967.

Frank Roth's. 24-line statement for exhibition catalogue. New York: Martha Jackson Gallery, 1967.

An Exhibition of Recent Accumulations by Arman. Introduction for exhibition catalogue. New York: Sidney Janis Gallery, 1968.

Arman. A 59-line statement for exhibition catalogue. New York: Sidney Janis Gallery, 1968.

Racelle Strick. 14-line statement for exhibition catalogue. Bridgehampton, New York: The Benson Gallery, 1968.

Linda Lindeberg. Statement for exhibition catalogue. New York: Stanley Moss & Co., 1969.

Larry Rivers and The Marlborough Gallery Invite You to the Opening of Larry's Exhibition Which Will Cover His Work over the Past Five Years. Invitation. Text by John Ashbery. New York, New York: Frank O'Hara Foundation, 1970.

Alex Katz, edited by Irving Sandler and Bill Berkson. Contains the review of Katz by Ashbery which appeared in *Art News* in Oct, 1970. London, New York and Washington: Praeger Publishers, 1971.

Jon Carsman. Statement for exhibition catalogue. New York: Graham Gallery, 1971.

Recent Paintings by Robert Dash: November 5 - November 28, 1971. Foreword for exhibition catalogue. Allentown, Pennsylvania: Allentown Art Museum, 1971.

Robert Dash. Foreword for exhibition catalogue. Pennsylvania: Allentown Art Museum, 1971.

Stephen Antonakos. 5-line statement for exhibition catalogue. Oshkosh, Wisconsin: Allen Priebe Art Gallery, Wisconsin State University, 1971.

O'Hara, Frank. *The Collected Poems of Frank O'Hara*, edited by Donald Allen. Introduction. New York: Knopf, 1971.

John MacWhinnie. 23-line statement for exhibition catalogue. New York: Borgenicht Gallery, 1974.

Yves Tanguy. Essay entitled "Tanguy – the Geometer of Dreams". New York: Acquavella Galleries Inc, 1974.

Brainard-Freeman Notebooks, edited by Phil Smith. Introductions by John Ashbery and Phil Demeyes. New York: Gegenschein, 1975.

Lucas, E.V. and George Morrow. *What a Life: an Autobiography*. Introduction. New York: Dover Publications, 1975.

Mark Tobey. Introduction for exhibition catalogue. New York: M. Knoedler, 1976.

Roussel, Raymond. *How I Wrote Certain of My Books*, translated by Trevor Winkfield. Contains "On Raymond Roussel". New York: Sun, 1977.

Apparitions: Poems. Northridge, California: Lord John Press, 1981.

Fairfield Porter (1970-1975): Realist Painter in an Age of Abstraction. Contains "Fairfield Porter". New York: New York Graphics Society, 1982: 7-13; reprinted in RS: 313-317.

Louisa Matthiasdottir. Introduction. New York: R. Schoelkopf Gallery, 1982.

Kitaj, R. B. *Kitaj: Paintings, Drawings, Pastels*. Essay. Washington, D.C.: Smithsonian Institution, 1981; New York: Thames and Hudson, 1983.

"Schubert's Unfinished". *Quarterly Review of Literature Poetry Series, 40th Anniversary Issue: David Schubert: Works and Days*, edited by Theodore Weiss and Reneé Weiss (1983).

"Red's Hero Sandwich". *Red Grooms, a Retrospective, 1956-1984: Essays by Judith E. Stein, John Ashbery, and Janet K. Cutler*. Philadelphia: Pennsylvania Academy of the Fine Arts, 1985: 15-17.

Foucault, Michel. *Death and the Labyrinth: the World of Raymond Roussel*, translated by Charles Ruas. Contains "On Raymond Roussel" (the same essay appeared in the 1977 edition of Raymond Roussel's *How I Wrote Certain of My Books*, above, and was reprinted from "Re-Establishing Raymond Roussel" in *Portfolio and ArtNews Annual* 6 (Autumn, 1962). Garden City, New York: Doubleday, 1986; London: The Athlone Press, 1987.

Jane Freilicher Paintings. Contains "Jane Freilicher". New York: Taplinger Publishing Company, 1986; reprinted in RS: 239-245.

Nell Blaine Sketchbook. Contains "Nell Blaine". New York: The Arts Publisher, 1986; reprinted in RS: 236-235.

Allain, Marcel and Pierre Souvestre. *Fantomas*. Introduction. New York: Morrow, 1986; London: Picador, 1987.

Joe Brainard: Selections from the Butts Collection at UCSD. La Jolla, California: Mandeville Gallery, University of California, San Diego, 1987.

Artist Books of Kaldewey Press: the Metropolitan Museum of Art, Thomas J. Watson Library, New York, September 6-December 2, 1988. Text, John Ashbery ... [et al]. Illustrations, Carl Apfelschnitt ... [et al]. Poestenkill, New York: Kaldewey Press, 1988.

Poets on Painters: Essays on the Art of Painting by Twentieth-Century Poets, edited by J.D. McClatchy. Contains "Respect for Things as They Are" (this is the same article that appeared as "Fairfield Porter" in *Fairfield Porter (1970-1975)* above). Berkeley, Los Angeles and London: University of California Press, 1988: 247-254.

A Joseph Cornell Album. New York: Da Capo Press, 1989.

Jane Hammond: New Paintings 1990: Wetterling Gallery, Gothenburg, December 15-January 27, 1990-91.

Essay. Göteborg: Wetterling Gallery, 1990.

Bridge Book. Minneapolis: Walker Art Center and Minnesota Center for Book Arts, 1991.

Morrel, Owen. *Owen Morrel: April 25-June 1, 1991*. Introduction. New York: Philippe Staib Gallery, 1991.

Ellsworth Kelly: Plant Drawings. Essay. New York, New York: Matthew Marks Gallery, 1992.

Joan Mitchell 1992. Foreword. New York: Robert Miller Gallery, 1993.

Ford, Mark. *Soft Sift*. Foreword. New York: Harcourt Brace, 1993.

Fisher, Sandra and Thomas Meyer. *Monotypes & Tracings: German Romantics*. Introduction. London: Enitharmon Press, 1994.

Jane Freilicher: March 1995. Essay. New York: The Fischbach Gallery, 1995.

Kertess, Klaus. *Whitney Museum of American Art. 1995 Biennial Exhibition*. With contributions by John Ashbery... [et al]. New York: Whitney Museum of American Art; distributed by Harry N. Abrams, 1995.

Roussel, Raymond. *How I Wrote Certain of My Books and Other Writings*, edited by Trevor Winkfield. Introduction (the same essay appeared as "On Raymond Roussel" in the 1977 edition of Raymond Roussel's *How I Wrote Certain of My Books*, and in Michel Foucault's *Death and the Labyrinth*, above, and was reprinted from "Re-Establishing Raymond Roussel" in *Portfolio and ArtNews Annual* 6 (Autumn, 1962). Introduction. Boston: Exact Change, 1995.

Mapplethorpe, Robert. *Pistils*. Essay. London: Jonathan Cape, 1996; New York: Random House, 1996.

The Heavy Bear: Delmore Schwartz's Life Versus His Poetry: a Lecture Delivered at the Sixty-Seventh General Meeting of the English Literary Society of Japan on 21st May 1995. Tokyo: English Literary Society of Japan, 1996.

Joe Brainard Retrospective: March 20 through April 19, 1997. Preface. New York: Tibor de Nagy Gallery, 1997.

The Phoenix Book Shop: a Nest of Memories, edited by Bob Wilson, Kenneth Doubrava, John LeBow. Contains pieces by Ashbery and others. With essays by Hilton Kramer and Karen Wilkin. Candia, New Hampshire: John LeBow, 1997.

Tibor de Nagy Gallery: the First Fifty Years, 1950-2000. Foreword. New York: Tibor de Nagy Gallery, 2000.

Ford, Mark. *Raymond Roussel and the Republic of Dreams*. Preface. London: Faber & Faber, 2000; New York: Cornell University Press, 2001.

Jane Hammond: the John Ashbery Collaboration, 1993–2001. With texts by John Ashbery, Ingrid Schaffner and Jill Snyder. Cleveland, Ohio: Cleveland Center for Contemporary Art, 2001.

Lewallen, Constance. *Joe Brainard: a Retrospective*. With essays by John Ashbery and Carter Ratcliff. Berkeley: University of California, Berkeley Art Museum; New York: Granary Books in association with Mandeville Special Collection Library [undated].

INTERVIEWS

"Is Today's Artist With or Against the Past?" (Interview with Stuart Davis). AN (Summer, 1958): 32-35, 59-61.

"Henri Michaux: Painter Inside Poet". AN 61.1 (Mar, 1961): 30-31, 64-65; reprinted in John Ashbery, *Reported Sightings*. Cambridge, Massachusetts: Harvard University Press, 1989: 396-400.

"Under the Mattress?" (Interview with Jean Dubuffet). Newsweek 59.9 (Feb 26, 1962): 84.

John Ashbery and Kenneth Koch: a Conversation. Tucson, Arizona: Interview Press, 1965.

"John Ashbery Interviewing Harry Mathews". *Review of Contemporary Fiction* 7.3 (Fall, 1987): 36-48.

RECORDINGS

AUDIO

Poetry Reading. John Ashbery with Richard Eberhart, Frank O'Hara, Lyon Phelps. Recorded on Feb 26, 1951 at Christ Church Parish House, Cambridge, Massachusetts. Massachusetts: Lamont Poetry Room, Harvard College Library.

Folder 1. John Ashbery with James Schuyler, Frank O'Hara, Daisy Aldan, Kenneth Koch, Grace Hartigan and Leon Hecht. Archive of Recorded Poetry and Literature (Library of Congress), 1953.

John Ashbery at the Living Theater. Recorded on Sep 16, 1963, for Harvard University. Boston, Massachusetts: Fassett Recording Studio, 1963.

Poetry Reading. John Ashbery with Barbara Guest. Recorded on Dec 1, 1966 at the Academy of American Poets. Massachusetts: Lamont Poetry Room, Harvard College Library.

Taken from a Poetry Reading given by Mr Ashbery on April 7, 1967 in Willard Straight Hall at Cornell University. Uris Library Listening Rooms, Cornell University, Ithaca, New York.

The Poetry of John Ashbery. Recorded on Mar 27, 1967, at the YM-YWHA Poetry Center, New York. New York: J. Norton, distributed by Poets' Audio Center, Washington, D.C., 1967.

Disconnected; the Dial-a-Poem Poets. New York: Giorno Poetry Systems, 1974.

John Ashbery and Kenneth Koch: a Conversation. Hollywood, California: Center for Cassette Studies, 1970.

John Ashbery, James Wright, Peter Davidson, Donald Hall, Anne Sexton and Adrienne Rich Reading Their Poems, edited by Paul Kresh. Produced by Arthur L. Klein. New Rochelle, New York: Spoken Arts, 1970.

The Poetry of John Ashbery. McGraw-Hill Sound Seminars, 1970.

John Ashbery Reading at San Diego State. With Gary Snyder. San Diego State University, 1973.

John Ashbery Reading His Poems with Comment in the Recording Studio on Jan 16, 1973. Library of Congress, Washington D.C., 1973.

John Ashbery and John Hollander Reading from Their Poetry. Recorded on Nov 11, 1973, at Modern Poetry Association's 19th Annual Poetry Day, Chicago. Chicago: Radio Station WFMT.

[John Ashbery Interviewed by David Kermani, Jun 2, 1974]. Oral History Collection, Columbia University, New York.

[John Ashbery Interviewed by Margaret Kaminski, May, 1974]. *Meet the Author Series*, Detroit Public Library, Michigan.

[John Ashbery Reading from His Poetry on Apr 28, 1975]. New York: Radio Station WBAI.

Poetry Reading. Introduction by David Lehman. Clinton, New York: M. G. Butler, 1976.

John Ashbery Reading from Houseboat Days. Recorded on May 27, 1977, at the Revelle Formal Lounge, University of California, San Diego, 1977.

John Ashbery. San Diego State University, 1978.

Poetry Reading. Recorded on Nov 9, 1978 at Harvard University. Massachusetts: Lamont Poetry Room, Harvard College Library.

What Is Poetry? New York: Encyclopedia Americana / CBS News Audio Resource Library #02782, 1978.

A Tribute to W.H. Auden. John Ashbery with others. Recorded on Oct 18, 1983, at Guggenheim Museum, New York. New York: Academy of American Poets.

Self-Portrait in a Convex Mirror. San Francisco: Arion Press, 1984. Includes original prints by Richard Avedon ... [et al]; together with a foreword by the poet, a recording of his reading of the poem and, on the album, an essay by Helen Vendler.

Memorial Service for Elizabeth Bishop. John Ashbery with others. Recorded on Oct 21, 1979, at the Agassiz Ballroom, Harvard University. Massachusetts: Lamont Poetry Room, Harvard College Library.

John Ashbery Reading at University of California, San Diego, May 9, 1985. Selections from *Three Poems, A Wave* and unpublished poems, 1985.

Attitudes Toward the Flame: Two Contemporary Poets. John Ashbery, Robert Creeley. Los Angeles: Museum of Contemporary Art, 1986.

John Ashbery. Kansas City, Missouri: New Letters, 1986.

The Work of John Ashbery. Sydney: ABC Radio, 1988.

The Songs We Know Best. Washington, D.C.: Watershed, 1989.

John Clare's Inquisitive Eye. The first of Ashbery's Charles Eliot Norton Lectures, Nov 6, 1989. Massachusetts: Lamont Poetry Room, Harvard College Library.

Olives and Anchovies: the Poetry of Thomas Lovell Beddoes. The second of Ashbery's Charles Eliot Norton Lectures, Nov 29, 1989. Massachusetts: Lamont Poetry Room, Harvard College Library.

John Ashbery, Nov. 1 1990, Poetry Collection. Introduction by Carl Dennis. Buffalo, New York: Poetry / Rare Books Collection at the State University of New York at Buffalo, 1990.

The Bachelor Machines of Raymond Roussel. The third of Ashbery's Charles Eliot Norton Lectures, Feb 14, 1990. Massachusetts: Lamont Poetry Room, Harvard College Library.

Why Do You Need to Know about the Poetry of John Wheelwright? The fourth of Ashbery's Charles Eliot Norton Lectures, Mar 7, 1990. Massachusetts: Lamont Poetry Room, Harvard College Library.

Reading Laura Riding. The fifth of Ashbery's Charles Eliot Norton Lectures, Mar 21, 1990. Massachusetts: Lamont Poetry Room, Harvard College Library.

Schubert's Unfinished. The sixth and last of Ashbery's Charles Eliot Norton Lectures, Apr 9, 1990. Massachusetts: Lamont Poetry Room, Harvard College Library.

Poets in Person. John Ashbery with David Bromwich, and Sharon Olds with Alicia Ostriker. Chicago: Modern Poetry Association, 1991.

April Galleons: Selections. John Ashbery reads from his collection, *April Galleons*. New York: [unnamed publisher], 1992.

A Sixtieth Anniversary Reading: with Chancellors of the American Academy of Poets. John Ashbery with Anthony Hecht, Daniel Hoffman, John Hollander, Richard Howard, Stanley Kunitz, William Meredith, W.S. Merwin, David Wagoner and Richard Wilbur. Recorded in the Library of Congress Montpelier Room, Washington, D.C., Sep 29, 1994. Recorded for the Archive of Recorded Poetry and Literature. Washington, D.C.: Academy of American Poets, 1994.

John Ashbery. Recorded on Mar 8, 1994, at the New School, New York. New York: Academy of American Poets, 1994.

John Ashbery. Introduced by David Lehman. New York: Academy of American Poets, 1994.

John Ashbery. "Voice of the Poet" series. Random Audio, 2001.

John Ashbery and Tony Towle Reading Their Poems in the Mumford Room, Library of Congress, Nov. 8, 2001. Washington, D.C.: Library of Congress, 2001.

The Kelly Writers House Fellows Program – John Ashbery. A recording of the Mar 26, 2002, audiocast conversation with John Ashbery, moderated by Al Filreis. http://www.english.upenn.edu/~whfellow/ashbery.html.

VIDEO

The Poetry of John Ashbery. Guilford, Connecticut: J. Norton, 1967.

Poulin Jnr., A. "The Poetry of John Ashbery". Videotaped on Nov 27, 1972 at Brockport Writers' Forum, State University of New York at Brockport.

John Ashbery Reading His Poems with Comment in the Recording Laboratory, Jan 16, 1973. Recorded for the Archive of Recorded Poetry and Literature. Contains selections from *Some Trees, The Tennis Court Oath, Rivers and Mountains, The Double Dream of Spring* and *Three Poems.*

[John Ashbery Reading from His Poetry at the San Francisco Museum of Art, May 16, 1973]. Videotape Lending Library of the Poetry Center, San Francisco State University, 1973.

Poetry Reading, Nov. 27, 1974. Recorded at the University of California, San Diego. Ashbery reads from *Double Dream of Spring, Some Trees, Self-Portrait in a Convex Mirror* and *Three Poems.*

Poetry Reading, May 14 and June 7, 1975. Introduction by Susan Howe. Recorded at WBAI Radio, New York City. Ashbery reads from *Self-Portrait in a Convex Mirror.*

John Ashbery and Charles Simic Reading and Discussing Their Poems. Recorded Nov 24, 1975, in the Coolidge Auditorium at the Library of Congress in Washington, D.C. Sponsored by the Gertrude Clarke Whittall Poetry and Literature Fund, Library of Congress, Washington, D.C. Recorded for the Archive of Recorded Poetry and Literature.

John Ashbery Reading from Houseboat Days. Recorded May 27, 1977, at the Revelle Formal Lounge, University of California, San Diego.

John Ashbery: Outtakes from the Film Series, USA: Poetry. Produced and edited by the American Poetry Archive, The Poetry Center at San Francisco State University. 2nd ed. San Francisco: The Archive, 1978.

John Ashbery Reading at San Diego State, October 12, 1978. Introduction by Fred Moramarco. Selections from *Three Poems, Self-Portrait in a Convex Mirror* and *Houseboat Days.*

Poetry and the People: John Ashbery Reading. Salem, Oregon: Chemeketa Community College, 1978.

Poetry Reading, June 1979. John Ashbery and Ann Lauterbach. Introduction by Susan Howe. Recorded at WBAI Radio, New York City. Ashbery and Lauterbach read from Ashbery's long poem "Litany".

Memorial Service for Elizabeth Bishop. Recorded Oct 21, 1979, at the Agassiz Ballroom, Harvard University. Ashbery reads Bishop's "A Miracle for Breakfast".

John Ashbery Reading at University of California, San Diego, May 9, 1985. Selections from *Three Poems, A Wave* and unpublished poems.

The Spoken Arts Treasury of 100 Modern American Poets Reading Their Poems. Vol. 17, edited by Paul Kresh. Produced by Arthur L. Klein. New Rochelle, New York: Spoken Arts, 1985.

WQXR Salute to the Arts. John Ashbery and Ned Rorem. Introduced by June LeBell and Ethel Lynn Chase. Recorded Apr 30, 1986, in New York. Sponsored by the Academy of American Poets. On deposit at the Woodberry Poetry Room, Harvard College Library.

John Ashbery and David Bottoms Reading Their Poetry. Recorded Feb 24, 1987, in the Coolidge Auditorium at the Library of Congress in Washington, D.C. Sponsored by the Gertrude Clarke Whittall Poetry and Literature Fund, Library of Congress, Washington, D.C. Recorded for the Archive of Recorded Poetry and Literature.

Poetry Reading, Nov. 20, 1989. James Schuyler and John Ashbery. Recorded at the Poetry Centre, New York City.

The Songs We Know Best. John Ashbery reads and comments on his own poetry. J. Norton Publishers' Tape Library. Guildord, CT: Jeffrey Norton, 1988.

John Ashbery, 12-5-84, Reading. San Francisco, California: The American Poetry Archive, The Poetry Center, San Francisco State University, 1990.

Harvard College Library, the Woodberry Poetry Room, 1931-1991, 60th Anniversary. John Ashbery, Stratis Haviaras, Seamus Heaney, Lucy Brock-Broido, Richard Wilbur, James Merrill, Jayne Anne Phillips, celebrate the Woodberry Poetry Room and its former curator Jack Sweeney with poems, prose and reminiscences. Woodberry Poetry Room, Harvard College Library, 1991.

A Sixtieth Anniversary Reading: with Chancellors of the Academy of American Poets. Recorded in the Library of Congress Montpelier Room, Washington, D.C., Sep 29, 1994. Recorded for the Archive of Recorded Poetry and Literature. Washington, D.C.: Library of Congress Magnetic Recording Laboratory, 1994.

Robert Creeley, a 70th Birthday Celebration: Memories of October Readings. Introduction by Susan Howe for a talk with artist Jim Dine and conversation with Robert Creeley, hosted by Charles Bernstein, and the October 12th reading by John Ashbery with an introduction by Susan Schultz. Video production by Vincent Gregory. Buffalo, New York: Vincent Gregory, 1996.

The Poetry and Dance Festival, Tribute to Lincoln Kirstein. Presented by the Poetry Society of America and the Dance Collection of the New York Public Library for the Performing Arts, 1996.

John Ashbery and Barbara Guest. Thin Air Video Presents: Poetry Video Documentation by Mitch Corber. New York: Thin Air Video, 1997.

John Ashbery: Reading, 9-13-90, and in Conversation with Kevin Killian. The American Poetry Archive, The Poetry Center, San Francisco State University. San Francisco, California: The Archive, [1990].

Something Wonderful May Happen: New York School of Poets and Beyond. David Lehman and Charles Bernstein interview two of the original New York School of Poets, John Ashbery and Kenneth Koch, who also read from their works. Interviews filmed at Joe's Pub, New York City, 2001. New York: Filmmakers Library, 2001.

The Kelly Writers House Fellows Program – John Ashbery. A digital recording of the reading from *Your Name Here* and *As Umbrellas Follow Rain* given by Ashbery on Mar 25, 2002. http://www.english.upenn.edu/ ~ whfellow/ashbery.html.

TRANSLATIONS OF BOOKS BY OTHERS

Melville. Jean-Jacques Mayoux. Evergreen Profile Book 9. New York and London: Grove Press, Inc. and Evergreen Books, Ltd., 1960.

Murder in Montmartre. Noël Vexin. Translated by John Ashbery (using pseudonym of Jonas Berry) and Lawrence G. Blockman. New York: Dell, 1960.

The Deadlier Sex. Geneviève Manceron. Translated by John Ashbery (using pseudonym of Jonas Berry) and Lawrence G. Blockman. New York: Dell, 1961.

Alberto Giacometti. Jacques Dupin. Paris: Maeght Éditeur, 1962.

EDITED AND CO-EDITED WORKS

The Harvard Advocate (CXXXI.3 - CXXXIII.1, Dec, 1947 - Sep, 1949). With others. Cambridge, Massachusetts. Periodical.

One Fourteen (VI.8 - VII.5 (?), Sep, 1952 - Jul/Aug, 1953?). New York: Oxford University Press. Periodical.

Locus Solus (1-5, Winter, 1961 - Summer (?) 1962). With Kenneth Koch, Harry Mathews and James Schuyler. Lans-en-Vercours (Isère), France: Locus Solus Press, 1961-1962. Periodical.

Art and Literature: an International Review (1-12: Mar, 1964 - Spring, 1967). With Anne Dunn, Rodrigo Moynihan and Sonia Orwell. Lausanne, Switzerland: Societe Anonyme d'Editions Litteraires et Artistiques.

Art News (LXIV.9 - LXXI.5 (Jan, 1966 - Sep, 1972). With Harris Rosenstein. New York: Newsweek.

The Grand Eccentrics. With Thomas B. Hess. New York: Collier Books, 1966.

The Academy: Five Centuries of Grandeur and Misery: from the Carracci to Mao Tse-tung. With Thomas B. Hess. New York: MacMillan Company, 1967.

Avant-Garde Art. With Thomas B. Hess. New York: Macmillan, 1968; London: Collier-Macmillan, 1968.

Light: from Aten to Laser. With Thomas B. Hess. New York: Macmillan, 1969.

Narrative Art. With Thomas B. Hess. New York: Macmillan, 1970.

Poetry Pilot (Sep, 1970). New York: Academy of American Poets.

Academic Art. With Thomas B. Hess. New York: Collier Books, 1971; London: Collier-Macmillan, 1971.

Art of the Grand Eccentrics. With Thomas B. Hess. New York: Macmillan, 1971.

Painterly Painting. With Thomas B. Hess. New York: Newsweek, 1971.

SECONDARY WORKS

BOOKS

Blasing, Mutlu Konuk. *Politics and Form in Postmodern Poetry: O'Hara, Bishop, Ashbery, and Merrill.* New York: Cambridge University Press, 1995.

Bloom, Harold. *John Ashbery.* New York: Chelsea House, 1985.

Cazé, Antoine. *John Ashbery.* Paris: Belin, 2000.

Herd, David. *John Ashbery and American Poetry.* Manchester: Manchester University Press, 2000; and as *John Ashbery and American Poetry: Fit to Cope with Our Occasions.* New York: Palgrave, 2000.

Lehman, David, Editor. *Beyond Amazement: New Essays on John Ashbery.* Ithaca and London: Cornell University Press, 1980. Bibliography, pages 285-286.

—. Editor. *John Ashbery*. Ithaca, New York: Cornell University Press, 1979.

Malanga, Gerard. *John Ashbery, 1970*. Binghamton, New York: Bellevue Press, 1979.

Reichardt, Ulfried. *Innenansichten der postmoderne: zur dichtung John Ashberys, A. R. Ammons', Denise Levertovs und Adrienne Richs*. Würzburg: Königshausen & Neumann, 1991. (Revision of The Author's Thesis (Doctoral) – Freie Universität Berlin, 1988).

Schultz, Susan M., Editor. *The Tribe of John Ashbery and Contemporary Poetry*. Tuscaloosa: University of Alabama Press, 1995.

—. Editor. *John Ashbery's Influence on Contemporary Poetry*. *Verse* (John Ashbery Special Number) 8.1 (Spring, 1991).

Shapiro, David. *John Ashbery: an Introduction to the Poetry*. New York: Columbia University Press, 1979.

Shoptaw, John. *On the Outside Looking Out: John Ashbery's Poetry*. Cambridge, Massachusetts: Harvard University Press, 1994.

ARTICLES, DISCUSSIONS, ENTRIES, ESSAYS

"A Last Word from a Poet". *Forbes* 150.6 (Sep 14, 1992): 193.

Alberola-Crespo, Nieves. "Carnival and Decadence in 'Description of a Masque'". *Irish Journal of American Studies* 8 (1999): 225-240.

—. "Reflejos de expressionismo abstracto en la obra de John Ashbery". *Proceedings of the 20th International AEDEAN Conference*. Barcelona: University of Barcelona, 1997.

Alféri, Pierre. "Un calligrame". *L'Oeil de Boeuf* 22 (a special issue devoted to John Ashbery) (Paris) (Dec, 2000): 61.

Allen, Gilbert. "When Paraphrase Fails: the Interpretation of Modern American Poetry". *College English* 43.4 (Apr, 1981): 363-370.

Altieri, Charles. "Ashbery as Love Poet". In *The Tribe of John Ashbery and Contemporary Poetry*, edited by Susan M. Schultz. Tuscaloosa: University of Alabama Press, 1995.

—. "Contemporary Poetry as Philosophy: Subjective Agency in John Ashbery and C. K. Williams". *Contemporary Literature* 33.2 (Summer, 1992): 214-242.

—. "John Ashbery and the Challenge of Postmodernism in the Visual Arts". *Critical Inquiry* 14.4 (Summer, 1988): 805-830.

—. *Self and Sensibility in Contemporary American Poetry*. Cambridge and New York: Cambridge University Press, 1984.

—. "Motives in Metaphor: John Ashbery and the Modernist Long Poem". *Genre* 11 (Winter, 1978): 653-687.

Applewhite, James. "Painting, Poetry, Abstraction, and Ashbery". *Southern Review* 24 (Spring, 1988): 272-290.

Armantrout, Rae. Not *"Literary Practitioners of Deconstruction"*. Tenerife, Spain: Secretariado de Publicaciones, Universidad de La Laguna, 1989.

Ashton, Dore. *The New York School: a Cultural Reckoning*. New York: Viking, 1973.

Atlas, James. "New Voices in American Poetry". *New York Times* 129 (Feb 3, 1980): s6 p16.

Attridge, Derek. "Rhythm in English Poetry". *New Literary History* 21 (Autumn, 1990): 1015-1037.

Auden, W.H. Foreword. *Some Trees*. New Haven, Connecticut: Yale University Press, 1956. 11-16.

Auslander, Philip. *The New York School Poets as Playwrights: O'Hara, Ashbery, Koch, Schuyler, and the Visual Arts*. New York: Peter Lang, 1989.

Bachinger, Katrina. "Setting Allegory Adrift in John Ashbery's *Mountains and Rivers*, James Joyce's *Portrait of the Artist as a Young Man*, and Vincent O'Sullivan's *Let the River Stand*". In *Trends in English and American Studies: Literature and the Imagination*, edited by Sabine Coelsch-Foisner, Wolfgang Goertschacher and Holger Klein. Lewiston, New York: Mellen, 1996.

Bacigalupo, Massimo. "A Poetry Reading in Genoa". *RSA Journal* 3 (1992): 23-32.

Barrett, Ed. "Crossroads in the Past: Techie". *Field: Contemporary Poetry and Poetics* 65 [Special Issue: John Ashbery: A Symposium] (Fall, 2001): 31-35.

Bayley, John. "The Poetry of John Ashbery". In John Bayley. *Selected Essays*. Cambridge: Cambridge University Press, 1984; reprinted in *Modern Critical Views: John Ashbery*, edited by Harold Bloom. New York: Chelsea House Publishers, 1985: 195-205.

Benfey, Christopher. "The Limits of Fun". *New Republic* (Jan 4-11, 1999): 37+.

—. "Portraits and Puzzles". *New Republic* 204.24 (Jun 17, 1991): 42-48.

Bennett, Guy. "Traduction de la poésie/poésie de la traduction". *L'Oeil de Boeuf* 22 (a special issue devoted to John Ashbery) (Paris) (Dec, 2000): 71.

Bensko, J. "Reflexive Narration in Contemporary American-Poetry: Some Examples from Mark Strand, John Ashbery, Norman Dubie and Louis Simpson". *Journal of Narrative Technique* 16.2 (1986): 81-96.

Bergan, Brooke. "'A Wedge in Time': the Politics of Photography". *Antioch Review* 48.4 (Fall, 1990): 309-324.

Bergman, David. Introduction to John Ashbery's *Reported Sightings: Art Chronicles 1957-1987*, edited by David Bergman. New York: Knopf, 1989: xi-xxiii.

—. "Choosing Our Fathers: Gender and Identity in Whitman, Ashbery and Richard Howard". *American Literary History* 1.2 (Summer, 1989): 383-403.

Bernstein, Charles. "Afterword: the Influence of Kinship Patterns upon Perception of an Ambiguous Stimulus". In *The Tribe of John Ashbery and Contemporary Poetry,* edited by Susan M. Schultz. Tuscaloosa: University of Alabama Press, 1995.

Berger, Charles. "Vision in the Form of a Task: *The Double Dream of Spring*". In *Beyond Amazement: New Essays on John Ashbery,* edited by David Lehman. Ithaca and London: Cornell University Press, 1980: 163-208; reprinted in *Modern Critical Views: John Ashbery,* edited by Harold Bloom. New York: Chelsea House Publishers, 1985: 145-178.

Bernard, Sarah. "Little Darlings: Poet John Ashbery Gets Inspired by ... Henry Darger's Visions of Girlish Apocalypse?". *New York* 32.13 (Apr 5, 1999): 14.

Berrigan, Ted. "The Business of Writing Poetry: Vol. 1" in *Talking Poetics from Naropa Institute: Annals of the Jack Kerouac School of Disembodied Poetics,* edited by Anne Waldman, Anne Webb and Allen Ginsberg. Boulder, Colorado: Shambhala, 1978.

Berry, Jonas. "Ashbery, John (Lawrence) 1927-". *Contemporary Authors,* New Revision Series 102. Detroit: Gale Group, 2002: 40-51.

"Between the Lines". *New York* 13 (May 12, 1980): 9.

Bienvenu, Roberta. "'The Whole Is Admirably Composed': John Ashbery's Autobiographical Project". *Crazyhorse* 51 (Wintrer, 1996): 70-83.

"Biographie de John Ashbery". *L'Oeil de Boeuf* 22 (a special issue devoted to John Ashbery) (Paris) (Dec, 2000): 30.

Blasing, Mutlu Konuk. *Politics and Form in Postmodern Poetry: O'Hara, Bishop, Ashbery, and Merrill.* Cambridge, England; New York: Cambridge University Press, 1995.

Bloom, Harold. "The Breaking of Form". In *Modern Critical Views: John Ashbery,* edited by Harold Bloom. New York: Chelsea House Publishers, 1985. 115-126.

—. Introduction to *Modern Critical Views: John Ashbery,* edited by Harold Bloom. New York: Chelsea House Publishers, 1985: 1-16.

—. "John Ashbery: the Charity of the Harsh Moments". *Salmagundi* 22-23 (1973): 103-131; reprinted in *American Poetry Since 1960: Some Critical Perspectives,* edited by Robert B. Shaw; reprinted in *Figures of Capable Imagination.* New York: Seabury Press, 1976. 169-209; reprinted in *Modern Critical Views: John Ashbery,* edited by Harold Bloom. New York: Chelsea House Publishers, 1985: 49-79.

—. "Measuring the Canon: 'Wet Casements' and 'Tapestry'". In *Modern Critical Views: John Ashbery,* edited by Harold Bloom. New York: Chelsea House Publishers, 1985: 217-232.

Bogan, Louise. *A Poet's Alphabet: Reflections on the Literary Art and Vocation,* edited by Robert Phelps and Ruth Limmer. New York: McGraw-Hill, 1970.

Boyers, Robert. "A Quest Without an Object". *Times Literary Supplement* (Sep 1, 1978): 962-963.

Bradley, George. "Foreword: a Short Article or Poem in Response to the Work". In *The Tribe of John Ashbery and Contemporary Poetry,* edited by Susan M. Schultz. Tuscaloosa: University of Alabama Press, 1995.

Breslin, Paul. "Warpless and Woofless Subtleties". *Poetry* (Oct, 1980).

Bromwich D. "John Ashbery: the Self Against Its Images". *Raritan* 5.4 (1986): 36-58; reprinted in David Bromwich, *Skeptical Music: Essays on Modern Poetry.* Chicago and London: Chicago University Press, 2001: 185-204.

—. "Poetic Invention and the Self-Unseeing". *Grand-Street* 7.1 (Autumn, 1987): 115-129; reprinted in David Bromwich, *Skeptical Music: Essays on Modern Poetry.* Chicago and London: Chicago University Press, 2001: 19-31.

Brossard, Olivier. "Entretien avec John Ashbery". *L'Oeil de Boeuf* 22 (a special issue devoted to John Ashbery) (Paris) (Dec, 2000): 7.

Brown, Dennis. "John Ashbery's 'A Wave' (1983). Time and Western Man". In *Poetry and the Sense of Panic: Critical Essays on Elizabeth Bishop and John Ashbery,* edited by Lionel Kelly. Amsterdam and Atlanta: Rodopi, 2000: 65-73.

Brown, Merle. "Poetic Listening". *New Literary History* 10 (1978): 125-139.

Brownstein, M.L. "Postmodern Language and the Perpetuation of Desire". *Twentieth-Century Literature* 31.1 (Spring, 1985): 73-88.

Carney, Raymond. "John Ashbery". *Dictionary of Literary Biography,* Vol. 5.1. Detroit: Gale Group, 1980: 14-20.

Carroll, Paul. "If Only He Had Left from the Finland Station". In *The Poem in Its Skin.* Chicago and New York: Follett Publishing Company, 1968: 6-26.

Carvalho, Sílvia Maria de Magalhães. *The Desire to Communicate: Reconsidering John Ashbery and the Visual Arts.* Frankfurt am Main; New York: Peter Lang, 2000.

—. "The Indifference of Two True Aesthetes: Marcel Duchamp and John Ashbery". In *Pioneering North America: Mediators of European Culture and Literature,* edited by Klaus Martens and Andreas Hau. Wutzburg: Konigshausen & Neumann, 2000.

Caws, Mary-Anne. "Strong-Line Poetry: Ashbery's Dark Edging and the Lines of the Self". In *The Line of Postmodern*

Poetry, edited by Robert J. Frank and Henry M. Sayre. Urbana: University of Illinois, 1988.

—. "A Slant on Surrealism: Aesthetics as Preparation". *Proceedings of the 10th Congress of the International Comparative Literature Association* 2 (1985).

Cazé, Antoine. "D'un regard critique sur l'Amérique en general à travers la poésie en particulier". *L'Oeil de Boeuf* 22 (a special issue devoted to John Ashbery) (Paris) (Dec, 2000): 83.

Champion, Miles. *PN Review* 21.1 (Sep-Oct, 1994): 40-41.

Clark, Kevin. "John Ashbery's 'A Wave': Privileging the Symbol". *Papers on Language and Literature* 26.2 (Spring, 1990): 271-279.

Clary, Killarney. "In Doubt and Thus Alive". *Yale Review* 79 (Spring, 1990): 323-327.

Cohen, Keith. "Ashbery's Dismantling of Bourgeois Discourse". In *Beyond Amazement: New Essays on John Ashbery*, edited by David Lehman. Ithaca and London: Cornell University Press, 1980: 128-149.

Colbert, Benjamin. "Romantic Entabglements: Ashbery and the Fragment". In *Poetry and the Sense of Panic: Critical Essays on Elizabeth Bishop and John Ashbery*, edited by Lionel Kelly. Amsterdam and Atlanta: Rodopi, 2000: 41-51.

Connor, Steven. "Points of Departure: Deconstruction and John Ashbery's 'Sortes Vergilianae'". In *Contemporary Poetry Meets Modern Theory*, edited by Anthony Easthope and John Thompson. Hemel Hempstead: Harvester Wheatsheaf, 1991: 5-18.

Contemporary Literary Criticism. Detroit: Gale, Volume 2, 1974; Volume 3, 1975; Volume 4, 1975; Volume 6, 1976; Volume 9, 1978; Volume 13, 1980; Volume 15, 1980; Volume 25, 1983; Volume 41, 1988; Volume 77, 1993.

Cook, Albert. "Expressionism Not Wholly Abstract: John Ashbery". *American Poetry* 2.2 (Winter, 1985): 53-70.

Corn, Alfred. "A Magma of Interiors". In *Modern Critical Views: John Ashbery*, edited by Harold Bloom. New York: Chelsea House Publishers, 1985: 81-89.

Costello, Bonnie. "John Ashbery's Landscapes". In *The Tribe of John Ashbery and Contemporary Poetry*, edited by Susan M. Schultz. Tuscaloosa: University of Alabama Press, 1995.

—. "John Ashbery and the Idea of the Reader". *Contemporary Literature* 23.4 (Fall, 1982): 493-514.

Cott, Jonathan. "The New American Poetry". In *The New American Arts*, edited by Richard Kostelanetz. New York: Horizon, 1965: 146-152.

Cottom, Daniel. "Ashbery's 'Down by the Station Early in the Morning'". *Explicator* 52.4 (Summer, 1994): 245-248.

—. "'Getting It': Ashbery and the Avant-Garde of Everyday Language". *SubStance* 23.1 (1994): 3-23.

Crase, Douglas. "The Prophetic Ashbery". In *Beyond Amazement: New Essays on John Ashbery*, edited by David Lehman. Ithaca and London: Cornell University Press, 1980: 30-65; reprinted in *Modern Critical Views: John Ashbery*, edited by Harold Bloom. New York: Chelsea House Publishers, 1985: 127-143.

Dacey, Philip. "Lovers: Poetry and Music". *Mid-American Review* 11.1 (1991): 234-237.

Davie, Donald. "Poetry as 'Taking a Stand'". *Shenandoah* 29.2 (1978): 45-52.

Dayan Joan. "Finding What Will Suffice: John Ashbery's 'A Wave'". *Modern Language Notes* 100.5 (1985): 1045-1079.

Dewey, Anne. "The Relation Between Open Form and Collective Voice: The Social Origin of Processual Form in John Ashbery's *Three Poems* and Ed Dorn's *Gunslinger*". *Sagetrieb* 11.1-2 (Spring-Fall, 1992): 47-66.

Di Piero, W.S. "Lowell and Ashbery". *Southern Review* 14 (1978): 359-367.

—. "John Ashbery: the Romantic as Problem Solver". *American Poetry Review* (Jul-Aug, 1973): 39-42.

Dictionary of Literary Biography, Volume 5, *American Poets Since World War II*. Detroit: Gale, 1978.

Dictionary of Literary Biography, Volume 165, *American Poets Since World War II*, Fourth Series. Detroit: Gale, 1996.

Dictionary of Literary Biography Yearbook, 1981. Detroit: Gale, 1982.

Digby A. "Three Modern American Acquisitions (By the British Library, Mark Twain's 'Memory Builder', Ezra Pound's A 'Lume Spento', and John Ashbery's 'Turandot and Other Poems')". *British Library Journal* 23.1 (Spring, 1997): 102-104.

Donaldio, Stephen. "Some Younger Poets in America". In *Modern Occasions*, edited by Philip Rahv. New York: Farrar, Strauss and Giroux, 1966: 241-243.

Donoghue, Denis. "Sign Language". *New York Review of Books* 26.21-22 (Jan 24, 1980): 36-39.

DuBois, Andrew Lee. "John Ashbery's Harvard Education, 1945-1949". *Harvard Review* 22 (Spring, 2002).

Edelman, Lee. "The Pose of Imposture: Ashbery's 'Self-Portrait in a Convex Mirror'". *Twentieth-Century Literature* 32 (Spring, 1986): 95-114.

Edenfield, Olivia Carr. "Ashbery's 'Untilted'". *Explicator* 56.1 (Fall, 1997): 41-44.

Ehrenpreis, Irvin. "Boysenberry Sherbet". *New York Review of Books* (Oct 16, 1975): 3-4.

Eichbauer, Mary E. *Poetry's Self-Portrait: the Visual Arts as Mirror and Muse in René Char and John Ashbery*. New York: Peter Lang, 1992.

Engel, Bernard. "On John Ashbery's 'Self-Portrait in a Convex Mirror'". *Notes on Modern American Literature* 2 (1977): item 4.

Epstein, Andrew. "Frank O'Hara's Translation Game". *Raritan* 19.3 (Winter, 2000): 144-161.

Ernest, John. "Fossilized Fish and the World of Unknowing: John Ashbery and William Bronk". In *The Tribe of John Ashbery and Contemporary Poetry,* edited by Susan M. Schultz. Tuscaloosa: University of Alabama Press, 1995.

Erwin, John W. "The Reader Is the Medium: Ashbery and Ammons Ensphered". *Contemporary Literature* 21 (Autumn, 1980).

Evans, Cynthia. "John Ashbery: 'A Moment Out of the Dream'". *American Poetry Review* 8 (1979).

Everett, Barbara. "Distraction vs Attraction". *London Review of Books* 24.12 (Jun 27, 2002): 7-10.

Everett, Nicholas. "Ashbery's Humour". *PN Review* 21.1 (Sep-Oct, 1994): 44-45.

Federman, Raymond. "Self, Voice, Performance, in Contemporary Writing". In *Coherence,* edited by D. Wellman. Cambridge, Massachusetts: OARS, 1981.

Fein, Esther B. "End Notes" (John Ashbery wins Antonio Feltrinelli International Prize for Poetry). *New York Times* 142 (Nov 18, 1992): B4(N), C26(L).

Fink, Thomas A. "The Poetry of David Shapiro and Ann Lauterbach: After Ashbery". *American Poetry Review* 17 (Jan-Feb, 1988): 27-32.

—. "The Comic Thrust of Ashbery's Poetry". *Twentieth-Century Literature* 30 (Spring, 1984): 1-14.

—. "'Here and There': the Locus of Language in John Ashbery's 'Self-Portrait in a Convex Mirror'". *Contemporary Poetry* 4.3 (1982): 47-64.

Finkelstein, Norman. "'Still Other Made-Up Countries': John Ashbery and Donald Revell". *Verse* 8.1 (Spring, 1991): 33-35.

Fite, David. "John Ashbery: the Effort to Make Sense". *Missouri Review* 2.2-3 (Spring, 1979): 123-130.

—. "On the Virtues of Modesty: John Ashbery's Tactics Against Transcendence". *Modern Language Quarterly* 42.1 (March, 1981): 65-84.

Ford, Mark. "John Ashbery and Raymond Roussel". *Verse* 3.1 (Nov, 1986): 13-23.

—. "A New Kind of Emptiness". *PN Review* 21.1 (Sep-Oct, 1994).

—. "Ashbery, John (1927-)". In *Oxford Companion to 20th-Century Poetry,* edited by Ian Hamilton. Oxford and New York: Oxford University Press, 1996: 18-19.

—. "Mon opinion à l'heure actuelle". *L'Oeil de Boeuf* 22 (a special issue devoted to John Ashbery) (Paris) (Dec, 2000): 56.

—. "Mont d'Espoir or Mount Despair: Early Bishop, Early Ashbery, and the French". *PN Review* 23.4 (Mar-Apr, 1997); reprinted in *Poetry and the Sense of Panic: Critical Essays on Elizabeth Bishop and John Ashbery,* edited by Lionel Kelly. Atlanta: Rodopi, 2000: 9-27.

Forrest-Thomson, Veronica. *Poetic Artifice: a Theory of Twentieth-Century Poetry.* Manchester: Manchester University Press, 1978.

Francis, Richard. "Weather and Turtles in John Ashbery's Recent Poetry". *PN Review* 21.1 (Sep-Oct, 1994): 45-47.

Fredman, Stephen. *Poet's Prose: the Crisis in American Verse.* Cambridge; New York: Cambridge University Press, 1983; 2nd ed. Cambridge; New York: Cambridge University Press, 1990.

—. "An Open, Habitable Space: Poetry 1991". *Contemporary Literature* 33.4 (Winter, 1992): 712(24).

—. "Bishop and Ashbery: Two Ways out of Stevens". *The Wallace Stevens Journal* 19.2 (Fall, 1995): 201-218.

—. "John Ashbery's New Voice". *Regions of Unlikeness: Explaining Contemporary Poetry.* Lincoln: University of Nebraska Press, 1999: 73-112.

Gardini, Nicola. "Éloge de la poésie mineure". *L'Oeil de Boeuf* 22 (a special issue devoted to John Ashbery) (Paris) (Dec, 2000): 107.

Gardner, Thomas. "Bishop and Ashbery: Two Ways Out of Stevens." *The Wallace Stevens Journal* 19.2 (Fall, 1995): 201-218.

Gery, John. " The Anxiety of Affluence: Poets after Ashbery". *Verse* 8.1 (Spring, 1991): 28-32.

—. "Ashbery's Menagerie and the Anxiety of Affluence". In *The Tribe of John Ashbery and Contemporary Poetry,* edited by Susan M. Schultz. Tuscaloosa: University of Alabama Press, 1995.

Getz, Thomas H. "The Self-Portrait in the Portrait: John Ashbery's 'Self-Portrait in a Convex Mirror' and Henry James's 'The Liar'". *Studies in the Humanities* 13.1 (Jun, 1986): 42-51.

—. "En Route to Annihilation, John Ashbery's 'Shadow Train'". *Concerning Poetry* 20 (1987): 99-116.

Gilbert, Roger. "A.R. Ammons and John Ashbery: the Walk as Thinking". In *Critical Essays on A.R. Ammons,* edited by Robert Kirschten. New York: G.K. Hall; London: Prentice Hall International, 1997.

Gilson, Annette. "Disseminating 'Circumference': the Diachronic Presence of Dickinson in John Ashbery's 'Clepsydra'". *Twentieth-Century Literature* 44.4 (Winter, 1998): 484-505.

Govrin, Nurit. "Milim Mehapshot Mashma'ut". *Monthly of the Association of Hebrew Writers* 55.4-5 (1982): 30-31.

Gray, Jeffrey. "Ashbery's 'The Instruction Manual'". *Explicator* 54.2 (Winter, 1996): 117-120.

Gregerson, Linda. "Among the Wordstruck". In *Negative Capability: Contemporary American Poetry,* edited by Linda Gregerson. Ann Arbor: University of Michigan Press, 2001.

Gregson, Ian. "The Influence of John Ashbery in Britain". *PN Review* 21.1 (Sep-Oct, 1994): 52-53.

—. "Epitaphs for Epigones: John Ashbery's Influence in England". *Bete Noire* 4 (Winter, 1987): 89-94.

Guillory, Daniel L. "'Leaving the Atocha Station': Contemporary Poetry and Technology". *TriQuarterly* 52 (Fall, 1981): 165-182.

Hamilton, David. "On 'Can You Hear, Bird,' by John Ashbery". *Iowa Review* 26.3 (Fall, 1996): 201(3).

Hamilton, Sharon. "Modern Poetry and Rock 'n Roll: Comparing John Ashbery and *Led Zeppelin*". *Mid-Atlantic Almanack* 7 (1998): 67-77.

Harmon, William. "Orphic Bankruptcy, Deficit Spending". *Parnassus* 8.1 (1980): 213-220.

Harris L. "Affronted by Ashbery" (A reader's response to the book review by James Fenton of John Ashbery's *Selected Poems*). Letter. *New York Times Book Review* (Feb, 1986): 40.

Heffernan, James A.W. *Museum of Words: the Poetics of Ekphrasis from Homer to Ashbery.* Chicago and London: University of Chicago Press, 1993.

—. "Entering the Museum of Words: Ashbery's 'Self-Portrait in a Convex Mirror'". In *Pictures into Words: Theoretical and Descriptive Approaches to Ekphrasis*, edited by V. Robillard and E. Jongeniel. Netherland: VU University Press, 1999.

Henry, Gerrit. "It's Delightful, It's Delicious, It's Deluxe (Collaboration of Painter and Poet on a Book)" *Print Collector's Newsletter* 15 (May-Jun, 1984): 45-47.

—. "The System". *Art International* 15 (Oct, 1971): 75.

Herbert, W.N. "Ashbery and O'Hara: Their Respective Selves". *Verse* 3.3: 24-32.

—. "Variable Coins". *PN Review* 83.3: 15-16.

Herd, David. "John Ashbery: 'Self-Portrait in a Convex Mirror'". In *A Companion to Twentieth-Century Poetry,* edited by Neil Roberts. Oxford: Blackwell, 2001.

—. "Occasions for Solidarity: Ashbery, Riley, and the Tradition of the New". *Yearbook of English Studies* 30 (2000): 234-249.

—. "'And Time Shall Force a Gift on Each': Ashbery, Pasternak and the Expression of the Avant Garde". *Critical Quarterly* 40.4 (Winter, 1998): 47-64.

Hilbert, Ernest. "Bold Type: Essay on John Ashbery". http://www.randomhouse.com/boldtype/0701/ashbery/ essay.html.

Hoeppner, Edward Haworth. *Echoes and Moving Fields: Structure and Subjectivity in the Poetry of W. S. Merwin and John Ashbery.* Lewisburg, Pennsylvania: Bucknell University Press; London; Cranbury, New Jersey: Associated University Presses, 1994.

—. "Visual Gestalt and John Ashbery's 'Europe'". *Concerning Poetry* 20 (1987): 87-97.

—. "Shadows and Glass: Mirrored Selves in the Poetry of W. S. Merwin and John Ashbery". *Philological Quarterly* 65 (Summer, 1986): 311-334.

Holden, Jonathan. "A Tone Poem: Rude Colour". *Field: Contemporary Poetry and Poetics* 65 [Special Issue: John Ashbery: A Symposium] (Fall, 2001): 38-42.

—. "Syntax and the Poetry of John Ashbery". *American Poetry Review* 8.4 (Jul-Aug, 1979): 37-40.

—. "Visual Gestalt and John Ashbery's Europe". *Concerning Poetry* 20 (1987): 87-97.

Hollander, John. "The Lenore Marshall Prize". *Nation* 241 (Oct 19, 1985): 386(3).

—. "A Poetry of Restitution". *Yale Review* 70 (Winter, 1981): 161(25); reprinted in John Hollander, *The Work of Poetry.* New York: Columbia University Press, 1997: chapter 3.

—. "Soonest Mended". In *Modern Critical Views: John Ashbery,* edited by Harold Bloom. New York: Chelsea House Publishers, 1985: 207-215.

Hoover, Paul. "Fables of Representation: Poetry of the New York School". *American Poetry Review* 31.4 (Jul-Aug, 2002): 20(11).

Horvath B. "Dwelling in Persuasion - John Ashbery's Dream of Life". *Ball State University Forum* 25.4 (1984): 55-62.

Howard, Richard. "Sortes Vergilianae". *Poetry* 117 (Oct, 1970): 50-53; reprinted in Richard Howard, *Alone with America: Essays on the Art of Poetry in the United States Since 1950.* New York: Atheneum, 1980: 18-37.

—. "*Three Poems* by John Ashbery". *Poetry* (Aug, 1972): 296-298; reprinted in Richard Howard, *Alone with America: Essays on the Art of Poetry in the United States Since 1950.* New York: Atheneum, 1980: 47-49.

—. "*Houseboat Days* by John Ashbery". *New York Arts Journal* (1977); reprinted in Richard Howard, *Alone with America: Essays on the Art of Poetry in the United States Since 1950.* New York: Atheneum, 1980: 52-56.

—. "John Ashbery". In *Modern Critical Views: John Ashbery,* edited by Harold Bloom. New York: Chelsea House Publishers, 1985: 17-47.

—. and Mott, M. "Comment". *Poetry* 127 (Mar, 1976): 349-351.

—. and Murray, P. "Comment". *Poetry* 120 (Aug, 1972): 296-268.

Howell, Anthony. "Ashbery in Perspective". *PN Review* 21.1 (Sep-Oct, 1994): 56-57.

Hughes, S. John. "Insights and Oversights in the Poetic Vision". *Saturday Review* 53 (Aug 8, 1970): 33.

Hulse, Michael. "John Ashbery". *PN Review* 21.1 (Sep-Oct, 1994): 58-59.

"I Would Like to Have Written ...". *New York Times* 131 (Dec 6, 1981): s7, 7.

Imbriglio, Catherine. "'Our Days Put on Such Reticence': the Rhetoric of the Closet in John Ashbery's *Some Trees*". *Contemporary Literature* 36.2 (Summer, 1995): 249-288.

Jackson, Richard. "Nomadic Time: the Poetry of John Ashbery". In Richard Jackson, *The Dismantling of Time in*

Contemporary Poetry. Tuscaloosa: University of Alabama Press, 1988: 141-186.

—. "Many Happy Returns: the Poetry of John Ashbery". *Ploughshares* 12.3 (Fall, 1986): 3-13.

—. "John Ashbery's *A Wave*: Winner of Poetry Prize". (Leonore Marshall Poetry Prize) *New York Times* 135 (Oct 11, 1985): 29(N), C28(L).

—. "Writing As Transgression: Ashbery's Archaeology of the Moment". *Southern Humanities Review* 13.3 (1978): 279-284.

Johnson, Patricia A. "The Speculative Character of Poetry". *CEA Critic* 49.2-4 (Winter-Summer, 1986-1987): 18-24.

Jones, Peter. "John Ashbery, Born 1927". In Peter Jones, *An Introduction to Fifty American Poets*. London and Sydney: Pan Books, 1979: 334-339.

Kalstone, David. "John Ashbery: Self-Portrait in a Convex Mirror". In David Kalstone, *Five Temperaments*. New York: Oxford University Press, 1977: 170-203; reprinted in *Modern Critical Views: John Ashbery*, edited by Harold Bloom. New York: Chelsea House Publishers, 1985: 91-114.

—. "Reading John Ashbery's Poems". *University of Denver Quarterly* 10.4 (1976): 6-34.

Kaneseki, Hisao. "Kaiga to Shi: John Ashbery no Baai". *Eigo Seinen*: 108-109.

Kavanagh, P.J. "The Subjective School". *Spectator* (Feb 11, 1989): 43.

Kazin, Alfred. "Robert Lowell and John Ashbery: the Difference Between Poets". *Esquire* 89 (Jan, 1978): 20+.

Keeling, John. "The Moment Unravels: Reading John Ashbery's 'Litany'". *Twentieth-Century Literature* 38.2 (Summer, 1992): 125-151.

Keller, Lynn. *Re-Making It New: Contemporary Poetry and the Modernist Tradition*. Cambridge: Cambridge University Press, 1987.

—. "'Thinkers Without Final Thoughts': John Ashbery's Evolving Debt to Wallace Stevens". *English Literary History* 49 (Spring, 1982).

Kelly, Lionel, Editor. *Poetry and the Sense of Panic: Critical Essays on Elizabeth Bishop and John Ashbery*. Atlanta, Georgia: Rodopi, 2000.

Keniston, Ann. "'The Fluidity of Damaged Form': Apostrophe and Desire in Nineties Lyric". *Contemporary Literature* 42.2 (Summer, 2001): 294(31).

Kennedy, Robert C. "John Ashbery". *Art International* 17.2 (Feb, 1973): 62-68.

Kermani, David. "Pourquoi je n'ai pas réactualisé la bibliographie d'Ashbery au cours des vingt-cinq dernières années". *L'Oeil de Boeuf* 22 (a special issue devoted to John Ashbery) (Paris) (Dec, 2000): 101.

Kevorkian, Martin. "John Ashbery's 'Flow Chart': John Ashbery and the Theorists on John Ashbery Against the Critics Against John Ashbery". *New Literary History* 25.2 (Spring, 1994): 459-476.

Kinzie, Mary. "'Irreference': the Poetic Diction of John Ashbery, Part II: Prose, Prosody, and Dissembled Time". *Modern Philology* 84 (May, 1987): 382-400.

—. "Styles of Avoidance; 'Irreference': the Poetic Diction of John Ashbery, Part I". *Modern Philology* 84 (Feb, 1987): 267-281.

Koch, Kenneth. *Rose, Where Did You Get That Red?* New York: Random House, 1973.

Koch, Stephen. "Games of the Poet". *Nation* 203 (Dec 12, 1966): 649-650.

—. "The New York School of Poets: the Serious at Play". *New York Times Book Review* (Feb 11, 1968): 4-5.

Koethe, John. "The Absence of a Noble Presence". In *The Tribe of John Ashbery and Contemporary Poetry*, edited by Susan M. Schultz. Tuscaloosa: University of Alabama Press, 1995; reprinted in John Koethe, *Poetry at One Remove: Essays*. Ann Arbor: University of Michigan Press, 2000: 52-61.

—. "The Metaphysical Subject of John Ashbery's Poetry". In *Beyond Amazement: New Essays on John Ashbery*, edited by David Lehman. Ithaca and London: Cornell University Press, 1980: 87-100; reprinted in John Koethe, *Poetry at One Remove: Essays*. Ann Arbor: University of Michigan Press, 2000: 15-28.

Kostelanetz, Richard. "How to Be a Difficult Poet". *New York Times Magazine* (May 23, 1976): 18-33; reprinted in Richard Kostelanetz. *The Old Poetries and the New*. Ann Arbor: University of Michigan Press, 1979.

Kramer, Lawrence. *Music and Poetry: the Nineteenth Century and After*. Berkeley: University of California Press, 1984.

—. "'Syringa': John Ashbery and Elliott Carter". In *Beyond Amazement: New Essays on John Ashbery*, edited by David Lehman. Ithaca and London: Cornell University Press, 1980: 255-271.

Kunow, Rudiger. "'You Have It but You Don't Have It': John Ashbery's Guarded Affirmations of Life". In *Affirmation and Negation in Contemporary American Culture*, edited by Gerhard Hoffman and Alfred Hornung. Heidelberg: Carl Winter Universitätsverlag, 1994: 251-271.

Larrissy, Edward. "'Is Anything Central': Ashbery and the Idea of a Centre". In *Poetry and the Sense of Panic: Critical Essays on Elizabeth Bishop and John Ashbery*, edited by Lionel Kelly. Amsterdam and Atlanta: Rodopi, 2000: 75-85.

Lauterbach, Ann. "'A Blessing in Disguise': Enlightened Trust". *Field: Contemporary Poetry and Poetics* 65 [Special Issue: John Ashbery: A Symposium] (Fall, 2001).

Leary, Paris and Robert Kelly, Editors. *A Controversy of Poets*. New York: Doubleday, 1965.

Leckie, Ross. "Art, Mimesis and John Ashbery's 'Self Portrait in a Convex Mirror'". *Essays in Literature* 19.1 (Spring, 1992): 114-131.

Leddy, Michael. "Lives and Art: John Ashbery and Henry Darger". *Jacket* 17 (2002). http://jacketmagazine.com/ 17/leddy-ashb.html.

Lehman, David. *The Last Avant-Garde: the Making of the New York School of Poets*. New York: Doubleday, 1999.

—. "John Ashbery: the Pleasures of Poetry". *New York Times Magazine* (Nov 16, 1984): 84-89.

—. Introduction. In *Beyond Amazement: New Essays on John Ashbery*, edited by David Lehman. Ithaca and London: Cornell University Press, 1980: 15-29.

—. "The Shield of a Greeting: the Function of Irony in John Ashbery's Poetry". In *Beyond Amazement: New Essays on John Ashbery*, edited by David Lehman. Ithaca and London: Cornell University Press, 1980: 101-127.

Lepkowski, Frank J. "John Ashbery's Revision of the Post-Romantic Quest: Meaning, Evasion, and Allusion in 'Grand Galop'". *Twentieth-Century Literature* 39.3 (Fall, 1993): 251-265.

Lieberman, Laurence. "Unassigned Frequencies: Whispers out of Time". *American Poetry Review* (Mar-Apr, 1977): 4-18; reprinted in Laurence Lieberman, *Unassigned Frequencies*. Chicago: University of Illinois Press, 1977: 3-61.

Lindop, Greville. "On Reading John Ashbery". *PN Review* 4 (1977): 30-32.

Logan, William. "Author! Author!" *New Criterion* 19.4 (Dec, 2000): 65.

Lolordo, Nick. "Charting the Flow: Positioning John Ashbery". *Contemporary Literature* 42.4 (Winter, 2001): 750-774.

Londry, Michael. *Harvard Review* 17 (Fall, 1999): 85-92.

Longenbach, James. "Ashbery and the Individual Talent". *American Literary History* 9.1 (Spring, 1997): 103-127.

Looper, Travis. "Ashbery's 'Self-Portrait'". *Papers on Language and Literature* 28.4 (Fall, 1992): 451-456.

Lundquist, Sara L. "Légèreté et richesse: John Ashbery's English 'French Poems'". *Contemporary Literature* 32.3 (Fall, 1991): 403-421.

Machiz, Herbert. *Artist's Theatre. Four Plays. Try! Try!, by Frank O'Hara. The Heroes, by John Ashbery. The Bait, by James Merrill. Absalom, by Lionel Abel*. New York: Grove Press, 1960.

Malamud, Randy. "Truman Capote, 1924-1984; Supplement III, Part I: John Ashbery to Walker Percy". In *American Writers: a Collection of Literary Biographies*, edited by Lea Baechler and A. Walton Litz. New York: Scribner, 1991.

Malinowska, Barbara. *Dynamics of Being, Space, and Time in the Poetry of Czeslaw Milosz and John Ashbery*. New York: Peter Lang, 2000.

—. "Oscillation of Ergon and Parergon: Dynamic Framing Devices and Their Relations in John Ashbery's Poetry". In *Salzburg Studies in English Literature* 77:3 Salzburg, Austria: Institut für Anglistik und Amerikanistik, Universität Salzburg; Lewiston, New York: E. Mellen Press, 1993.

Martens, Klaus. "Skulptur aus Momenten über drei Gedichten von John Ashbery". *Amerikanstudien* 32.2 (1987): 155-167.

—. "Rage for Definition: the Long Poem as 'Sequence'". *Poetry and Epistemology: Turning Points in the History of Poetic Knowledge: Papers from the International Poetry Symposium, Eichstatt, 1983*. Regensburg, 1986: 350-365.

—. "Does It Emerge? Or Do We Enter in?: Aspekte des Verhaltnisses und neuester amerikanischer Lyrik als 'Horspiel'". In *Anglistentag* (1985), edited by B. Carstensen and H. Grabes. Giessen, Germany: Hoffmann, 1986.

—. "Language as Heuristic Process: the Ulysses Motif in Stevens and Ashbery". In *Poetic Knowledge: Circumference and Centre*, edited by R. Hagenbuchle and J. Swann. Bonn: Bouvier, 1980.

Mathews, Harry. "Autobiography, From The Way Home". *L'Oeil de Boeuf* 22 (a special issue devoted to John Ashbery) (Paris) (Dec, 2000): 43.

Mazur, Krystyna. "The 'Unfamiliar Stereotype': Repetition in the Poetry of John Ashbery". In *Poetry and the Sense of Panic: Critical Essays on Elizabeth Bishop and John Ashbery*, edited by Lionel Kelly. Amsterdam and Atlanta: Rodopi, 2000: 115-117.

McCabe, Susan. "Stevens, Bishop, and Ashbery: a Surrealist Lineage". *Wallace Stevens Journal* 22.2 (Fall, 1998): 148-168.

McCarthy, Penny. "About Ashbery". *PN Review* 21.1 (Sep-Oct, 1994): 63-64.

McCorkle, James. "Nimbus of Sensations: Eros and Reverie in the Poetry of John Ashbery and Ann Lauterbach". *The Tribe of John Ashbery and Contemporary Poetry*, edited by Susan M. Schultz. Tuscaloosa: University of Alabama Press, 1995.

—. *The Still Performance: Writing, Self, and Interconnection in Five Postmodern American Poets*. Charlottesville: University Press of Virginia, 1992.

McDowell, Edwin. "Ashbery and Chappell Win Yale's Bollingen Poetry Prize". *New York Times* 134 (Jan 16, 1985): 17(N), C15(L).

McDowell, Robert. "How Good Is John Ashbery?". *American Scholar* 56.2 (Spring, 1987): 275-278.

McGuinness, Patrick. "Ashbery". *PN Review* 21.1 (Sep-Oct, 1994): 64-66.

McHale, Brian. "How (Not) to Read Postmodernist Long Poems: the Case of Ashbery's 'The Skaters'" (Harshav Festschrift Issue 1). *Poetics Today* 21.3 (Fall, 2000): 561(30).

—. "Making (Non)Sense of Postmodernist Poetry". In *Language, Text, and Context: Essays in Stylistics*, edited by M. Toolan. London: Routledge, 1992.

Mead, Philip. "Memoranda of Our Feelings: John Ashbery's *A Wave*". *Scripsi* 4.1: 103-119.

Meyers, John Bernard, Editor. *The Poets of the New York School*. Philadelphia: University of Pennsylvania Press, 1969.

Middleton, Christopher. "Language Woof-Side Up". *New York Times Book Review* (Jun 17, 1984).

Miklitsch, Robert. "John Ashbery". *Contemporary Literature* 21.1 (Winter, 1980): 118-135.

Milesi, Laurent. "Figuring Out Ashbery: 'The Skaters'". *Revue Française d'Etudes Americaines* 67 (Jan, 1996): 45-57.

Miller, Chris. "Ashbery: 'What's Keeping Us Here?'". *PN Review* 21.1 (Sep-Oct, 1994): 67-68.

Miller, Stephen Paul. "Periodizing Ashbery and His Influence". In *The Tribe of John Ashbery and Contemporary Poetry*, edited by Susan M. Schultz. Tuscaloosa: University of Alabama Press, 1995.

—. "'Self-Portrait in a Convex Mirror', the Watergate Affair, and Johns's Crosshatch Paintings: Surveillance and Reality-Testing in the Mid-Seventies". *Boundary 2* 20.2 (Summer, 1993): 84-115.

Miller, Susan Hawkins. "Psychic Geometry: John Ashbery's Prose Poems". *American Poetry* 3.1 (Fall, 1985): 24-42.

Mills-Courts, Karen. *Poetry as Epitaph: Representation and Poetic Language*. Baton Rouge: Louisiana State University Press, 1990.

Mohanty S. and J. Monroe. "John Ashbery and the Articulation of the Social". *Diacritics: a Review of Contemporary Criticism* 17.2 (1987): 37-63.

Molesworth, Charles. *The Fierce Embrace: a Study of Contemporary American Poetry*. Columbia, Missouri: University of Missouri Press, 1979.

—. "'This Leaving-Out Business': the Poetry of John Ashbery". *Salmagundi* 38-39 (Summer-Fall, 1977): 20-41.

Monroe, Jonathan. "Idiom and Cliché in T.S. Eliot and John Ashbery". *Contemporary Literature* 31.1 (Spring, 1990): 17-36.

Mooneyman, Laura. "'As New Wak't': Wallace Stevens's 'Chocorua to Its Neighbour' and John Ashbery's 'Spring Day'". *South Atlantic Review* 55.2 (May, 1990): 117-129.

Moramarco, Fred. "Coming Full Circle: John Ashbery's Later Poetry". In *The Tribe of John Ashbery and Contemporary Poetry*, edited by Susan M. Schultz. Tuscaloosa: University of Alabama Press, 1995.

—. "John Ashbery and Frank O'Hara: the Painterly Poets". *Journal of Modern Literature* 5.3 (Sep, 1976): 436-462.

—. "The Lonesomeness of Words: a Revaluation of *The Tennis Court Oath*". In *Beyond Amazement: New Essays on John Ashbery*, edited by David Lehman. Ithaca and London: Cornell University Press, 1980: 150-162.

Morse, Jonathan. "Typical Ashbery". In *The Tribe of John Ashbery and Contemporary Poetry*, edited by Susan M. Schultz. Tuscaloosa: University of Alabama Press, 1995.

Mottram, Eric. "John Ashbery: 'All in the Refined Assimilable State'". *Poetry Information* 20.1 (Winter, 1979-1980): 31-48.

Mueller Robert. "John Ashbery and the Poetry of Consciousness: 'Self-Portrait in A Convex Mirror'". *Centennial Review* 40.3 (Fall, 1996): 561-572.

"Multiples and Objects and Books". *Print Collector's Newsletter* 15 (May-Jun, 1984): 67.

Munn, Paul. "Vestigial Form in John Ashbery's 'A Wave'". *New Orleans Review* 19.1 (Spring, 1992): 19-22.

Murphy, Margueritte S. *A Tradition of Subversion: the Prose Poem in English from Wilde to Ashbery*. Amherst: University of Massachusetts Press, 1992.

—. "John Ashbery's 'Three Poems': Heteroglossia in the American Prose Poem". *American Poetry* 7.2 (Winter, 1990): 50-63.

"Naming the Land". *Harper's Magazine* 269 (Aug, 1984): 37+.

Nason, Richard W. *Boiled Grass and the Broth of Shoes: Reconstructing Literary Deconstruction*. Jefferson, North Carolina: McFarland & Co., 1991.

"News Notes". *Poetry* 180.2 (May, 2002): 107+.

Nicholls, Peter. "John Ashbery and Language Poetry". In *Poetry and the Sense of Panic: Critical Essays on Elizabeth Bishop and John Ashbery*, edited by Lionel Kelly. Amsterdam and Atlanta: Rodopi, 2000: 155-167.

Norton, Jody. "'Whispers Out of Time': the Syntax of Being in the Poetry of John Ashbery". *Twentieth-Century Literature* 41.3 (Fall, 1995): 281-305.

O'Hara, Frank. "Rare Modern". *Poetry* (Feb, 1957): 310-313.

Olson, John. "The Haunted Stanzas of John Ashbery". *Talisman* 23-26 (2001-2002): 98-106.

Opello, Olivia. "John Ashbery; the Reader's Dilemma". *Publications of the Mississippi Philological Association* (1987): 79-87.

Packard, William, Editor. *The Craft of Poetry*. New York: Doubleday, 1964.

Paddon S. "John Ashbery and Haavikko, Paavo, Architects of the Postmodern Space in Mind and Language". *Canadian Review of Comparative Literature* 20.3-4 (Sep-Dec, 1993): 409-416.

"Paying Attention". *Economist* (US) 320.7724 (Sep 14, 1991): 108.

Perl, Jed. "Cabinet of Wonders". *On Paper* 2.5 (May-Jun, 1998): 4-5.

Perloff, Marjorie. "Ashbery, John (Lawrence)". *Contemporary Poets*, 6th ed. New York: St Martin's Press, 1996: 33-36.

—. "Barthes, Ashbery, and the Zero Degree of Genre". In Marjorie Perloff, *Poetic License: Essays on Modernist and Postmodernist Lyric*. Evanston, Illinois: Northwestern University Press, 1990: 267-284.

—. "'Homeward Ho!': Silicon Valley Pushkin". *American Poetry Review* (Nov-Dec, 1986): 37-46.

—. "'Mysteries of Construction': the Dream Songs of John Ashbery". In Marjorie Perloff, *The Poetics of Indeterminacy*. Princeton: Princeton University Press, 1981: 248-287.

—. "'Fragments of a Buried Life': John Ashbery's Dream Songs". In *Beyond Amazement: New Essays on John Ashbery*, edited by David Lehman. Ithaca and London: Cornell University Press, 1980: 66-86.

—. "Contemporary/Postmodern: the 'New' Poetry". *Bucknell Review* 25.2 (1980): 171-180.

—. "'Tangled Versions of the Truth': Ammons and Ashbery at Fifty". *American Poetry Review* (Sep-Oct, 1978): 5-11.

—. "'Transparent Selves': the Poetry of John Ashbery and Frank O'Hara". *Yearbook of English Studies* 8 (1978): 171-196.

Perkins, David. "Meditations on the Solitary Mind: John Ashbery and A.R. Ammons". In David Perkins, *A History of Modern Poetry: Modernism and After*. Cambridge: Harvard University Press: 619-620, 623-624, 632.

Pilling, John. "The 'Hybrid Mix' of Ashbery's *Three Poems*, or, How Not to Be French". In *Poetry and the Sense of Panic: Critical Essays on Elizabeth Bishop and John Ashbery*, edited by Lionel Kelly. Amsterdam and Atlanta: Rodopi, 2000: 119-125.

—. "Secret Sorcery: Early Ashbery". *PN Review* 21.1 (Sep-Oct, 1994): 38-40.

—. "The Other John Ashbery". *PN Review* 17.1 (Sep-Oct, 1990): 44-46.

Polletta, Gregory T. "Ashbery's Poetry and the Scenarios of Strangeness in Contemporary Criticism". In *On Strangeness*, edited by Margaret Bridges. Tübingen: Narr, 1990.

Prince, F.T. "In a Glass Darkly". *PN Review* 21.1 (Sep-Oct, 1994): 37-38.

Printz-Pahlson, Goran. "Surface and Accident: John Ashbery". *PN Review* 12.2: 34-36.

—. "Om John Ashbery". *Artes* 6 (1982): 28-33.

Prinz, Jessica. "The Non-book: New Dimensions in the Contemporary Artist's Book". *Visible Language* 25 (Spring, 1991): 289-302.

Quinn, Justin. "John Ashbery, Nature Poet". *PN Review* 21.1 (Sep-Oct, 1994): 68-70.

Quinney, Laura. *The Poetics of Disappointment: Wordsworth and Ashbery*. Charlottesville: University of Virginia Press, 1999.

Raaberg, G. Owen. "Surrealist Strategy in Mythic and Ironic Modes: the Poetry of Octavio Paz and John Ashbery". *Proceedings of the 10th Congress of the International Comparative Literature Association* 2 (1985): 321-326.

Ramke, Bin. "Just Someone to Say Hi To: Say Hello to the Nice Man". *Field: Contemporary Poetry and Poetics* 65 [Special Issue: John Ashbery: A Symposium] (Fall, 2001): 31-35.

—. "How French Is It? Recent Translations and Poems by John Ashbery". *Denver Quarterly* 29.3 (Winter, 1995): 118-124.

Rand, Richard. "'Sortes Vergiliane'". In *Contemporary Poetry Meets Modern Theory*, edited by Anthony Easthope and John Thompson. Toronto: University of Toronto Press, 1991.

Rapaport, Herman. "Deconstructing Apocalyptic Rhetoric: Ashbery, Derrida, Blanchot". *Criticism* 27.4 (Fall, 1985): 387-400.

Rawson, Claude. "Bards, Boardrooms and Blackboards: John Ashbery, Wallace Stevens and the Academization of Poetry". *PN Review* 21.1 (Sep-Oct, 1994): 71-74.

Reed J. "Blue-Sonata, the Poetry of John Ashbery". *Poetry Review* 81.1 (1991): 63-64.

—. *Blue Sonata: the Poetry of John Ashbery*. Privately printed, 1994.

Reichardt, Ulfried. "Umgangssprache und Altagsmythen in John Ashbery's Dichtung: Spiel oder Kritik?". *AAA: Arbeiten aus Anglistik und Amerikanistik* 15.1 (1990): 39-50.

—. *Innenansichten der Postmoderne: zur Dichtung Jonh Ashberys, A.R. Ammons, Denise Lvertovs und Adrienne Richs*. Wurzburg: Konigshausen & Neumann, 1991.

—. "John Ashbery" *Metzler Lexikon amerikanischer Autoren*, edited by Bernd Engler and Kurt Müller. Stuttgart, Weimar: Metzler, 2000: 34-36.

Revell, Donald. "Invisible Green V". *American Poetry Review* 31.2 (Mar, 2002): 23+.

—. "Purists Will Object: Some Meditations on Influence". In *The Tribe of John Ashbery and Contemporary Poetry*, edited by Susan M. Schultz. Tuscaloosa: University of Alabama Press, 1995.

—. "John Ashbery's Tangram". *Notes on Modern American Literature* (1977): item 12.

Richman, Robert. "Our 'Most Important' Living Poet". *Commentary* 74 (Jul, 1982): 62-68.

Rigsbee, David. "Notes on the Obscurity of John Ashbery". *Pembroke Magazine* 16 (1984): 49-53.

—. "Against Monuments: a Reading of Ashbery's 'These Lacustrine Cities'". In *Beyond Amazement: New Essays on John Ashbery*, edited by David Lehman. New York and London: Cornell University Press, 1980: 209-223.

Robinson, Peter. "'As My Way Is': John Ashbery's Gift". *PN Review* 21.1 (Sep-Oct, 1994): 71-74.

131

Roger, Oliver. "Poet in the Theatre". In *Conversations on Art and Performance,* edited by Bonnie Marranca and Gautam Dasgupta. Baltimore: Johns Hopkins, 1999.

Rognoni, Francesco. "Distanza e circondamento: un' introduzione all' opera di John Ashbery". *Confronto Letterario* 10.20 (Nov, 1993): 395-412.

Romano, John. "New Laureates". *Commentary* 60 (Oct, 1975): 54-58.

Ross, Andrew. *The Failure of Modernism: Symptoms of American Poetry.* New York: Columbia University Press, 1986.

—. "Taking *The Tennis Court Oath*". In *The Tribe of John Ashbery and Contemporary Poetry,* edited by Susan M. Schultz. Tuscaloosa: University of Alabama Press, 1995.

—. "Doubting John Thomas". In Andrew Ross, *The Failure of Modernism: Symptoms of American Poetry* (New York, 1986): chapter 6.

—. "The Alcatraz Effect: Belief and Postmodernity". *SubStance* 13.1 (1984): 71-84.

Rubinstein, Raphael. "A Muse in the Room, or Poets Are Poor". *Art Journal* 52.4 (Winter, 1993): 67-69.

Rust, Rob. "Kjaerlighetens politikk: To samta". *Vagant* 3-4 (1998), supplement: 77-86.

Saez, Richard. "'To Regain Wholeness': the Many and the One in Elliott Carter's Songs". *Parnassus* (Fall-Winter, 1982): 289-333.

Sailer, Susan Shaw. "On the Redness of Salmon Bones, the Communicative Potential of Conger Eels, and Standing Tails of Air: Reading Postmodern Images". *Word and Image* 12.3 (Jul-Sep, 1996): 308-325.

St. John, David. "'Illustration': Lustre". *Field: Contemporary Poetry and Poetics* 65 [Special Issue: John Ashbery: A Symposium] (Fall, 2001).

Salusinsky, Imre. "The Genesis of Ashbery's 'Europe'". *Notes on Modern American Literature* 7.2 (Fall, 1983): Item 12.

Sandbach, Shimon. "Keats, Altered by the Present". *Comparative Literature* 35.1 (Winter, 1983): 43-54.

Sartorius, Joachim. "Urinoir, Jar, Hasard". *Kunstforum International* 139 (Dec, 1997-Mar, 1998): 176-181.

Sayre, Henry M. "'A Recurring Wave / of Arrival': Ashbery's Endings". *Poet and Critic* 11.3 (1979): 39-44.

Schmidt, Michael. *Lives of the Poets.* London: Weidenfeld & Nicolson, 1998: 717-722.

—. "Editorial". *PN Review* 21.1 (Sep-Oct, 1994).

Schulman, Grace. "To Create the Self". *Twentieth-Century Literature* 23 (Oct, 1977): 299-313.

Schultz, Susan M. "'Returning to Bloom': John Ashbery's Critique of Harold Bloom". *Contemporary Literature* 37.1 (Spring, 1996): 24-48.

—. "Introduction". In *The Tribe of John Ashbery and Contemporary Poetry,* edited by Susan M. Schultz. Tuscaloosa: University of Alabama Press, 1995.

—. "'The Lyric Crash': the Theatre of Subjectivity in John Ashbery's *Three Poems*". *Sagetrieb* 12.2 (Fall, 1993): 137-148.

—. "Houses of Poetry after Ashbery: the Poetry of Ann Lauterbach and Donald Revell". *Virginia Quarterly Review* 67.2 (Spring, 1991): 294 + .

Shapiro, David. "Art as Collaboration: Towards a Theory of Pluralist Aesthetics". In *Artistic Collaboration in the Twentieth Century,* edited by Cynthia Jafee McCabe. Washington D.C.: Smithsonian Institute Press, 1984: 45-62.

—. "Urgent Masks: an Introduction to John Ashbery's Poetry". *Field* 5 (Fall, 1971): 32-45.

Shapiro, Marianne. "John Ashbery: the New Spirit". *Water Table* 1 (Fall, 1980): 58-73.

Shaw, Robert B., Editor. *American Poetry Since 1960: Some Critical Perspectives.* Manchester: Carcanet Press, 1973.

Shetley, Vernon Lionel. *After the Death of Poetry: Poet and Audience in Contemporary America.* Durham: Duke University Press, 1993.

—. "Language on a Very Plain Level". *Poetry* (Jul, 1982).

Shoptaw, John Clark. "The Music of Construction: Measure and Polyphony in Ashbery and Bernstein". In *The Tribe of John Ashbery,* edited by Susan M. Schultz. Tuscaloosa: University of Alabama, 1995.

—. *On the Outside Looking Out: John Ashbery's Poetry.* Cambridge, Massachusetts: Harvard University Press, 1994.

—. "James Merrill and John Ashbery". In *The Columbia History of American Poetry,* edited by Jay Parini and Brett C. Millier. New York: Columbia University Press, 1993.

—. "Investigating *The Tennis Court Oath*". *Verse* 8.1 (Spring, 1991): 61-72.

Silverberg, Mark. "Laughter and Uncertainty: John Ashbery's Low-Key Camp". *Contemporary Literature* 43.2 (Summer, 2002): 285-316.

Simon, John. "Partying on Parnassus: the New York School of Poets". *New Criterion* 17.2 (Oct, 1998): 31; reprinted in John Simon, *Dreamers of Dreams: Essays on Poets and Poetry.* Chicago: Ivan R. Dee, 2001: 32-45.

—. "More Brass Than Enduring". *Hudson Review* (Autumn, 1962).

Simpson, Louis. "Dead Horses and Live Issues". *Nation* (Apr 24, 1967): 520-522.

Sloan, Benjamin. "Ashbery's 'Down by the Station Early in the Morning'". *Explicator* 52 (Summer, 1994): 245-8.

—. "*Houseboat Days* and 'Houses Founded on the Sea': an Example of Emerson as Source for Ashbery". *Notes* on *Contemporary Literature* 23.5 (May, 1993): 5-6.

Smith, Dinitia. "Poem Alone" (Profile of John Ashbery). *New York* 24.20 (May 20, 1991): 44-52.

Smith, Frank. "Dedans merci, *sort of*". *L'Oeil de Boeuf* 22 (a special issue devoted to John Ashbery) (Paris) (Dec, 2000): 150.

Sokolsky, Anita. "'A Commission That Never Materialized': Narcissism and Lucidity in Ashbery's 'Self-Portrait in a Convex Mirror'". In *Modern Critical Views: John Ashbery*, edited by Harold Bloom. New York: Chelsea House Publishers, 1985. 233-250.

Sommer, Piotr. "An Interview in Warsaw". In *Code of Signals: Recent Writings in Poetics*, edited by M. Palmer. Berkeley: North Atlantic, 1983.

Spurr, David. "John Ashbery's Poetry of Language". *Centennial Review* 25 (1981).

Staiger, Jeff. "The Hitherside of History: Tone, Knowledge, and Spirit in John Ashbery's 'The System'". *Texas Studies in Literature and Language* 39.1 (Spring, 1997): 80-95.

Stamelman, Richard. "Critical Reflections: Poetry and Art Criticism in Ashbery's 'Self-Portrait in a Convex Mirror'". *New Literary History* 15 (Spring, 1984): 607-630.

Stein, Judith E. "The Word Made Image". *Art in America* 83.5 (May, 1995): 98-101.

Stein, William B. "Stevens and Ashbery: the Wrinkles in the Canvas of Language". *Wallace Stevens Journal* 3.3-4 (1979): 55-69.

Stepanchev, Stephen. *American Poetry Since 1945: a Critical Survey*. New York: Harper, 1965.

Stewart, Susan. "The Last Man". *American Poetry Review* 17 (Sep-Oct, 1988): 9-16.

Stitt, Peter. "John Ashbery: the Poetics of Uncertainty". In Peter Stitt, *Uncertainty and Plenitude: Five Contemporary Poets*. Iowa City, Iowa: University of Iowa Press, 1997: 19-49.

Sutton, Walter. *American Free Verse: the Modern Revolution in Poetry*. New York: New Directions, 1973.

Sweet, David. "Plastic Language: John Ashbery's 'Europe'". *Word and Image* (Apr-Jun, 2002): 153 + .

—. "'And *Ut Pictura Poesis* Is Her Name': John Ashbery, the Plastic Arts, and the Avant-garde". *Comparative Literature* 50.4 (Fall, 1998): 316-332.

—. "Parodic Nostalgia for Aesthetic Machismo: Frank O'Hara and Jackson Pollock". *Journal of Modern Literature* (Summer, 2000): 375.

Tabbi, Joseph. "Hypertext Hotel Lautréamont". *SubStance* 26.1 (82) (1987): 34-55.

Takachi, Junichiro. "Something Different and New: Questions to John Ashbery". *Eigo-Seinen* (Tokyo): 271-274.

Truchlar, L. "Das Kalkul der Vision: John Ashbery als Lyriker". In *Essays in Honour of Erwin Sturzl on His 60th Birthday*, edited by James Hogg [et al]. Salzburg: University of Salzburg, 1980.

Turco L. "John Ashbery Handbook Forms". *New Orleans Review* 19.1 (Spring, 1992): 5-8.

Upton, Lee. "Get Me Rewrite: I Want Candy". *Field: Contemporary Poetry and Poetics* 65 [Special Issue: John Ashbery: A Symposium] (Fall, 2001).

Vendler, Helen. "Ashbery's Aesthetic: Reporting on Fairfield Porter and Saul Steinberg". *Harvard Review* 22 (Spring, 2002).

—. "Scoops from the Tide Pools: the Allegories and Mimicries of Mark Ford". *Times Literary Supplement* 4996 (Jan 1, 1999): 11.

—. "John Ashbery, Louise Glück." In *The Music of What Happens: Poems, Poets, Critics*. Cambridge: Harvard University Press, 1988.

—. "Understanding Ashbery". *New Yorker* 57 (Mar 16, 1981): 108 + ; reprinted in *Modern Critical Views: John Ashbery*, edited by Harold Bloom. New York: Chelsea House Publishers, 1985: 179-194.

Vermaelen, Dennis. "Syringa ou les fragments d'Orphée: Actes du colloque tenu à Tours (30 novembre - 2 decembre 2000). In *Présence de 'l'Antiquité grecque et romaine au XXe siècle*, edited by Rémy Poignault. Tours: Centre des Recherches Andre Piganiol, 2002.

Vincent, John. "Reports of Looting and Insane Buggery Behind Altars: John Ashbery's Queer Politics". *Twentieth-Century Literature* 44.2 (Summer, 1998): 155-175.

Walker, David. "'Summer': Cryptography, Desire and the Secret Language of Nature". *Field: Contemporary Poetry and Poetics* 65 [Special Issue: John Ashbery: A Symposium] (Fall, 2001).

Walker, Jeffrey S. "Classical Rhetoric and/or the Modern Lyric: a Contra-Fiat". *American Poetry* 4.3 (Spring, 1987): 2-18.

Walsh R. "Art Work to John Ashbery's Poem 'Self Portrait In A Convex Mirror'". *AN* 83.8 (1984): 105-106.

Wamsley, Howard. "Speeding Hackney Cabriolet". *Poetry* 109 (Dec, 1966): 185-187.

Ward, David. "Dam and River: Two Ways to Art in the 1950s". *PN Review* 26.1 (Sep-Oct, 1999): 28-31.

Ward, Geoffrey. *Statutes of Liberty: the New York School of Poets*. New York: St. Martin's Press, 1993; Basingstoke: Macmillan, 1993; New York: Palgrave, 2001.

—. "'Whatever Saves': Syntax in Ashbery and James". *Cambridge Quarterly* 28.2 (Jun, 1999): 91 + .

—. "Why It's Right There in the Proces Verbal: the New York School of Poets". *Cambridge Quarterly* 21.3 (1992): 273-282.

Wasserman, Rosanne. "Marianne Moore and the New York School: O'Hara, Ashbery, Koch". *Sagetrieb* 6.3 (Winter, 1987): 67-77.

Wesling, Donald. "Late Capitalist Lyric: Politics in American Poetry (and Poetics) Since 1945". In *Cross-Cultural*

Studies: American Canadian and European Literatures, 1945-1985, edited by Mirko Jurak. Ljubljana: English Department, 1988.

Wheale, Nigel. "'The All, the All' in the Poetry of John Ashbery". *Poetry Review* 69.3 (1980): 56-60.

Williams, Ned B. "Ashbery's 'The Grapevine'". *Explicator* 49.4 (Summer, 1991): 251-254.

Wilson, Rob. "John Ashbery's Post-Industrial Sublime". *Verse* 8.1 (Spring, 1991): 48-52.

Winkfield, Trevor. "Pleins feux sur les pommes". *L'Oeil de Boeuf* 22 (a special issue devoted to John Ashbery) (Paris) (Dec, 2000): 53.

Winter, Max. "Of Stopgaps and Things Past: John Ashbery's Twentieth-Century Book of Poetry". *Denver Quarterly* 36.3-4 (Fall-Winter, 2002): 109-112.

Wisner-Broyles, A., Editor. *Poetry Criticism: Excerpts from Criticism of the Works of the Most Significant and Widely Studied Poets of World Literature.* Vol. 26. Detroit: Gale, 1999.

Wolf, Leslie. "The Brushstroke's Integrity: the Poetry of John Ashbery and the Art of Painting". In *Beyond Amazement: New Essays on John Ashbery,* edited by David Lehman. Ithaca and London: Cornell University Press, 1980: 224-254.

Yacobi, Tamar. "Ashbery's 'Description of a Masque': Radical Interart Transfer Across History". *Poetics Today* 20.4 (Winter, 1999): 673 + .

Yaguchi, Yorihumi. "Nihon de no John Ashbery". *Eigo-Seinen* (Tokyo): 275-276.

Zinnes, Harriet. "John Ashbery: the Way Time Feels as It Passes". *Hollins Critic* 29.3 (Jun, 1992): 1-13.

Zverev, Alexei. "Poetry at Mayakovsky's Place". *Soviet Life* 2 (Feb, 1991): 54 + .

INTERVIEWS

"An Interview with John Ashbery". In *American Writing Today,* edited by Richard Kostelanetz. Washington: US International Communications Agency, 1982.

Ash, John. "John Ashbery in Conversation with John Ash". *PN Review,* 46, 12.2: 31-34.

Bergman, David. "Building the Nest of Ninnies: a Conversation with John Ashbery". *Lambda Book Report* 6.4 (Nov, 1997): 24.

Berkson, Bill. "The Art of Poetry XIII". This interview was to have been published in *The Paris Review* in 1970, but Ashbery disliked the piece, and it never appeared. According to David Kermani's *John Ashbery: a Comprehensive Bibliography* (1976) (H2c), two sets of page proofs and three photocopies were then known to exist.

Bleikasten, André. "Entretien avec John Ashbery". *La Quinzaine Littéraire,* Feb, 1993: 16-28.

Bloom, Janet and Robert Losada. "Craft Interview with John Ashbery". *New York Quarterly* 9 (Winter, 1972): 11-33; reprinted in *The Craft of Poetry: Interviews from the* New York Quarterly, edited by William Packard. Garden City: Doubleday, 1964: 111-132.

Blythe, Caroline. "Speaking in Tongues: an Interview with John Ashbery". *Oxford Poetry* 6:2 (Winter 1991): 56-62.

Boddy, Kasia. *PN Review* 25.3 (Jan-Feb, 1999): 18-21.

Bracho, Edmundo. "Lejos del dogma: Entrevista con John Ashbery". *Quimera* 122 (1994): 24-31.

Cohen, Scott. "Ashbery Explains It". *Interview* 20.6 (Jun, 1990): 74.

De Jongh, Nicholas. "Waving Not Drowning: an Interview with John Ashbery". *Guardian* (May 9, 1987): 15.

Gangel, Sue. "John Ashbery Interviewed by Sue Gangel". *American Poetry Observed: Poets on Their Work,* edited by Joe David Bellamy. Urbana and Chicago: University of Illinois Press, 1984: 9-20.

Gardener, Raymond. "Interview with John Ashbery". *Guardian* (Apr 19, 1975): 8.

Giles, Paul. "The Poetry of John Ashbery". *Oxford Poetry* 1.3 (Spring 1984).

Gruen, John. *The Party's Over Now; Reminiscences of the Fifties – New York 's Artists, Writers, Musicians and Their Friends.* Includes reminiscences by and about Ashbery. New York: Viking, 1972: 155-160 and *passim.*

Henry, Gerrit. "Visiting John Ashbery". *Culture Hero; a Fanzine of Stars of the Super World* (New York) 1.4 (Mar, 1970?): 17.

—. "In Progress". *Spectator* (Jul 31, 1979): 1.

Herd, David. "John Ashbery in Conversation with David Herd". *PN Review* 21.1 (Sep-Oct, 1994): 32-37.

Hilringhouse, Mark. "A Conversation with John Ashbery". *Soho News* (Dec, 1981): 15-16.

Jackson, Richard. "The Immanence of a Revelation (John Ashbery)". *Poetry Miscellany.* Chattanooga, Tennessee: University of Tennessee at Chattanooga, 1982: 3-10; reprinted in *Acts of Mind: Conversations with Contemporary Poets,* edited by Richard Jackson. Alabama: University of Alabama Press, 1983: 69-77.

Kane, Daniel. "Daniel Kane Interviews the Poet John Ashbery, February 22, 1999". http://www.writenet.org/poetschat/poetschat_jashbery.html.

Kermani, David. [John Ashbery interviewed by David Kermani, Jun 2, 1974]. Oral History Collection, Columbia University, New York.

Kimberley, Nick. "An Interview with John Ashbery". *City Limits* (May 16, 1986): 29.

Koch, Kenneth. *John Ashbery and Kenneth Koch (A Conversation).* Tucson, Arizona: Interview Press, 1965.

Koethe J. "An Interview with John Ashbery". *Sub-Stance* 37.3 (1983): 178-186.

Kostelanetz, Richard. "How to Be a Difficult Poet". *New York Times Magazine* (May 23, 1976): 18-33; reprinted in Richard Kostelanetz. *The Old Poetries and the New*. Ann Arbor: University of Michigan Press, 1979.

Labrie R. "John Ashbery – An Interview". *American Poetry Review* 13.3 (May—Jun 1984): 29-33.

Lopes, Rodrigo Garcia. "Notes about the Process: an Interview with John Ashbery". *Hayden's Ferry Review* 12 (1993): 27-33.

Munn P. "An Interview with John Ashbery". *New Orleans Review* 17.2 (1990): 59-63.

Murphy, John. "John Ashbery, an Interview". *Poetry Review* 75.2 (Aug, 1985): 20-25.

Osti, Louis A. "The Craft of John Ashbery". *Confrontation* 9 (Fall, 1974): 84-96.

"Paying Attention: an Interview with John Ashbery". *Economist* (Sep 14, 1991): 136.

Poulin Jnr., A. "The Experience of Experience: a Conversation with John Ashbery". *Michigan Quarterly* 22.3 (Summer, 1981): 242-255.

Rehak, Melanie. "Questions for John Ashbery". *New York Times Magazine* (Apr 4, 1999): 15.

Smith, Lee. "Back to School: an Interview with John Ashbery". *Bookforum* (Fall, 2000): 36-38.

Stitt, Peter. "The Art of Poetry XXXIII: John Ashbery". *Paris Review* 25 (Winter, 1983): 31-59; reprinted as "John Ashbery" in *Poets at Work: The Paris Review Interviews*, edited by George Plimpton. New York: Viking, 1989: ch. 15.

Tranter, John. "John Ashbery Interviewed by John Tranter New York City, May 1988". *Jacket* (a free, internet-only quarterly review) 2 (Jan, 1998). http://jacketmagazine.com/02/jaiv1988.html.

—. "An Interview with John Ashbery". *Scripsi* 4.1 (Jul, 1986): 93-102; reprinted as "John Ashbery Interviewed by John Tranter New York City, 20 April 1985" in *Jacket* (a free, internet-only quarterly review) 2 (Jan, 1998). http://jacketmagazine.com/02/jaiv1985.html.

Walsh, Robert. "Artful". *Interview* 19.9 (Sep, 1989): 34.

DISSERTATIONS AND THESES

Alberola Crespo, Nieves. *La voz poética de John Ashbery: una paradójica bipolaridad*. Ph.D. Dissertation, Alicante: Universidad de Alicante, 1994.

Anderson, Matthew Daniel. *Modernity and the Example of Poetry: Readings in Baudelaire, Verlaine and Ashbery*. Ph.D. Dissertation, Yale University, 1999.

Auslander, Philip. *The Pop Sensibility in Theatre: Plays by the Poets of the New York School*. Ph.D. Dissertation, Cornell University, 1983.

Avrich, Jane. *'The Poem Is You': Author-Reader Relationships in the Poetry of John Ashbery*. A.B. Honours Thesis, Harvard University, 1988.

Barr, Burlin. *Lyrical Contact Zones: Cinematic Representation and the Transformation of the Exotic*. Dissertation, Cornell University, 1999.

Boyd, Mary Kay. *John Ashbery's Slightly Rumpled Realism*. Master's Thesis, Florida Atlantic University, 1989.

Ciocco, Jamie. *Living into the Layers: John Ashbery's Poetry of the Subjective Present*. A.B. Honors Thesis, Harvard University, 1994.

Clark, Kevin. *American Catharsis: the Evolution and Practice of the Contemporary Long Poem*. Ph.D. Dissertation, University of California Davis, 1986.

Debrot, Jacques Louis. *Picture Poetry: the Visual Arts and American Avant Garde*. Ph.D. Dissertation, Harvard University, 2001.

DuBois, Andrew Lee. *As Variously as Possible: a Contemporary Poetics*. Ph.D. Dissertation, Duke University, 1996.

Eichbauer, Mary E. *The Visual Arts as a Myth of Poetic Origins in Rene Char and John Ashbery*. Ph.D. Dissertation, University of California, Los Angeles, 1985.

Epstein, Andrew. *Against Fixity: Individualism and Friendship in Twentieth-Century America*. Ph.D. Dissertation, Columbia University, 2000.

Fink, Thomas A. *"These Decibels": the Poetry of John Ashbery*. Ph.D. Dissertation, 1981.

Ford, Mark. *A Critical Study of the Poetry of John Ashbery*. Ph.D. Dissertation, University of Oxford, 1991.

Franzek, Phyllis Jean. *Political Poetics: Revisionist Form in Adrienne Rich, John Ashbery, Charles Wright, and Jorie Graham*. Ph.D. Dissertation, University of Southern California, 1995.

Fredman, Stephen. *Sentences: Three Works of American Prose Poetry*. Ph.D. Dissertation, Stanford University, 1980.

Gardner, Thomas. *A Created I: the Contemporary American Long Poem*. Ph.D. Dissertation, University of Wisconsin—Madison, 1982.

Gillespie, Dennis P. *Augustine and America: Five Contemporary Autobiographical Works*. Ph.D. Dissertation, 1989.

Gray, Jeffrey. *Travel and the Trope of Vulnerability in the Poetry of Elizabeth Bishop, Robert Lowell, Frank Bidart, and John Ashbery*. Ph.D. Dissertation, University of California, Riverside, 1994.

Grotjohn, Robert. *'For Those Who Love to Be Astonished': the Prose Long Poem as Genre*. Ph.D. Dissertation,

University of Wisconsin—Madison, 1991.

Hainly, Bruce. *How to Proceed in Everything I can Think of*. Ph.D. Dissertation, Yale University, 1993.

Harter, Lisa Reidy. *"Self-Portrait in a Convex Mirror": John Ashbery as a Decadent Late Romantic*. Masters Thesis, George Mason University, 1994.

Hettich, Michael. *Contemporary Action Poets: Frank O'Hara and John Ashbery*. Ph.D. Dissertation, University of Miami, 1992.

Hoeppner, Edward Haworth. *Icon and Hyperbola: Strategies for Verse in the Poetry of W.S. Merwin and John Ashbery*. Ph.D. Dissertation, University of Iowa, 1984.

Imbriglio, Catherine. *In and Out of the Stockade: Recontextualising John Ashbery's Poetry*. Ph.D. Dissertation, Brown University, 1995.

Johnson, Geoffery M. *John Ashbery and Wassily Kandinsky: the Abstract Concerns of Text and Image*. Master's Thesis, San Diego State University, 1992.

Levin, Amy Karen. *The Idea Beckons: Visual and Verbal Art in Ashbery's 'Shadow Train.'* Master's Thesis, University of Colorado at Boulder, 1982.

Londry, Michael John. *New York Poets at Harvard: a Critical Edition of the Early Harvard Advocate Writings of John Ashbery, Kenneth Koch, and Frank O'Hara, 1947-1951*. Masters Thesis, University Of Alberta, 1997.

Lundergan, Robert. *Reading Ashbery, Reading Heidegger*. Master's Thesis, California State University, Chico, 1989.

Lyons, Neva Gibson. *The Poetry of John Ashbery*. Thesis, University of Oklahoma, 1977.

Malinowska, Barbara. *Dynamics of Being, Space and Time in the Poetry of Czeslaw Milosz and John Ashbery*. Ph.D. Dissertation, University Of South Florida, 1994.

Marshall, Thomas Christopher. *Figure in the Landscape: a Romantic Motif in the Poetry of John Ashbery*. Masters Thesis, San Diego State University, 1981.

Mazur, Krystyna. *Poetry and Repetition: Walt Whitman, Wallace Stevens and John Ashbery*. Ph.D. Dissertation, Cornell University, 2000.

McGuirk, Keven Vincent. *Lyric Trials – Lyric and Rhetoric in Contemporary Poetry: Seamus Heaney, Adrienne Rich, A.R. Ammons and John Ashbery*. Ph.D. Dissertation, University of Western Ontario, 1993.

Miller, Stephen Paul. *Three Self-Consuming Mechanisms of the Mid-seventies: John Ashbery's 'Self-Portrait in a Convex Mirror', the Watergate Affair, and Jasper Johns's Crosshatch Paintings*. Ph.D. Dissertation, New York University, 1990.

Miller, Susan Hawkins. *The Poetics of the Postmodern American Prose Poem*. Ph.D. Dissertation, University of Oregon, 1981.

Munn Paul Tyner. *The Determinate Lyric, from John Donne to John Ashbery*. Ph.D. Dissertation, University of Minnesota, 1988.

Murphy, John. *Aspects of the Self in the Poetry of Robert Lowell, Frank O'Hara and John Ashbery*. Ph.D. Dissertation, University of Essex, 1990.

Osborn, Andrew Langworthy. *Admit Impediment: the Use of Difficulty in Twentieth-Century American Poetry*. Ph.D. Dissertation, University Of Texas At Austin, 2000.

Picard, Christopher L. *The Way of These Lines: the Poetry and Poetic of John Ashbery*. Ph.D. Dissertation, Brown University, 1985.

Pies, Stacy-Ellen. *The Poet or the Journalist: Stephane Mallarmé, John Ashbery and the Poeme Critique*. Ph.D. Dissertation, City University of New York, 1993.

Quamme, Margaret A. *The Interaction of Lyric and Narrative in the Long Modern American Poem*. Ph.D. Dissertation, Brown University, 1991.

Quinney, Laura. *A Chorus of Similes; the Verse of John Ashbery*. Ph.D. Dissertation, 1980.

Rapisarda, Martin. *The Articulation of Difference in John Ashbery's Poetry*. Ph.D. Dissertation, 1987.

Reeck, Matthew Stefan. *Identifying the Individual Styles of John Ashbery and James Merrill*. Masters Thesis, University Of Kansas, 2001.

Reichardt, Ulfried. *Innenansichten der postmoderne: zur dichtung John Ashberys, A. R. Ammons', Denise Levertovs und Adrienne Richs*. Ph.D. Dissertation, Universität Berlin, 1988; a revised version published by Königshausen & Neumann in Würzburg in 1991.

Revell, Donald G. *A Chorus of Similes: the Verse of John Ashbery*. Ph.D. Dissertation, State University Of New York At Buffalo, 1980.

Ring, Robert. *An Open Possibility: John Ashbery and the Postmodern Prose Poem*. Masters Thesis, Oklahoma State University, 1998.

Rodewald, Beate. *The Present Is Clearly Here to Stay: a Reconsideration of Surrealism and the Work of John Ashbery*. Ph.D. Dissertation, Kent State University, 1992.

Ryoo, Gi Taek. *Self, Object, and Language: Contemporary Poetics and Poetry: (Robert Creeley, John Ashbery)*. Ph.D. Dissertation, State University of New York at Binghamton, English, General Literature and Rhetoric Department, 2000.

Shapiro, David. *The Meaning of Meaninglessness: the Poetry of John Ashbery*. Thesis, Columbia University, 1973.

Shoptaw, John Clark. *Living Within the System: an Introduction to the Later Poetry of John Ashbery*. Ph.D. Dissertation, Harvard University, 1987.

Silverberg, Mark. *Beyond Radical Art: the New York School of Poets and the Neo Avant Garde*. Ph.D. Dissertation, Dalhousie University, 2000.

Sloan, Benjamin. *Set Free on an Ocean of Language That Comes to Be Part of Us: John Ashbery and the Influence of Emerson, Whitman, James, and Stevens*. Ph.D. Dissertation, City University of New York, 1990.

Stover, Betty-Lou. *The Age of Deconstruction*. Ph.D. Dissertation, Wayne State University, 1991.

Swiggart, Katherine Anne. *Extreme Measures: Exaggeration in the Poetry of Sylvia Plath, Anthony Hecht, Frank Bidart, and John Ashbery*. Ph.D. Dissertation, UCLA, 2001.

Tarver, John M. *A Close Reading of John Ashbery's 'Self-Portrait in a Convex Mirror.'* Master's Thesis, Louisiana State University, Baton Rouge, 1984.

Timmons, Jeffrey Wayne. *Theory and Poetry: John Ashbery's 'Self-Portrait in a Convex Mirror.'* Master's Thesis, Portland State University, 1994.

Tuttle, William C. *The Never-Resting Mind: the Meditative Mode in Twentieth-Century American Poetry*. Ph.D. Dissertation, State University of New York, Buffalo, 1997.

Updyke, Cory. *Ashbery: the Modern Voice*. Ph.D. Dissertation, Westminster College, 1997.

Welker, Rosanne Lynn. *Toward an Aesthetic Appreciation of the L = A = N = G = U = A = G = E + D John Ashbery*. Master's Thesis, University of Virginia, 1989.

Wisse, William R. *The Scheme of Common Language: a Comparison of John Ashbery and Amy Gerstler*. Masters Thesis, McGill University, 1994.

Wu, Shu-Ching. *Experiencing the Shuttling Process of Communication in Ashbery's Poems: Metaphor and Metonymy*. Master's Thesis, North Carolina State University, 2002.

Zimmer, William Norbert. *On and off the Scaffolding: the Plotting of the Self in Major Works of the New York Schools of Painting and Poetry*. Master's Thesis, University of Texas at Austin, 1975.

MUSICAL SETTINGS

Carter, Elliott. *Music of Elliott Carter*. New York: CRI, 1991. Musical Recording.

Carter, Elliott. *Syringa*. Poem by John Ashbery; texts in Classical Greek by Aeschylus ... [et al]. New York: Associated Music Publishers, 1980. Score.

Corigliano, John. *How Like Pellucid Statues, Daddy. Or Like a – an Engine*. Text by John Ashbery. New York: G. Schirmer, 1995. Score.

Dashow, James. *Ashbery Setting*. Text from "Clepsydra". For soprano, flute, and piano. Score privately printed by the composer, 1972.

Second Voyage. Text by John Ashbery. New York: Composers Recordings, Inc., 1982. Musical Recording. (CD, CRI SD 456.)

Klein, Joseph. *Three Haiku, after John Ashbery*. For mezzo-sporano and percussion, 1989. Manuscript score.

Reif, Paul. *White Roses*. Text by John Ashbery. For soprano and piano. New York: Seesaw Music Corp, c.1970. Score.

Reynolds, Roger. *Whispers out of Time*. For string orchestra. A response to poet John Ashbery's "Self-Portrait in a Convex Mirror". New York: C.F. Peters Corp. (Edition Peters no. 67261), 1989. Score.

Rorem, Ned. *Some Trees: Three Poems for Three Voices*. Words by John Ashbery. For soprano, mezzo-soprano, bass-baritone, and piano. New York: Composers Recordings Inc, CRI 238 USD. New York: Boosey & Hawkes, 1970. Score.

Salzman, Eric. *Foxes and Hedgehogs; Verses and Cantos*. Text from "Europe". For four voices and instruments with electronic extensions. Score unpublished but available from Quogue Music, New York, 1972.

Stewart, Don. *Never Seek to Tell Thy Love*. For Soprano, Flute, Clarinet / Bass Clarinet, Violin, Cello, Percussion and Piano: op. 39. Poem by John Ashbery. Tunbridge, Vermont: Trillenium Music Co., 1999. Score.

BOOK REVIEWS

SOME TREES (1956)

Arrowsmith, William, *Hudson Review* (Summer, 1956).

O'Hara, Frank. *Poetry* (Feb, 1957): 312.

THE TENNIS COURT OATH (1962)

Duyn, Mona Van. *Poetry* 100:6 (Sep, 1962): 390-395.

Flaccus, Kimball. *Voices* (Sep-Dec, 1962): 42.

Flint, R.W. *Partisan Review*, 29.2 (Spring, 1962): 290-294.
John, G.D. *Christian Science Monitor* (Sep 6, 1962).
Kennedy, X.J. *New York Times Book Review* (Jul 15, 1962).
Morse, Samuel French. *Virginia Quarterly* 38.2 (Winter, 1962): 324-330.
Schevill, James. *Saturday Review* (May 5, 1962): 24.
Simon, John. *Hudson Review* (Autumn, 1962): 455.
Tobin, E. *Spirit* (Jul, 1962): 91.

RIVERS AND MOUNTAINS (1966)

Howard, Richard, *Poetry* (1970).
Nation (Dec 12, 1966).
New York Review of Books (Apr 14, 1966).

SELECTED POEMS (1967)

Thwaite, Anthony. *Times Literary Supplement* 3420 (Sep 14, 1967): 820.

A NEST OF NINNIES (1969, 1987)

Koethe, John. *Poetry* 118.1 (Oct, 1970): 54-59.
Phillips, Alice H.G. "Relatively Relaxed".*Times Literary Supplement* 4399 (Jul 24, 1987): 801.
Lambda Book Report 6.4 (Nov, 1997): 44.

FRAGMENT (1969)

Nation (Apr 14, 1969).
New Yorker (Mar 24, 1969).
New York Times Book Review (Jun 8, 1969).
Yale Review (Oct, 1969).

THE DOUBLE DREAM OF SPRING (1970)

Avant, J.A. *Library Journal* (Jan 1, 1970).
Helms, Alan. *Partisan Review* 39.4 (Fall, 1972): 621-626.
Hughes, J.W. *Saturday Review* (Aug 8, 1970): 34.
Kalstone, David. *New York Times Book Review* (Jul 5, 1970).
Mazzocco, Robert. *New York Review of Books* (Dec 13, 1973): 45-47.

THREE POEMS (1972)

Dale, Peter. "Three Poets: Can Belief and Form Come in Bags of Tricks?" *Saturday Review* 55.28 (Jul 8, 1972): 57-58.
DiPiero, W.S. "John Ashbery: The Romantic as Problem Solver". *American Poetry Review* 2.4 (Jul-Aug, 1973): 39-42.
Donadio, Stephen. "Poetry and Public Experience". *Commentary* 55.2 (Feb, 1973): 63-72.
Helms, Alan. "Growing Up Together". *Partisan Review* 39.4 (Fall, 1972): 621-626.
Hollo, Anselm. "'Gifts to Our Spirit': John Ashbery's Three Poems". *Crazy Horse* 14 (Nov, 1973): 17-18.
Hornick, Lita. *World* 29 (Apr, 1974): 101-104.
Howard, Richard. "Pursuits and Followings". *Poetry* 120.5 (Aug, 1972): 296-303.
Koethe, John. "Ashbery's Meditations". *Parnassus* 1.1 (Fall-Winter 1972): 89-93; reprinted in John Koethe, *Poetry at One Remove: Essays*. Ann Arbor: University of Michigan Press, 2000: 10-14.
Mazzocco, Robert. "Very Different Cats". *New York Review of Books* (Dec 13, 1973): 45-47.
Murray, Michele. *National Catholic Reporter* (Mar 24, 1972): 14.
O'Conner, Patricia T. *New York Times Book Review* (Dec 28, 1986): 28.

O'Donnell, Dan. *Scholastic* 114.12 (Mar 30, 1973): 37-38.

SELF-PORTRAIT IN A CONVEX MIRROR (1975, 1977)

Auster, Paul. *Harper* (Nov, 1975): 106.

Bell, Pearl K. *New Leader* (May 26, 1975).

Brinnin, J.M. *New York Times Book Review* (Aug 2, 1975).

Corn, Alfred. *Parnassus* 1 (Fall, 1975); reprinted as "A Magma of Interiors" in Harold Bloom, *Modern Critical Views: Contemporary Poets.* New York and Philadelphia: Chelsea House, 1986: 235-244.

Didsbury, Peter. *Poetry Review* 68.1 (Apr, 1978): 62-67.

Howard, Richard. "*Self-Portrait in a Convex Mirror* by John Ashbery". *Poetry* (Mar, 1976): 349-351; reprinted in Richard Howard, *Alone with America: Essays on the Art of Poetry in the United States Since 1950.* New York: Atheneum, 1980. 49-52.

Kalstone, David. "Quicksilver Distortions". *Times Literary Supplement* 3838 (Jul 25, 1975): 834.

Larrissy, Edward. *Critical Quarterly* 20.2 (Summer, 1978): 88-91.

Moramarco, Fred. "John Ashbery and Frank O'Hara: the Painterly Poets". *Journal of Modern Literature* 5.3 (Sep, 1976): 436-462.

Madigan, Michael. *Library Journal* 100.10 (May 15, 1975): 990.

THE VERMONT NOTEBOOK (1975, 2001)

Publishers Weekly, 2001.

Perl, Jed. *New Republic* (Dec 17, 2001)

HOUSEBOAT DAYS (1977, 1979)

Boyars, Robert. "A Quest Without an Object". *Times Literary Supplement* 3987 (Sep 1, 1978): 962.

Breslin, Paul. *Poetry* 137 (Oct, 1980): 42 + .

Howes, Victor. *Christian Science Monitor* (Oct 12, 1977).

Johnson, Rosemary. *Parnassus* 6.2 (1978): 118-124.

Larissy, Edward. "Taking in Everything". *Times Literary Supplement* 4016 (Mar 14, 1980): 301.

Logan, William. *Library Journal* 102.17 (Oct 1, 1977): 2068.

Morrison, Blake. *New Statesman* 99 (Jan 4, 1980): 22 + .

Pettingell, Phoebe. *New Leader* (Nov 7, 1977).

Shattuck, Roger. "Poet in the Wings". *New York Review of Books* 25.4 (Mar 23, 1978): 38-40.

White, Edmund. *Bookletter* (1977).

THREE PLAYS (1978, 1988)

Luddy, Thomas E. *Library Journal* 103.6 (Mar 15, 1978): 681.

Norfolk, Lawrence. "Forever Coming Closer". *Times Literary Supplement* 4446 (Jun 17, 1988): 681.

AS WE KNOW (1979, 1981)

Breslin, Paul. *Poetry* 137 (Oct, 1980): 42 + .

Bromwich, David. *New York Times* 129 (Jan 6, 1980): s7, p6.

Donoghue, Denis. "Sign Language". *New York Review of Books* 26.21-22 (Jan 24, 1980): 36-39.

Logan, William. *Washington Star* (Feb 10, 1980); reprinted in William Logan, *Reputations of the Tongue: on Poets and Poetry.* Gainesville: University Press of Florida, 1999: 37-40.

McNeil, Helen. "Between Brass and Silver". *Times Literary Supplement* 4079 (Jun 5, 1981): 644.

Parisi, Joseph. *Chicago Tribune Book World* (Jan 27, 1980).

White, Edmund. *Washington Post Book World* (Nov 25, 1979).

Yeaton, Diane. *American Poetry Review* 10.1 (Jan-Feb, 1981): 34-36.

Williamson, Michael. *Library Journal* 104.21 (Dec 1, 1979): 2574.

Shadow Train (1981, 1982)

Donoghue, Denis. *New York Times* 130 (Sep 6, 1981): s7, p6.
Beaver, Harold. *Parnassus* 9.2 (Fall-Winter, 1981): 54-61.
Gioia, Dana. *Hudson Review* (Winter, 1981-82) ; reprinted in Dana Gioia, *Can Poetry Matter?* St Paul, Minnesota: Graywolf Press, 1992: 184-186.
Logan, William. *Chicago Tribune* (1980); reprinted in William Logan, *All the Rage*. Ann Arbor, Michigan: Michigan University Press, 1998: 53-57.
Morrison, Blake. "Missing One Another". *Times Literary Supplement* 4149 (Oct 8, 1982): 1105.
Pettingell, Phoebe. *New Leader* 64 (Jun 29, 1981): 15+.
Shetley, Vernon. *Poetry* 140 (Jul, 1982): 236+.
Stuttaford, Genevieve. *Publishers Weekly* 219 (Apr 3, 1981): 65.
Vendler, Helen. *New York Review of Books* (Jul 16,1981).
Yenser, Stephen. *Yale Review* 71 (Autumn, 1981): 116+.
Young, David. *Washington Post Book World* (Jun 7, 1981).
Williamson, Michael. *Library Journal* 106.7 (Apr 1, 1981): 799.

A Wave (1984)

Crase, Douglas. *Nation* 239 (Sep 1, 1984): 146+.
Hainsworth, Peter. "Changing Unchanging". *Times Literary Supplement* 4264 (Dec 21, 1984): 1466.
Hudzik, Robert. *Library Journal* 109.8 (May 15, 1984): 984.
Lehman, David. *Newsweek* 104 (Jul 16, 1984): 78.
McClatchy, J.D. *Poetry* 145.2 (Feb, 1985): 301+.
Mead, Philip. *Scripsi* 4.1 (Jul, 1986): 103-119.
Middleton, Christopher. *PN Review* 21.1 (Sep-Oct, 1994): 41-42.
New York Times Book Review, 1984.
Publishers Weekly 225 (Apr 13, 1984): 57+.
Romer, Stephen. *New Statesman* 109 (Jan 18, 1985); 32.
Stitt, Peter. *Georgia Review* 38 (Fall, 1984): 628-638.
Vendler, Helen. *New York Review of Books* 31 (Jun 14, 1984): 32+.
Ward, Geoffrey. *Cambridge Quarterly* 14.2 (1985): 163-173.

Selected Poems (1985, 1986, 1987, 1991)

Fenton, James. *New York Times Book Review* 90 (Dec 29, 1985): 10.
Hudzik, Robert. *Library Journal* 111 (Jan, 1986): 88.
Jarman, Mark. *Hudson Review* 39 (Summer, 1986): 334-347.
Jenkins, Alan. *Sunday Times* (Apr 27, 1986): 32.
Kakutani, Michiko. *New York Times* 135 (Dec 7, 1985): 13(N), 18(L).
O'Conner, Patricia T. *New York Times Book Review* (Dec 28, 1986): 28.
Rawson, Claude. "A Poet in the Postmodern Playground". *Times Literary Supplement* 4344 (Jul 4, 1986): 723-724.
Romer, Stephen. *Times Literary Supplement* 4637 (Feb 14, 1992): 12.
Spurr, David. *Poetry* 148 (Jul,1986): 228+.
Stuttaford, Genevieve. *Publishers Weekly* 228 (Nov 15, 1985): 50.
Warren Rosanna. *Partisan Review* 54 (Winter, 1987): 157+.
Worsham, Fabian. *Southern Humanities Review* 22 (Winter, 1988): 94-96.

April Galleons (1987, 1988)

Beaver, Harold. *New York Times Book Review* (Apr 3, 1988): 12.
Boening, John. *World Literature Today* 63.1 (Winter, 1989): 103.
Choice (1987).
Ford, Mark. *London Review of Books* (Jan 19, 1989).
Hudzik, Robert. *Library Journal* 112.17 (Oct 15, 1987): 83.
Jackson, Richard. *Georgia Review* 42.4 (Winter, 1988): 856-866.
Norfolk, Lawrence. *Times Literary Supplement* 4446 (Jun 17, 1988): 681.
Pettingell, Phoebe. *New Leader* 70.18 (Nov 30, 1987): 17+.

Scammell, William. *Poetry Review* 78.1 (Spring, 1988): 48-49.
Shetley, Vernon. *Poetry* 152.2 (May, 1988): 109+.
Speirs, Logan. *English Studies* 71.1 (Feb, 1990): 61.
Stewart, Susan. *American Poetry Review* 17 (Sep-Oct, 1988): 9-16.
Stuttaford, Genevieve. *Publishers Weekly* 232.10 (Sep 4, 1987): 59.
Virginia Quarterly Review 64.2 (Spring, 1988): 63.
Yenser, Stephen. "Ashbery's Muse". *Partisan Review* 57 (Fall, 1990): 665-668.

The Best American Poetry: 1988

Guillory, Daniel L. *Library Journal* 114.1 (Jan, 1989): 88.
Kaganoff, Penny. *Publishers Weekly* 234.17 (Oct 21, 1988): 53.
Levy, Ellen. "The Age of Anthologies". *Nation* 248.21 (May 29, 1989): 747-748.
Porche, Verandah. "Home Is Where the Art Is". *Village Voice* 34.10 (Mar 7, 1989): S26.

Reported Sightings (1989, 1991)

Boening, John. *World Literature Today* 66.3 (Summer, 1992): 525-526.
Clary, Killarney. "In Doubt and Thus Alive". *Yale Review* 79.3 (Spring, 1990): 323-327.
Feld, Ross. *Parnassus: Poetry in Review* 18.2 (Fall, 1993): 359+.
Friend, Miles Edward. *Journal of Aesthetic Education* 26 (Fall, 1992): 117-118.
Harbison, Robert. "Thinking Prose". *New Statesman & Society* 3.87 (Feb 9, 1990): 38.
Perl, Jed. "The Dedicated Eye". *New Republic* 201.16 (Oct 16, 1989): 38-43.
Ratcliff, Carter. "Poet as Critic". *Art in America* 80.1 (Jan, 1992): 29+.
Skeats, Terry. *Library Journal* 114.14 (Sep 1, 1989): 188.
Solomon, Deborah. *New Criterion* 8 (Nov, 1989): 71-73.
Stuttaford, Genevieve. *Publishers Weekly* 236.2 (Jul 14, 1989): 62.
Walsh, Robert. "Artful". *Interview* 19.9 (Sep, 1989): 34.
Welish, Marjorie. "Writers on Art". *Partisan Review* 58.4 (Fall, 1991): 742+.
Wollheim, Richard. "Objects of Love". *Times Literary Supplement* 4547 (May 25, 1990): 553.

Flow Chart (1991)

Angel, Ralph. *American Poetry Review* 21.3 (May-Jun, 1992): 54+.
Bayley, John. "Richly Flows Contingency". *New York Review of Books* 38.14 (Aug 15, 1991): 3+.
Benfey, Christopher. "Portraits and Puzzles". *New Republic* 204.24 (Jun 17, 1991): 42-48.
Berger, Charles. "Poetry Chronicle". *Raritan: a Quarterly Review* 11.4 (Spring, 1992): 123+.
Blasing, Mutlu Konuk. *Michigan Quarterly Review* 31.3 (Summer, 1992): 425+.
Corn, Alfred. *Poetry* 159.3 (Dec, 1991): 169+.
Crawford, Robert. *Poetry Review* 81.4: 11-13.
Ford, Mark. "Free-Wheeling Towards the Abyss". *Times Literary Supplement* 4630 (Dec 27, 1991): 9.
Gardner, Thomas. *Contemporary Literature* 33.4 (Winter, 1992): 712+.
Herd, David. "House Guests". *New Statesman & Society* 5.231 (Dec 4, 1992): 39+.
Hosmer, Robert. "What We See and Feel and Are". *Southern Review* 28.2 (Spring, 1992): 431+.
Jarman, Mark. *Hudson Review* 45.1 (Spring, 1992): 158+.
Lawrence, Joseph. *Nation* 254.15 (Apr 20, 1992): 531+.
Lawson, Andrew. *Fragmente: a Magazine of Contemporary Poetics* 4 (Autumn-Winter, 1991): 102-112.
Logan, William. *Chicago Tribune* (Sep 8, 1991); reprinted in William Logan, *Desperate Measures*. Gainsville, Florida: University Press of Florida, 2002: 32-34.
Muratori, Fred. *Library Journal* 116.8 (May 1, 1991): 79.
Perloff, Marjorie. "The Forest of Agony and Pleasure". *New York Times Book Review* (Jun 16, 1991): 12.
Reilly, Evelyn. "Afloat". *Parnassus: Poetry in Review* 17.2/18.1 (Fall, 1992): 40+.
Stuttaford, Genevieve. *Publishers Weekly* 238.14 (Mar 22, 1991): 67.
Vendler, Helen. *New Yorker* 68.24 (Aug 3, 1992): 73+.
Virginia Quarterly Review 68.1 (Winter, 1992): 28.

Hotel Lautréamont (1992)

Berger, Charles. *Yale Review* 81.2 (Apr, 1993): 144+.

Everett, Nicholas. "Going with the Flow". *Times Literary Supplement* 4689 (Feb 12, 1993): 10.
Ford, Mark. *Scripsi* 8.3 (Apr, 1993): 225-233.
—. *New Republic* 212.9 (Feb 27, 1995): 34 + .
Gardner, James. "Check-out Time". *National Review* (Feb 15, 1993): 50.
Haines, John Meade. "In and Out of the Loop". *Hudson Review* 46.2 (Summer, 1993): 425-428.
Herd, David. "House Guests". *New Statesman & Society* 5.231 (Dec 4, 1992): 39 + .
Lepkowski, Frank J. *Library Journal* 117.14 (Sep 1, 1992): 179.
Logan, William. *Parnassus: Poetry in Review* 18.2 (Fall, 1993): 317 + ; reprinted in William Logan, *Desperate Measures*. Gainsville, Florida: University Press of Florida, 2002: 73-78.
Meyer, Steven. *Raritan: a Quarterly Review* 15.2 (Fall, 1995): 144-161.
Publishers Weekly 239.36 (Aug 10, 1992): 58.
Revell, Donald. "The Optical Margin: Five Poets". *Ohio Review* 50 (Spring, 1993): 121 + .
Seaman, Donna. *Booklist* 89.1 (Sep 1, 1992): 26.
Sleigh, Tom. "Now, Voyagers". *New York Times Book Review* (May 23, 1993): 15.
Wood, Michael. "Outside the Shady Octopus Saloon". *New York Review of Books* (May 27, 1993).

AND THE STARS WERE SHINING (1994)

Bedient, Calvin. *Poetry* 165.1 (Oct, 1994): 44 + .
Clover, Joshua. *Iowa Review* 25 (Winter, 1995): 177-183.
Cornis-Pope, Marcel. *World Literature Today* 69.3 (Summer, 1995): 552 + .
Dooley, David. *Hudson Review* 47.4 (Winter, 1995): 673 + .
Ford, Mark. *New Republic* 2112.9 (Feb 27, 1995): 34 + .
Gregerson, Linda. "Among the Wordstruck". *New York Times Book Review* (Oct 23, 1994): 3.
Herd, David. *Times Literary Supplement* 4788 (Jan 6, 1995): 22.
Horovitz, Michael. "Gnash Your Stark Theories". *New Statesman & Society* 7.312 (Jul 22, 1994): 45.
McQuade, Molly. *Publishers Weekly* 241.5 (Jan 31, 1994): 78.
Meyer, Steven. *Raritan: a Quarterly Review* 15.2 (Fall, 1995): 154 + .
Muratori, Fred. *Library Journal*, (Nov 15, 1995).
New York Review of Books, 1994
Seaman, Donna. *Booklist* 90.12 (Feb 15, 1994): 1053.

CAN YOU HEAR, BIRD (1995)

Boening John. *World Literature Today* 70.4 (Fall, 1996): 961.
Brainard, Dulcy. *Publishers Weekly* 242.39 (Sep 25, 1995): 49.
Ford, Mark. *Times Literary Supplement* 4859 (May 17, 1996): 26.
Hamilton, David. *Iowa Review* 26 (Fall, 1996): 201-203.
Logan, William. "Martyrs to Language". *New Criterion* 14 (Dec, 1995): 56-63; reprinted in William Logan, *Desperate Measures*. Gainsville, Florida: University Press of Florida, 2002: 127-129.
Muratori, Fred. *Library Journal* 120.19 (Nov 15, 1995): 78.
Seaman, Donna. *Booklist* 92.6 (Nov 15, 1995): 532.
Taylor, John. *Antioch Review* 56.4 (Fall, 1998): 501 + .
Yenser, Stephen. *Yale Review* 84 (Jan, 1996): 166-176.

PISTILS (1996)

Bryant, Eric. *Library Journal* 121.20 (Dec, 1996): 88.

THE MOORING OF STARTING OUT (1997)

Bedient, Calvin. *Boston Review* (Apr-May, 1998).
Glover, Michael. "From Urban Musing to Lonely Landscapes". *New Statesman* (Apr 24, 1998): 56.
Gray, Paul. *Time,* 1998.
Hoffert, Barbara. *Library Journal* 122.17 (Oct 15, 1997): 64 + .
Howes, Victor. *Christian Science Monitor* (Oct 12, 1977).
Jenkins, Nicholas. "A Life of Beginnings". *New York Times Book Review* 103 (Jan 4, 1998): 14.
Kirsch, Adam. *New Republic* 219.13 (Sep 28, 1998): 38 + .

Taylor, John. *Antioch Review* 56.4 (Fall, 1998): 501+.
Zawacki, Andrew. "A Wave of Music". *Times Literary Supplement* 4967 (Jun 12, 1998): 25.

WAKEFULNESS (1998)

Bakaitis, Vyt. *World Literature Today* 73.1 (Winter, 1999): 151.
Bedient, Calvin. *Nation* 266.20 (Jun 1, 1998): 27+.
Brownjohn, Alan. *Sunday Times* (Jan 10, 1999).
Burt, Stephen. *Yale Review* 86.4 (Oct, 1998): 152+.
Clark, Tom. San Francisco Chronicle (1998).
Kendall, Tim. "Uh Oh, No Last Words". *Times Literary Supplement* 4977 (Aug 21, 1998): 23.
Kirkus Reviews (1998).
Kirsch, Adam. *New Republic* 219.13 (Sep 28, 1998): 38+.
Lehman, David. "Spotlight on...National Poetry Month". *People* 49.14 (Apr 13, 1998): 41.
Logan, William. *New Criterion* (Jun, 1998): 61; reprinted in William Logan, *Desperate Measures*. Gainsville, Florida: University Press of Florida, 2002: 259-261.
Matterson, Steven. *Poetry Ireland Review*, 62 (1998): 114.
Muratori, Fred. *Library Journal* 123.4 (Mar 1, 1998): 91.
Publishers Weekly 245.13 (Mar 30, 1998): 77.
Seaman, Donna. *Booklist* 94.14 (Mar 15, 1998): 1197.
Shetley, Vernon. *Raritan* 18.4 (Spring, 1999): 130-144.
Silano, Martha. *Economist* (US) (Aug 15, 1998): 72.
Virginia Quarterly Review 75.1 (Winter, 1999): 28.
"War of words". *Economist* 348.8081 (Aug 15, 1998): 72.

GIRLS ON THE RUN (1999)

Bernard, Sarah. "Little Darlings". *New York* 32.13 (Apr 5, 1999): 14.
Gander, Forrest. *Jacket* 8 (1999). http://jacketmagazine.com/08/gand-r-ashb.html.
Glover, Michael. *Independent* (Nov 13, 1999).
Kirby, David. *New York Times Book Review* (Apr 11, 1999).
Leddy, Michael. *World Literature Today* 73.4 (Autumn, 1999): 740.
Manguso, Sarah. *Iowa Review* 30.1 (Spring-Summer, 2000): 178+.
Matterson, Stephen. *Poetry Ireland Review* 62.114 (2000).
Muratori, Fred. *Library Journal* 124.7 (Apr 15, 1999): 100.
Palattella, John. *Newsday*, 1999.
Publishers Weekly 246.8 (Feb 22, 1999): 87.
Rehak, Melanie. "A Child in Time". *New York Times Magazine* 71.7 (Apr 4, 1999): 6.
Rubinstein, Raphael. "Ashbery in Dargerland". *Art in America* 88.2 (Feb, 2000): 37+.
Seaman, Donna. *Booklist* 95.14 (Mar 15, 1999): 1271.
Sellar, Tom. "Realms of the Unreal". *Theater* 32.1 (2002): 100-109.
Shetley, Vernon. *Raritan: a Quarterly Review* 18.4 (Spring, 1999): 130+.
Virginia Quarterly Review 75.4 (Autumn, 1999): 138.
Wheatley, David. "Tidbit and Talkative". *Times Literary Supplement* 5074 (Jun 30, 2000): 25.
Yaffe, David. "The Vivian Chronicles". *Civilization* 6:2 (Apr/May 1999): 96.

YOUR NAME HERE (2000)

Bedient, Calvin. "Charms and Afflictions". *Salmagundi* 132 (Fall, 2001): 186-194.
Beskin, Lisa. *Boston Review* (Apr-May, 2001).
Chiasson, Dan. "Him Again: John Ashbery". *Raritan: a Quarterly Review* 21.2 (Fall, 2001): 139-145.
Christian, Graham. *Library Journal* 125.13 (Aug, 2000): 109.
Corbett, William. *Harvard Review* 22 (Spring, 2002).
Logan, William. *New Criterion* 19.4 (Dec, 2000).
Oser, Lee. *World Literature Today* 75.2 (Spring, 2001): 336.
Publishers Weekly 247.30 (Jul 24, 2000): 82.
Qureshi, Ramez. *Jacket* 18 (Aug, 2002). http://jacketmagazine.com/18/qureshi.html.

Seaman, Donna. *Booklist* 97.3 (Oct 1, 2000): 313.
Simic, Charles. "Tragicomic Soup". *New York Review of Books* 47.18 (Nov 30, 2000): 8+.

OTHER TRADITIONS (2000)

Antrim, Taylor. *New York Times Book Review* 105.46 (Nov 12, 2000): 27.
Bedient, Calvin. "Charms and Afflictions". *Salmagundi* 132 (Fall, 2001): 186-194.
Beskin, Lisa. *Boston Review* (Apr-May, 2001).
Cox, Craig and Chris Dodge. *Utne Reader* 102 (Nov/Dec, 2000): 115.
Corbett, William. *Harvard Review* 22 (Spring, 2002).
Dirda, Michael. *Washington Post Book World* (Oct 15, 2000)
Ford, Mark. "Life Without Eliot". *New Republic* (Jan 1, 2001): 30-32, 34-36.
Gibbons, James. "Eccentric Visions: Ashbery's Other Traditions". *Raritan: a Quarterly Review* 21.2 (Fall, 2001): 146-161.
Hightower, Scott. *Library Journal* 125.14 (Sep 1, 2000): 206.
Klatt, L.S. *Georgia Review* 55.1 (Spring, 2001): 180+.
Notes & Queries 49.3 (Sep, 2002): 433+.
Oser, Lee. *World Literature Today* 75.2 (Spring, 2001): 338.
Palattella, John. *London Review of Books* 23.11 (Jun 7, 2001).
Pasquin, Ethan. *Contemporary Poetry Review* (http://www.cprw.com/Paquin/influence.htm), 2001.
Salter Reynols, Susan. *Los Angeles Times Book Review*.
Simic, Charles. "Tragicomic Soup". *New York Review of Books* 47.18 (Nov 30, 2000): 8+.
Yezzi, David. *New Criterion* 19.6 (Feb, 2001): 75.
Zaleski, Jeff. *Publishers Weekly* 247.39 (Sep 25, 2000): 108.

AS UMBRELLAS FOLLOW RAIN (2001)

Corbett, William. *Harvard Review* 22 (Spring, 2002).
Publishers Weekly 249.3 (Jan 21, 2002): 87.

CHINESE WHISPERS (2002)

Clover, Joshua. "End of the Experiment". *Village Voice Literary Supplement* (Oct 9-15, 2002): 76.
Flamm, Matthew. *New York Times Book Review* (Dec 15, 2002): 28.
Gibbon, James. *Artforum* 9.4 (Winter, 2002): 23.
Hoffert, Barbara. *Library Journal* 127.17 (Oct 15, 2002): 77.
Noel Tod, Jeremy. *Guardian* (Feb 8, 2003): Review, 25.
"Reasons for Rhyme". *Economist* (Feb 8, 2003): 76.
Scharf, Michael. *Publishers Weekly* 249.33 (Aug 19, 2002): 81.
Seaman, Donna. *Booklist* 99.3 (Oct 1, 2002): 296-297.

AUDIO REVIEWS

ACADEMY OF AMERICAN POETS AUDIO ARCHIVE: JOHN ASHBERY

Ratner, Rochelle. *Library Journal* 120.15 (Sep 15, 1995): 112.

JOHN ASHBERY: THE SONGS WE KNOW BEST

Stearns, Melissa. *Library Journal* 115.3 (Feb 15, 1990): 232-233.

BIBLIOGRAPHIES

Berry, Jonas. "Ashbery, John (Lawrence) 1927-". *Contemporary Authors*, New Revision Series 102. Detroit: Gale Group, 2002: 41-42, 48-51.
Kermani, David K. *John Ashbery: a Comprehensive Bibliography (Including His Art Criticism, and with Selected*

Notes from Unpublished Materials). Foreword by John Ashbery. New York and London: Garland Press, 1976.

Perloff, Marjorie. "Ashbery, John (Lawrence)". *Contemporary Poets*, 6th ed. New York: St Martin's Press, 1996: 33-34.

Prestianni, Vince. "John Ashbery: an Analytic Bibliography of Bibliographies". *Sagetrieb* 11.1-2 (Spring-Fall, 1992): 235-236.

—. John Ashbery: *John Ashbery: an Analytic Bibliography of Bibliographies*. Orono: University of Maine, 1992.

Bibliographie. *L'Oeil de Boeuf* 22 (a special issue devoted to John Ashbery) (Paris) (Dec, 2000): 152.

Herd, David. *John Ashbery and American Poetry*. Manchester: Manchester University Press, 2000: 223-240; as *John Ashbery and American Poetry: Fit to Cope with Our Occasions*. New York: Palgrave, 2000: 223-240.

FORTHCOMING

An updated version of David Kermani's 1976 bibliography will appear in late 2003 as a work-in-progress at http://www.bard.edu

ARCHIVES WITH HOLDINGS OF ASHBERY'S CORRESPONDENCE

Bertolino, James. *Papers, 1968-1980*. Ohio University Library, Athens, Ohio, Department of Archives & Special Collections. Contains letters from a variety of literary figures, including John Ashbery.

Rapp & Carroll. *Letters Received from Poets, 1959-1969*. Rare Books Room, University Libraries, Pennsylvania State University, University Park, Pennsylvania. Contains letters from a variety of literary figures, including John Ashbery.

Eshleman, Clayton. *Clayton Eshleman Papers, 1958-1993: MSS 21*. Mandeville Department of Special Collections, University of California at San Diego. Contains a large file of correspondence from a variety of literary figures, including John Ashbery. http://orpheus.ucsd.edu/speccoll/testing/html/mss0021a.html

Hickman, Leland. *Leland Hickman Papers: MSS 186*. Mandeville Department of Special Collections, University of California at San Diego. Contains correspondence from a variety of literary figures, including John Ashbery. http://orpheus.ucsd.edu/speccoll/testing/html/mss0186a.html

Mottram, Eric. *MOTTRAM: 5/7/1-18 1958-1981*. King's College London Features letters and poems by JA, as well as notes and essays on JA written by Mottram. http://www.kcl.ac.uk/depsta/iss/archives/collect/1mo70-05a.html

Schuyler, James. *James Schuyler Papers: MSS 78*. Mandeville Department of Special Collections, University of California at San Diego. Contains correspondence from a variety of literary figures, including John Ashbery. http://orpheus.ucsd.edu/speccoll/testing/html/mss0078a.html

Wright, Charles. *Charles Wright Papers, 1990-1999: Accession #11437*. Special Collections Department, University of Virginia Library, Charlottesville, Virginia. Contains correspondence from a variety of literary figures, including John Ashbery. http://ead.lib.virginia.edu/vivaead/published/uva-sc/vivadoc.pl?file=viu01233.xml

THE ASHBERY ARCHIVE

The bulk of Ashbery's papers are held in the Houghton Library of the Harvard College Library, Harvard, Massachusetts (Harvard Depository AM6). The holding presently comprises 56 cartons and 3 portfolio boxes (71 linear feet), and is organized into nine series: (1) Letters to Ashbery, (2) Letters from Ashbery, (3) Other letters, (4) Compositions by Ashbery, (5) Organization files, (6) Compositions by others, (7) Biographical material concerning Ashbery, (8) Printed material by others, (9) Oversized material. Though arranged, this material is not fully catalogued.

THE CRITICS

SOME TREES (1956)

'I have no idea most of the time what Mr Ashbery is talking about ... beyond the communication of an intolerable vagueness that looks as if it was meant for precision ... What does come through is an impression of an impossibly fractured brittle world, depersonalized and discontinuous, whose characteristic emotional gesture is an effete and cerebral whimsy.' – William Arrowsmith, *Hudson Review*, 1956

'Faultless music, originality of perception – Mr Ashbery has written the most beautiful first book to appear in America since *Harmonium*.' – Frank O'Hara, *Poetry*, 1956

'A glance at the table of contents tells us, first of all, how thoroughly aware Ashbery is of his conventions – more than aware, elated to have them at hand: "Eclogue", "Canzone", "Sonnet", "Pantoum" and three sestinas dramatize this poet's fondness for the art's most intricate forms, and his facility with them. Other pieces are named for works of literature themselves – "Two Scenes", "Popular Songs", "The Instruction Manual", "Album Leaf", "Illustration", "A Long Novel", "A Pastoral" – suggesting that Ashbery has none of the advanced artist's habitual hostility to his own medium, for all his dissociative techniques and fragmenting designs ... Most of the poems in this book aim, as one firing buckshot may be said to aim, at a single target: the elusive order of existence which the poet knows to be there, just beyond reach ...' – Richard Howard, *Poetry*, 1970

THE TENNIS COURT OATH (1962)

'If a state of continuous exasperation, a continuous frustration of expectation, a continuous titillation of the imagination are sufficient response to a series of thirty-one poems, then these have been successful. But to be satisfied with such a response I must change my notion of poetry.' – Mona Van Duyn, *Poetry*, 1962

'... this extreme disjointedness proves to have a tonal unity in no way dependent on meter or even cadence conventionally understood, but rather on a cadence of feeling-sight.' – R.W. Flint, *Partisan Review*, 1962

'"I attempt to use words abstractly," [Ashbery] declares, "as an artist uses paint" ... If the reader can shut off that portion of the brain which insists words be related logically, he may dive with pleasure into Ashbery's stream of consciousness.' – X.J. Kennedy, *New York Times Book Review*, 1962

'The trouble with Ashbery's work is that he is influenced by modern painting to the point where he tries to apply words to the page as if they were abstract, emotional colours and shapes ... Consequently, his work loses coherence ... There is little substance to the poems in this book.' – James Schevill, *Saturday Review* 1962

'Mr Ashbery has perfected his verse to the point where it almost never deviates into –
nothing so square as sense! – sensibility, sensuality, or sentences.' – John Simon,
Hudson Review, 1962

'*The Tennis Court Oath* ... seems to me a fearful disaster ... Coming to this eagerly as
an admirer of *Some Trees*, I remember my outrage and disbelief at what I found ...' –
Harold Bloom, 'John Ashbery: the Charity of Harsh Moments', 1973

'*The Tennis Court Oath* is still a book that arouses passions in critics and readers,
some of whom have criticized its purposeful obscurity. For me it becomes
approachable, explicable, and even downright lucid when read with some of the
aesthetic assumptions of Abstract Expressionism in mind ... Pollock's drips, Rothko's
haunting, colour-drenched, luminous, rectangular shapes, and Gottlieb's spheres and
explosive strokes are here, in a sense, paralleled by an imagistic scattering and emotional
and intellectual verbal juxtaposition.' – Fred Moramarco, *Journal of Modern Literature*,
1976

RIVERS AND MOUNTAINS (1966)

' ... we are rarely able to respond to this *œuvre* in the way we do to the traditional
modes anchored in what Northrop Frye calls the seasonal myths, for recurrence and
the cyclical patterns of ritual simply do not apply to Ashbery's poetry in its characteristic
extension here. Nothing in *Rivers and Mountains* "depends on everything's recurring
till we answer from within" as Frost put it, "because," as Ashbery answers, "*all the true
fragments are here.*" In the first poems in the book, we find ... some more of those
apologies for the poems themselves, but they are no longer militant or even apologetic,
they are triumphant in accounting for the *over-all* texture of these anti-psychological
poems: "continuance quickens the scrap which falls to us ... a premise of so much that
is to come, extracted, accepted gladly but within its narrow limits no knowledge yet,
nothing which can be used." And again, most significantly: "*Each moment of utterance
is the true one; likewise none are true*". Existence is reported to be as ineffable as in
the poems of *Some Trees*, but no longer beyond the poet's grasp because he is no
longer grasping ...' – Richard Howard, *Poetry*, 1970

A NEST OF NINNIES (1969, 1987)

'When the poets John Ashbery and James Schuyler first published their collaborative
novel in 1969, the New York school was at its airiest. The novel's characters are
shallow, but interestingly capricious, the prose is sprightly, and the plot crammed
with amusing coincidences, odd romances, swift scene changes and festive occasions
... W.H. Auden was sure that the book, with its happy air of total inconsequentiality,
was "destined to become a minor classic".

   ...
   The book was highly artificial when it was first written, and seems that much more
removed from life twenty years later ...' – *Times Literary Supplement*, 1987

FRAGMENT (1969)

'"Fragment" ... [is] ... for me, Ashbery's finest work. Enigmatically autobiographical, even if it were entirely fantasy, the poem's fifty stately ten-line stanzas, orotundly Stevensian in their rhetoric, comment obliquely upon a story never told, a relationship never quite a courtship, and now a nostalgia. Studying this nostalgia, in his most formal and traditional poem, more so than anything even in *Some Trees*, Ashbery presents his readers, however faithful, with his most difficult rumination. But this is a wholly Stevensian difficulty, neither elliptical nor obscure, but a ravishing simplicity that seems largely lacking in any referential quality. I have discussed the poem with excellent and sympathetic students who continue to ask: "But what is the poem *about?*" The obvious answer, that to some extent it is "about" itself, they rightly reject, since whether we are discussing Shelley, Stevens, or Ashbery, this merely distances the same question to one remove. But though repeated readings open up the referential aspect of "Fragment", the poem will continue to inspire our uneasiness, for it is profoundly evasive.' – Harold Bloom, 'The Charity of Hard Moments', 1976

THE DOUBLE DREAM OF SPRING (1970)

'Emotion has been intellectualized to the extent that it is almost nonexistent.' – J.A. Avant, *Library Journal*, 1970

'The Doris Day of modernist poetry, [Ashbery] plays nasty Symbolist-Imagist tricks on his audience while maintaining a facade of earnest innocuousness ... [Some of his lines] have about as much poetic life as a refrigerated plastic flower ... [and some] are trite and silly ... [His failure] is the price he has paid for uncritically accepting the Symbolist-Imagist aesthetic. The contrived image and the pseudo-profound symbol may enable a poet to continue his poem, despite the flaccid state of his emotion ... but such a continuation may, in fact, embody a kind of poetic dishonesty. Ashbery is one of the inheritors of Eliot's Symbolist Waste Land. Eliot, at least, was honest about the agony and emotional barrenness he tried to describe. Ashbery, a professional mindblower, inhabits a Technicolour Waste Land where he seems to feel completely at home.' – J.W. Hughes, *Saturday Review*, 1970

'Robbed of their solid properties, the smallest and surest of words become part of a new geography.' – David Kalstone, *New York Times Book Review* 1970

'In Ashbery there has always been a catlike presence, both in the poems themselves and in the person these poems reveal: tender, curious, cunning, tremendously independent, sweet, guarded. Above all, like a cat, Ashbery is a born hunter ... But the one prime act of the cat – to spring, to pounce, to make the miraculous leap – Ashbery, for me, has yet to perform.' – Robert Mazzocco, *New York Review of Books*, 1973

'There are three notes at the end of Ashbery's fourth volume of poems ... which help a lot, as the poet says, "to get over the threshold of so much unmeaning, so much / Being, preparing us for its event, the active memorial". Yes, precisely, that is what Ashbery's poems are, an active memorial to themselves, writhing in dissolute,

149

shimmering lines without emphases or repetitions around the column their own accumulation raises until "the convention gapes / prostrated before a monument disappearing into the dark". And if it is true that in reading poems which are habitually a gloss on their own singularity we need all the help we can get, it is also true that Ashbery wants us to enjoy our helplessness all the way: "these things are offered to your participation ... Each hastens onward separately / in strange sensations of emptiness, anguish, romantic / outbursts, visions and wraiths. One meeting cancels another ... becoming a medium in which it is possible to recognize oneself. Each new diversion adds its accurate touch to the ensemble, and so / a portrait is built up out of multiple corrections".

...

... the great innovation of Ashbery's poems is that they do not explain or symbolize or even refer to some experience the poet has had, something outside themselves in the world, something precedent. The poems are not about anything, they are something, they are their own creation, and it would be fair to say that the world is, instead, a comment on them, a criticism of them. For all his modesty and mildness, that is Ashbery's great Symbolist assertion – that the world may exist to conclude in a book.' – Richard Howard, *Poetry*, 1970

THREE POEMS (1972)

'*Three Poems* will excite aficionados of [Ashbery's] work, but it probably won't, as an introduction, win him new converts.' – Alan Helms, *Partisan Review*, 1972

'Worked in prose as demanding and thus as fecund as verse, John Ashbery's new book is a meditational masterpiece, calm in its encounters with minor fictions, desperate in pursuit of a supreme one. Its flutterings are those of the fledged imagination, its difficulties that of the truth.' – John Hollander, 1972

'There are several misconceptions about John Ashbery's work. He is often considered an anomaly – "daringly original", to be sure, but ultimately a kind of prestidigitator with his bag of tricks. This usually takes the form of praise: his language is dense but buoyant, he modulates it like a medium, and the logic of his poems is as invisible as it is hypnotic; finally, his entire work constitutes a sort of floating monument to itself, modernism's fullest flower. Versions of this view are held by both enthusiasts and detractors. Aside from its shallowness – since all that is true of virtually every great poet – it obscures the fact that one of the questions Ashbery takes most urgently is whether any expression can be adequate to the need that prompted it ... Looking at Ashbery's work in aesthetic terms alone makes about as much sense as taking Traherne's *Centuries of Meditation* (with which *Three Poems* has a great deal in common) as a response to the itch to meditate ...

...

Against Ashbery's the work of most other poets seems dismally contingent. Somehow it is just the even weight he allows each thing, the possibility of blending "in a union too subtle to cause any comment", that accounts for its stature. This is a vision as simple to understand as it is impossible to learn.' – John Koethe, *Parnassus*, 1972.

'Long stretches of "Self-Portrait" read like the bland prose of an uninspired scholar, complete with references and quotations. Bleached of feeling and poetic surprise, the words gasp for air, stutter, go dead.' – Pearl K. Bell, *New Leader*, 1975

'[A] collection of poems of breathtaking freshness and adventure in which dazzling orchestrations of language open up whole areas of consciousness no other American poet has even begun to explore ... The influence of films now shows in Ashbery's deft control of just those cinematic devices a poet can most usefully appropriate. Crosscut, flashback, montage, close-up, fade-out – he employs them all to generate the kinetic excitement that starts on the first page of his book and continues to the last.' – John Malcolm Brinnin, *New York Times Book Review*, 1975

'Ashbery's method is allusive, associative, and disjunctive, rather than logical, dramatic, or narrative. A typical extended poem will launch itself, or maybe wake up to find itself already in transit, throw out a fertile suggestion, make connections, go into reverse, change key, short-circuit, suffer enlightenment, laugh, nearly go over the edge, regard itself with disbelief, irony, and pathos, then sign off with an inconclusive gesture. The texture of many of the poems reminds me of Gaudí's mosaics in the Barcelona Parque Guell, where broken-up fragments of coloured tile with all kinds of figurations – Arabic-geometrical, floral, pictorial – are carefully reassembled in a new and satisfying whole ... It's possible of course to consider this kind of poetry not simply an 'imitation of consciousness' but rather a new synthetic kind of experience too underdetermined or maybe overdetermined to render consciousness accurately, and so existing on a purely contemplative, aesthetic plane. Obviously, these two efforts overlap and blend: "imitation" in art is never duplication, and it always involves some synthesis; but nothing lifelike can be synthesized in art unless it can seem to belong to consciousness. In the measure, then, that an imitation becomes more stylized and synthetic, its resemblance to anyone's consciousness proportionately decreases – it becomes more purely artful. I don't see the poems in *Self-Portrait* as all occupying a fixed point on the spectrum that moves from direct representation of a stream of consciousness to a purely composed and synthetic experience. It's like the new mixed suiting of materials – some are more synthetic than others. Nor would I assume that any of the poems were products of "automatic writing". If there's an automatic writer that can rap out phrases like the following, one wants the thing installed immediately: "This was one of those night rainbows / In negative colour. As we advance, it retreats; we see / We are now far into a cave, must be. Yet there seem to be / Trees all around, and a wind lifts their leaves, slightly".
      In a sense, all good writing is an "imitation of consciousness" insofar as that is compatible with the selectivity required for effective, beautiful communication. A special quality of consciousness as imitated by Ashbery, however, is its inclusiveness, or, more precisely, its magnification: into these poems come minute or translucent mental events that would escape a less acute gaze, an attention less rapt. It's the same degree of magnification, I think, used to apprehend the *tropismes* in Nathalie Sarraute's early fiction, although Ashbery lacks the fury and venom characteristic of her work. In this poetry, the unconscious – that misnomer – is in agreeable tension with the conceptual, composing mind; the free interweaving of the known and the about-to-

be-known makes for a rich experiential texture in which guesswork, risk, and discovery contribute almost a tactile quality to the overall patterning.' – Alfred Corn, *Parnassus*, 1975

'Whitman's invitation to American poets to loaf and invite their souls can't have had many responses more mysterious, peculiar, searching and beautiful than Ashbery's recent poems. Where he will go from there is, to use one of his titles, "no way of knowing". What is important is that Ashbery, who was on speaking terms with both the formalism of the American 1950s and the unbuttoned verse of the 1960s, is now bold and beyond them.' – David Kalstone: 'John Ashbery: Self-Portrait in a Convex Mirror', 1977

'How desperately, today, we need a poetry that will shame the slovenly readership out of us. Poetry must demand more from us if it is to make of us the kind of audience who will demand, in turn, loftiest vision – a readership who will settle for nothing less than to be uplifted in ardour of collaborative appreciation. John Ashbery is our gadfly. His new poetry creates discomforts, snares, inconveniences for readers to sting them into a more responsible mode of readership ...' – Laurence Lieberman, *American Poetry Review*, 1977

THE VERMONT NOTEBOOK (1975)

'"Did I know you, split-levels? What it's like to inhabit your dangerous divided spaces with views of celery plantations?" Long listed on the pages dedicated to "other books by John Ashbery" but largely unobtainable, *The Vermont Notebook*, the poet's wonderful 1975 collaboration with artist Joe Brainard (1942-1994), is finally seeing accessible print. Nearly 50 page-sized pen-and-ink drawings are matched with diary-like prose pieces, pairings that remain offhandedly perfect.' – *Publishers Weekly*, 1975

'You can feel [Ashbery's] impressions gathering, presented here at some point before they have assembled into the autonomy of his poems. Brainard's drawings ... do not have a magic that meets the prose ...' – Jed Perl, *New Republic,* 2001

HOUSEBOAT DAYS (1977)

'*Houseboat Days* is Ashbery's very best book, with many astonishing poems in it, some transcending even Ashbery's most beautiful earlier work. He and Elizabeth Bishop are our two living contemporaries who should be beyond all critical dispute.' – Harold Bloom, 1977

'Most of the poems in *Houseboat Days* which I can make out at all are ... deliberations on the meaning of the present tense, its exactions and falsifications, its promises and rewards. "There are no other questions than these, / half-squashed in mud, emerging out of the moment / we all live, learning to like it" – Ashbery is often painfully clear as to what he would wring from his evasive experience ("what I am trying to do is to illustrate opacity and how it can suddenly descend over us ... it's a kind of mimesis of how experience comes to me"), and the pain is there in the tone, now goofy and insolent, then again tender and self-deprecating, vulnerable but not without its gnomic assertions ("It is the nature of things to be seen only once"), various but without a consistent grimace ("It's all bits and pieces, spangles, patches, really; nothing / stands alone").' – Richard Howard, *New York Arts Journal*, 1977

'He's like a collage of Ovid and S.J. Perelman, as Kafka might have done it. He's a kaleidoscope of Daffy Duck and Amadis de Gaul, of root beer stands and lines from Sir Thomas Wyatt and old Scotch ballads, of art-deco and scrimshaw ... [D]oes he touch the heart? Does he know the passions? My dear. My dear. Really, sometimes you ask too much.' – Victor Howes, *Christian Science Monitor*, 1977

'[Ashbery] carries the saw that "poetry does not have subject matter because it is the subject" to its furthest limit. Just as we feel we are beginning to make sense of one of his poems, meaning eludes us again ... Still, we are somehow left with a sense that the conclusion is satisfactory, with a wondering delight at what we've heard ... *Houseboat Days* is evidence of the transcendent power of the imagination, and one of the major works of our time.' – Phoebe Pettingell, *New Leader*, 1977

'Ashbery is astonishingly original, and though his mannerisms have been widely imitated, he himself has imitated no one.' – Edmund White, *Bookletter*, 1977

As We Know (1979)

'To come to terms with John Ashbery's poetry is to come to terms with a sensibility deeply divided, nervously giddy, utterly fraudulent. How will those gimlet-eyed readers of the future judge our age's critical fascination with him? As a typical example of our culture's infatuation with fashion rather than meaning? As the inflation of a small, delicate talent for absurdity into a helium balloon six storeys high, fit only for Macey's Thanksgiving Day parade? Or as the rare recognition of an innovative genius by a time with little else to recommend it?
...
    The immediate pleasures of Ashbery's poems are so separate from textual analysis it is difficult not to be entranced by the surface – the wily gestures, the knowing tones, the great range of diction – and to dismiss a poem without attempting to dismantle it. Many of his poems yield to an analysis far less rigorous than that needed for Hart Crane or even Emily Dickinson. Unfortunately, most of them resolve into an aesthetics of perception that would little trouble and little interest a freshman philosophy class. Ashbery is so adept at creating the illusion of thought it is depressing to find his dressed-up ideas just sweet banalities.
    A poet can live on the banality of ideas far longer than he can live on the banality of expression. Ashbery's gift is a vague suggestiveness that is also a brilliant suggestiveness. When he writes, "Where day and night exist only for themselves / And the future is our table and chairs", he has supplied the small consolations of language (personification and metaphor being the core of etymology) in selfish nights and fateful

meals. The adversities of logic do not interest him (it would be unfair to say they elude him), and a poetry deprived of logic always devolves into suggestion ...

Ashbery is a brilliant example of a condition, a *fin de siècle* sensibility with the attention span of a stand-up comic. "Taglioni danced what Kant thought," a dance critic once wrote, and Ashbery writes what Wittgenstein thought as he watched his beloved cowboy movies.' – William Logan, *Washington Star*, 1980

'As these streams of everyday and extraordinary objects flow past us in no apparent order, but always in wondrously lyrical lines, the poems make their own curious kind of sense. After all, isn't this how we perceive "reality"? ... Ashbery's poems imply the improbability of finding ultimate significance amid the evanescence and transience of modern life. If, however, in the process of these poems the old order is lost or irrelevant, the longing for it or some kind of meaning is not.' – Joseph Parisi, *Chicago Tribune Book World*, 1980

'Since the death of Robert Lowell, the title of most important American poet has been on offer to John Ashbery. In "Litany", the magnificent long poem that begins *As We Know*, Ashbery has taken up that title while declining the magisterial stance that usually goes with even an unofficial laureateship.' – Helen McNeil, *Times Literary Supplement*, 1981

'It is worth quoting once more Keats's description of this world not as a vale of tears but as a vale of what he called "soul-making" ...: "I will call the *world* a School instituted for the purpose of teaching little children to read – I will call the *human heart* the *horn Book* used in that School – and I will call the *Child able to read, the Soul* made from that *school and its hornbook*. Do you not see how necessary a World of Pains and troubles is to school an Intelligence and make it a soul?" ...
...
I was only one of many readers put off, years ago, by the mixture of wilful flashiness and sentimentality in *The Tennis Court Oath* ... And I was impatient for some time after that because of Ashbery's echoes of Stevens, in forms done better, I thought, and earlier, by Stevens himself. Ashbery's mimetic ear, which picks up clichés and advertising slogans as easily as "noble accents and lucid inescapable rhythms" (as Stevens called them), is a mixed blessing in the new book (which has some undigested Eliot from the "Quartets" in it), as in the earlier ones. But though some superficial poems still appear in these new pages, poems of soul making and speculative classification – evident in *Rivers and Mountains* ... and taking expository form in the prose of *Three Poems* ... have been in the ascendant since *Self-Portrait in a Convex Mirror* ... and *Houseboat Days* ...' – Helen Vendler, *New Yorker*, 1981

Shadow Train (1981)

'*Shadow Train* will change no one's mind about John Ashbery's merits as a poet. His admirers will praise the new found discipline and concentration in this collection of sixteen-line "sonnet-like" poems. His detractors will grumble about the emperor's new briefs. And the rest will continue to play Pontius Pilate, washing their hands of the whole matter. Yet *Shadow Train* is an interesting book that can give a careful

reader a new understanding of Ashbery's strengths and weaknesses as a poet.
...

Despite the awards and the attention, [Ashbery] lacks the weight of the major poet his defenders claim he has become. Paradoxically, his work becomes more pleasurable and interesting the fewer claims one makes for it. He is a marvellous minor poet, but an uncomfortable major one.' – Dana Gioia, *Hudson Review*, 1981-82

'... his continual invention makes Ashbery the most stimulating (and occasionally most irritating) of our poets.' – William Logan, *Chicago Tribune*, 1980

'If, as is often said, British and American poets are no longer on speaking terms, their methods so different that they scarcely seem to be talking the same language, then it may be that John Ashbery must take some of the blame. In the 1950s and 1960s, the years of mid-Atlantic talents such as Auden, Lowell, Plath and Hughes, and of skilled critical mediators such as A. Alvarez and M.L. Rosenthal, it was possible to believe that our two poetic traditions were working hand in hand. The rise of Ashbery demonstrates how brief and illusory that reconciliation was and how much more, rightly or wrongly, the British continue to insist on reason and ready intelligibility in poetry.

With *Shadow Train*, Ashbery's relationship with British readers is likely to become even more troubled and mistrustful, for it's the most teasingly English of all his books. The form he has chosen to work with – the sequence of fifty sixteen-line sonnets – is one that was made famous by Meredith in *Modern Love*, and which Tony Harrison has just revived, to great acclaim, in *Continuous*. Given these two celebrated examples, the form inevitably arouses certain expectations: a confessional treatment of family, marriage, domestic intimacy; a seam of narrative; and an extreme formality of diction. Ashbery, though, refuses to deliver these: if there is a train of events it is, as the title implies, no more than shadowy; if there are emotional confessions, we don't really pick them up since there is no single narrator to unburden his loves and losses; and though there is a rigorous formality in one sense (four quatrains to each poem), it prevents neither the stumbling inarticulacy of the first line of the penultimate sonnet which reads *in toto* "The works, the days, uh", nor the colloquial gusto of "Or in My Throat": "That's why I quit and took up writing poetry instead. / It's clean, it's relaxing, it doesn't squirt juice all over / Something you were certain of a moment ago and now your own face / Is a stranger and no one can tell you it's true. Hey, stupid!" Already, five poems into the sequence, it is clear that Ashbery has appropriated the Meredithian mode for his own familiar and frustrating ends.' – Blake Morrison, *Times Literary Supplement*, 1982

'You must enjoy unpredictability if you are to like John Ashbery ... We must be ready for anything in reading [him] because this eclectic, dazzling, inventive creator of travesties and treaties is ready to and eager to include anything, say anything, go anywhere, in the service of an aesthetic dedicated to liberating poetry from predictable conventions and tired traditions.' – David Young, *Washington Post Book World,* 1981

'In *Shadow Train* ... however, the prevailing note is one of failure. There are good poems in ... [the book], and, as always, the writing is marked with intelligence and grace, but the dominant imagery is of staleness: the breeze on the face being not, now, the gusting of a new wind, but the recycled atmospherics of the air-conditioning system ... The uniformity of *Shadow Train*, the fifty poems of which are all four quatrains long, is a formal declaration that the poetry is less than fully receptive to the state of change which has hitherto provided its element.' – David Herd, *John Ashbery and American Poetry*, 2000

A Wave (1984)

'*A Wave* is John Ashbery's tenth book of poetry, and one of his best. Too much that he has written recently has been rather dull experiment. The quatrains of *Shadow Train* ... were all too often little more than lax five-finger exercises in superficially regular form, and *As We Know* ... was dominated by the sixty pages of "Litany", which, in spite of fascinating sections (particularly on literary criticism), suffered from the over-casual juxtaposition of the two monologues of which it was composed. Still, some of the shorter pieces in *As We Know* – say "Train Rising out of the Sea" or "Late Echo" – had pointed in a different direction. It is this which is now followed through in *A Wave* and reaches its high point in the long, absorbing poem which gives the collection its title.' – Peter Hainsworth, *Times Literary Supplement*, 1984

'"Recklessness," John Ashbery once observed, "is what makes experimental art beautiful." Ashbery ... might have had his own formidably original poetry in mind, for a policy of calculated recklessness is central to his artistry. Ashbery's latest collection characteristically throws caution to the winds in pursuit of things unattempted yet in prose or rhyme. The results are exhilarating. To top it off, the 21-page title poem is easily Ashbery's finest single achievement since "Self-Portrait in a Convex Mirror" won the Pulitzer Prize and vaulted him into national prominence. Ashbery's poems defy paraphrase ... Some of Ashbery's more solemn explicators miss – or undervalue – the strong element of humour in his work. There's a streak of sublime silliness in this book.' – David Lehman, *Newsweek*, 1984

'Reading John Ashbery's poems is a bit like playing hide-and-seek in a sprawling mansion designed by M.C. Escher ... Strictly speaking, hardly any of the titles of the forty four pieces in [this book] are thematic, so [the author's] themes and concerns have to be snatched more or less out of the air. His time of life (he will be 57 next month) is a concern – the backward look longer than the forward one. Others are the instability of his vibrant wealth of ideas; the opalescence of his kind of thinking, feeling and perceiving; the spectacular aesthetics of surfaces, multiple, overlapping, with "depths" apparent only as recessions in time as "the past absconds". And there is death to come, and love, painful or breathless, that comes or goes and still stays.' – *New York Times Book Review*, 1984

'Ashbery is not writing English again, and doing it with such authority you can't ignore what he really is writing – an American so roomy and sure that its appearance among us amounts to a national gift. "I guess I was trying to 'democratize' language" is the way Ashbery put it, referring in a recent interview to the prose-poem meditations in his *Three Poems*. Now, in his eleventh major collection and especially in its long title poem, he has placed the vast prose vistas of *Three Poems* within the lyric measures he realized most explicitly in *Houseboat Days*. In retrospect, it seems an inevitable triumph; and the trio of *Three Poems*, *Houseboat Days* and *A Wave* will probably be seen by his audience as the indispensable core of Ashbery's work.' – Douglas Crase, *Nation*, 1984

Selected Poems (1985)

'I still enjoy "The Skaters" (the version in this collection is abridged), although I treasure mainly its moments of absurd clarity. And I very much admire that didactic poem "Self-Portrait in a Convex Mirror" ... What I see now, where once I saw a relaxed and exquisite mockery, is an aesthetic loneliness, like the loneliness of secret work. I see a joke turn sour on the features, like one played once too often, with a little too much violence, like a joke that is meant to hurt. This vaunted depiction of consciousness, of experience, this nattering on the whole night, this derogation of sense: none of this helps with the question – what shall I do with my gift?' – James Fenton, *New York Times Book Review*, 1985

'John Ashbery is probably the most highly regarded living poet in America. He is, in more ways than one, the heir of Wallace Stevens, and like Stevens some three decades ago is acquiring a belated minority-following in Britain ... The *Selected Poems* ... is, like Stevens's corresponding volume, a highly personal stocktaking, which may disconcert the critics by its refreshing omission of some of the poems they most like to talk about ("They Dream only of America", for example, or "These Lacustrine Cities"). Ashbery is in many ways a critics' poet, like many modern and post-modern masters, the product of a culture whose reading is shaped in the seminar-room and which accepts "explication" (even defeated explication, which is a permanent invitation to more explication) as an essential part of its reading experience. This need not imply inauthenticity. It is a natural (and by no means the ugliest) product of the hegemony of university English departments over the literary consciousness of the more affluent regions of the Anglophone world, and deeply rooted in the economics of (especially) American publishers, which have identified even for imaginative writers the profitability of the teacherly text.' – Claude Rawson, *Times Literary Supplement*, 1986

'While Ashbery is usually thought of as a complex, insular poet, he often reveals a sense of childlike wonder at the world: "The spring, though mild, is incredibly wet. / I have spent the afternoon blowing soap bubbles". And if he is a writer who tackles eternal verities, the poet's selection of his verse for this collection shows that his immediate topics range from Popeye the Sailor to the Aquarian Age, Warren G. Harding and the weather. Ashbery recognizes that the creative artist today is "barely tolerated, living on the margin / in our technological society". Lyrics, long prose-poem meditations, haiku, conversational ramblings, and musings reminiscent of Wallace Stevens attest to the full range of his experimentalism. His themes are the growth of the self through pain, the possibilities for personal happiness, the distance between seeing and knowing.' – Genevieve Stuttaford, *Publishers Weekly*, 1985

APRIL GALLEONS (1987)

'From unlikely beginnings ("Song of the Windshield Wiper", "Alone in the Lumber Business", etc.) Ashbery's elusive, astonishingly inventive poems spring. In this first volume since *Selected Poems*, his seamless style allows a rich assemblage of voices to move nimbly between high comedy and low, among fable, memory, and meditation. Youthful experience is contrasted with a life in late middle age: " ... afraid to retrace steps / To the past that was only recently ours, / ... O in all your life were you ever teased / Like this, and it became your mind?" and while change remains a major theme, life rather than art becomes central.' – Robert Hudzik, *Library Journal*, 1987

'In one sense, this collection has a single subject, the workings of a mind – a witty, capacious, elegant mind willing to "tackle the infinite, basing our stratagem / On knowledge of one inch of it" ... As so often happens in reading an Ashbery poem, one's sense of it is deferred, but these later, more generous, and wise poems, are not so much baffling and dense as complex and fluid. In language, imagery, tone, and style, the poems are rich. They include lyric moments, flat assertions, oracular pronouncements, and wonderful humour. Ashbery plays with clichés, lines from old songs, and quips and makes serious judgments.' – *Choice*, 1987

'[This] is a book that needs to be lived with, that needs to be taken whole, before it can be judged. Not that the book fails to reward even the most cursory reading; Ashbery's rich humour (his comic gifts are still too little appreciated, I think) is still very much apparent, his talent for picking the provocatively unexpected word still very much alive. Reading through the volume as a whole, however, reveals the added pleasure that one of America's finest and most challenging poets is refusing to become a classic, is still growing, changing, and demanding that we as readers grow as well.' – Vernon Shetley, *Poetry*, 1988

REPORTED SIGHTINGS (1989)

'Ashbery has humour, discrimination, lucidity, an inner compass: all the attributes necessary to bring to life a whole gallery of artists ... This voice – clear, self-assured, amused but never taken in – can bring people and places to life with magical ease.' – Jed Perl, *New Republic*, 1989

'[Ashbery's] art criticism strives for accessibility. It's a mixture of gossip, reportage, artist's shoptalk, and barstool philosophizing, and at times it has a you-were-there vividness.' – Deborah Solomon, *New Criterion*, 1989

'Ashbery describes beautifully, but his description also functions as inquiry or retelling: in describing an image, he recounts the process of its making and the concerns that guided its maker ... Certainly, Ashbery offers new insights into well-known artists. But he also argues persuasively for our appreciation of a number of lesser-known figures.

We come away with much to look at anew.' – Jeremy Strick, *Newsday,* 1989

'A major achievement of Ashbery's is the way he suffuses his essays, even the most journeyman of them, with his own aesthetic. But this aesthetic is not easy to formulate, if only for the reason that ... for him the essence of art lies in the dialectic between the work of art as it objectively is and the spectator. For the true aesthetic effect Ashbery often uses the word "magic", and, as an example to make this over-familiar word precise, he quotes a painting of deer in the snow by Courbet and says it is "as though he continued to paint after he had obtained a satisfactorily realistic image". It is, of course, no part of Ashbery's claim that, when magic crowns the work, the primary painting must have realistic intentions, but his general point is that magic is always tangential to the original aim of the work. It is a "non-functional essential", and its pursuit leads the painter to press himself against "the limits of the visual".' – Richard Wollheim, *Times Literary Supplement,* 1990

FLOW CHART (1991)

'This is what real achievement in a contemporary poet consists of: he has laid down guidelines and made his mark on the language of the tribe.' – John Bayley, *New York Review of Books,* 1991

'*Flow Chart* shows us a John Ashbery at his most achingly vulnerable ... It is impossible to be certain of this early on, but the reach of *Flow Chart* suggests that it is Ashbery's most important book, and certainly his most human.' – Alfred Corn, *Poetry,* 1991

'*Flow Chart*, Ashbery's magnum opus, is ... the fullest demonstration to date of this poet's fascination with what Walter Pater described as "that strange, perpetual weaving and unweaving of ourselves" ... [Ashbery] is likely to be seen as the defining voice of his nation and time.' – Robert Crawford, *Poetry Review,* 1991

'John Ashbery's distinctiveness as a poet paradoxically resides in his ability to evade all single identities; like Whitman, he feels most fully himself when he contains multitudes ... [Ashbery] deploys a staggering variety of dictions, ranging from fragments of novelettish narratives to lyrical dream-visions, from the clichés of public speech to scraps of surrealist collage...' – Mark Ford, *Times Literary Supplement,* 1991

'From "The Skaters" (1966) to "A Wave" (1984), John Ashbery has produced a remarkable series of longer poems. But perhaps none is quite so various, so beautiful and so new as "Flow Chart", a very long poem that recalls Wordsworth's "Prelude".' – Marjorie Perloff, *New York Times Book Review,* 1991

'What is John Ashbery's ... *Flow Chart*? A two-hundred-and-fifteen-page lyric; a diary; a monitor screen registering a moving EEG; a thousand and one nights; Penelope's web unravelling; views from Argus's hundred eyes; a book of riddles; a ham-radio station; an old trunk full of memories; a rubbish dump; a Bartlett's *Familiar Quotations*; a Last Folio; a vaudeville act ... It makes Ashbery's past work (except for those poems in *The Tennis Court Oath* ...) seem serenely classical, well ordered, pure, shapely, and above all, short.' – Helen Vendler, *New Yorker*, 1992

'The appreciation of a poem by John Ashbery requires an act of faith, a surrender of the ordinary faculties of judgment. What you are to admire is a certain deposit of psychic life in each of these poems, a shifting, disengaged record of the poet's spiritual state at the moment of setting the words down on paper ... There was a time when I had more patience for this sort of thing than I now have. It is no longer enough.' – James Gardner, *National Review*, 1993

'[Ashbery is] extremely forgiving, a poet, like Wordsworth, of superb passages who doesn't insist that one dig out the gold in every line ...' – Tom Sleigh, *New York Times Book Review*, 1993

AND THE STARS WERE SHINING (1994)

'Readers have at times confused Ashbery's interest in examining the appearances of things with a lack of poetic depth. The reasons? Perhaps that Ashbery is typically intrigued by surfaces because his main theme is the perception of reality; and, being of a more lyrical than critical inclination, he pursues philosophical investigation in, by and through poetry, so that his poems tend to embody the idea that is their subject. In his sixteenth collection, Ashbery once again addresses his chosen theme – and others – through many tightly bound short poems and a longer piece in thirteen parts, the title poem. And while his main concern is the work of the imagination, he begins to sound a more narrative voice, while never allowing the poems to develop into true extended narratives. The poet is less reticent (though still far from explicit) in committing himself to the ideas sown in his work. Also, he takes up an unaccustomed subject: the discerning of a poem after the poet's passing, implying his own death. Characteristically, it is in his longer poems that Ashbery holds a situation up to the light and approaches it most variously and richly. Though readers may not grasp or even catch sight of every angle, they will be gripped.' *Publishers Weekly*, 1994

'These poems are perfect in their pitch, savvy in their metric and changeable pace. And in this, its fifth decade, John Ashbery's resilient body of work is astonishing most of all for its sheer (the poet will not feel flattered at first) good nature. The poems are supple, sceptical; they puncture our most tender complacencies, our most careful phraseologies; they show us for the rubes we are. But what might easily have been an exclusionary aesthetic is instead, and durably, invitational ... The key to this remarkable career appears to be a genuine capaciousness of spirit: learning without pedantry, copiousness without glut, facetiousness without the sneer; gifts to thank our lucky stars for.' – *New York Review of Books*, 1994

'"It / isn't possible to be young anymore", [Ashbery] says in this most autumnally crumbly of his books. "Yet the tree treats me like a brute friend; / my own shoes have scarred the walk I've taken" ... This moves brilliantly from "being done to" to "being accepted by" to "having done harm to". It's as deep as it is swift ... Still, the new book's not one of his strongest. Its "liberating whimsy" is less inspired than one could wish. The dazzle of, say, *Houseboat Days* ... is scarcely recalled. Partly the autumnal theme discourages it; partly it just isn't there. The focus lacks fierceness.' – Calvin Bedient, *Poetry*, 1994

'The often-cited "difficulty" of Ashbery's poetry lies in its refusal to separate clearly the intrinsic from the extraneous. It comes to us unlabeled and uncompromised: "an aesthetic remoteness blossoming profusely / but vaguely around what does / stand out here and there". But like abstract paintings that leave us awestruck for no easily articulated reason, the poems generate waves of infinitely ponderable possibilities. Enabled by Ashbery's mastery of syntax, haywire similes (summer takes spring away "like a terrier a lady has asked me to hold for a moment"), and linguistic congeniality ("Gosh, what a limited bunch of things to do there is"), they offer rich cascades of surprise, colloquies of disparate voices that may or may not emanate from the same consciousness. And as funny as Ashbery allows himself to be ("You don't learn the cancan at obedience school"), his oblique forays into the traditional poetic genres of elegy ("Others Shied Away") and meditation ("My Philosophy of Life") are genuinely affecting.' – Fred Muratori, *Library Journal*, 1995

Can You Hear, Bird (1995)

'The poems ... range across all manner of forms and styles, moods and voices. Some are more engaging than others (almost all Ashbery poems, even those which "do" nothing for us or leave us disoriented, are engaging).' – John Boening, *World Literature Review*, 1996

'Ashbery, recipient of the grandest of literary prizes, is as prolific as he is masterful. He is also insouciant, elegant, and blithely surreal. Here, in his seventeenth substantial poetry collection, he is also urbane and just a tad cynical. In "Atonal Music", he writes, "It's fine to reminisce, / but no one really cares about your childhood, / not even you". In "Dangerous Moonlight", one character tells another that they have "a million things to do / and restoring your peace of mind isn't one of them". As usual, Ashbery mixes his styles from classic forms to near prose, and glides effortlessly from the world at large to the world within. He is as adept at intoning the babble of mind as at limning the dynamism of a street scene or the quiet of a garden. As Ashbery assumes a variety of personas with all manner of attitudes in all kinds of situations, he gives voice to the perplexity we perceive all around us and seethe with within. Ashbery is a virtuoso all right, indefatigable and dazzling.' – Donna Seaman, *Booklist*, 1995

'There is nowhere that Ashbery's poetry can't sail, one feels, and nothing it can't do, apart of course, from "doing" anything ... Reading Ashbery – like reading the Gertrude Stein of *Tender Buttons* – is a continually surprising, exciting venture that proves the endlessness of the resources that we call language.' – Stephen Yenser, *Yale Review*, 1996

'... it is not because Ashbery is a "strong" poet (to use Harold Bloom's favoured term) that his work remains so inviting. It is rather because he is, in a special sense, an exemplarily weak one, full of representative doubts and anxieties, fond memories, misapprehensions and fears. His poetry appeals not because it offers wisdom in a packaged form, but because the elusiveness and mysterious promise of his lines reminds us that we always have a future and a condition of meaningfulness to start out toward.' – Nicholas Jenkins, *New York Times Book Review*, 1999

'Ashbery's poems do not evade the real; they deny it the power to prevent other realities from being conceived.' – Paul Gray, *Time, 1998*

'No one writing poems in the English language is likelier than Ashbery to survive the severe judgments of time ... He is joining that American sequence that includes Whitman, Dickinson, Stevens, and Hart Crane.' – Harold Bloom, 1998

'These new poems are major odes to the joy of imagining, to the mitigation of sameness. They have a clarity akin to radiance. In their exciting oscillations – between image and art, art and life – what lingers on, after their startlingness, is their truth. This is some of the most serious writing in, and of, America today.' – John Hollander, 1998

'*The Mooring of Starting Out* is filled with illustrations glimpsed through luminous, funny, formidably intelligent and often heartbreaking poems.' – Andrew Zawacki, *Times Literary Supplement*, 1998

WAKEFULNESS (1998)

'... Ashbery's work in its totality now represents something of a conundrum for American poetry – which is, of course, what it's meant to do. The poems laugh at us for expecting them to do anything more than laugh at us. This brilliant ruse is Ashbery's ultimate project.' – Tom Clark, *San Francisco Chronicle*, 1998

'Ashbery, like God, is most easily defined by negatives. His poems have no plot, narrative, or situation; no consistent emotional register or tone; no sustained mood or definite theme. They do not even have meaningful titles. So complete is Ashbery's abandonment of most of what we come to poetry for that his achievement seems, on first acquaintance, as though it must be similarly complete: a radical new extension of poetry's means and powers, or an audacious and wildly successful hoax.

Ashbery proves, better than any other poet, that a certain style of "difficulty" is not at all as difficult as it may seem ... Difficulty is only possible within a system of conventions, including the convention of meaning ... When a poet leaves conventions behind (which is not the same thing as playing with them or transcending them), a vast territory of verbiage is opened up, and he can journey anywhere.' – Adam Kirsch, *New Republic*, 1998

'Few poets have so cleverly manipulated, or just plain tortured, our soiled desire for meaning. [Ashbery] reminds us that most poets who give us meaning don't know what they're talking about.' – William Logan, *New Criterion*, 1998

'Exceptional in their daring wordplay and rhyme, teeming with the unexpected, the eccentric, and the downright freakish, these poems capture our attention by refusing to conform to narrative expectations. Here we enter the mind of an exacting genius, a mind so taken with the subtleties of language, with the way words are laid down, that when he states: "Each is truly a unique piece, / you said, or, perhaps, each / is a truly unique piece. I sniff the difference", we believe him.' – Martha Silano, *The Economist*, 1998

'Words are the ether of Ashbery's universe, and he is a receiver, perpetually tuned in to the clamour. He picks up random scraps of conversation, the inner mumbo-jumbo of the subconscious, and the more consolidated but still inconclusive syntax of thought, even as they break up in the static of interference and overlap. But Ashbery is a tireless recorder of atmospheric disturbances, a suave riddler, and a clever dramatist, spinning long-breathed poems that occupy the page like surreal collages. He swings easily from esoteric philosophy to ironic anecdotes, and he tosses out emotions like so much confetti. "No one takes hold anymore", he writes in "Palindrome of Evening", and so, he seems to say, listen but don't take it to heart, admire but don't covet, touch but don't clasp. Let it flow. And his graceful, sly, and tender poems glimmer and shift like aurora borealis in the mind's dark, making our synapses glow, not with reason and sense, but with impressions and sensibility.' Donna Seaman, *Booklist*, 1998

'Dizzying in their non-sense, Ashbery's centreless tropes sing their own disapproval: a warning to readers untutored in his churlish ways, this is poetry at its most demanding, and not always worth the candle.' – *Kirkus Reviews*, 1998

'Nuanced, subtle, and magnificent . . . a profound pleasure, the gift of a master.' – Harold Bloom, 1998

GIRLS ON THE RUN (1999)

'Ashbery's *Girls on the Run*, like its charming Peggy, is a poem both persnickety and "frequently at the heart of things". It will make its readers happier and wiser. This is our universal poet, as Walt Whitman was before him.' – Harold Bloom, 1999

'Like the details of the JFK assassination, John Ashbery's poems have been used to support every possible prejudice an observer might have. Some readers are convinced he's the greatest poet of our time, others that he's the poster boy for word-drunk self-indulgence, still others that the two positions aren't mutually exclusive. *Girls on the Run* won't change anyone's mind, though readers who put aside their biases for a moment will appreciate it for what it is, a tank of literary laughing gas that exhilarates and confounds in roughly equal measure.' – David Kirby, *New York Times Book Review*, 1999

'Ashbery dips his bucket into the well for his 19th volume, and emerges with a book-length poem inspired by the lusty dreamlike work of "outsider" artist Henry Darger. While the poem resembles a story, full of figures of fun like Dimples, Jane, Persnickety, and others with prurient appellations, *Girls on the Run* is a non-story. Rather, it's a jubilantly mannerist series of occasions. Events happen: "Hungeringly, Tidbit approached the crone who held the bowl, / . . . . drank the honey. It had good things about it. / Now, pretty as a moment, / Tidbit's housecoat sniffed the indecipherable". Meta-commentary, which describes the poem's total aesthetic, accompanies these happenings. For example, "See, they need to have a storyline. Sexy. So it appears. / The seven colors are remanded". As in his last volume, *Wakefulness*, this latest poem is far from autumnal. It's an unexpected supreme collection, a surrealist comic effort with panel after panel of loopy, glorious lines: "Slush and feathers. The hippo trod on a pine needle, they all sank back into relief / Everywhere we go is something to eat / and fat disappointment, tears in the rain. Somebody is coming over the radio. / A lull"; "Sometimes they were in sordid situations; / at others, a smidgen of fun would intrude on our day, / which exists to be intruded upon anyway". As vital, rambunctious, inventive, and outsiderish as ever.' – *Kirkus Reviews,* 1999

'Ashbery seeks the beauty of the literal, of a poem as enigmatic in meaning as it is acute in phrasing and music . . . Ashbery's is an art so intellectually precise that its ideas cannot be pried loose from its words.' – John Palattella, *Newsday,* 1999

YOUR NAME HERE (2000)

'One piece of Ashbery's genius is the way he's able to handle nostalgia as an object, deftly turning it this way and that in order to travel deeper ranges of time and of loss. And he explores the mechanisms of time and memory without ever sentimentalizing. *Your Name Here* is, simply, a beautiful book, funny and terrifying, as ingenious, strange, and shocking as Ashbery's work has always been. Its frequently elegiac, even sorrowful tone in no way diminishes the energy and inventiveness present in every poem. As he says, "We should all be so lucky as to get hit by the meteor / of an idea once in our lives".' – Lisa Beskin, *Boston Review,* 2001

'One of the enduring volumes in the language.' – Harold Bloom, 2000

'In *Your Name Here* (a witty title that reminds us of all the sneaky things he can do with language), Ashbery has started making sense. This will come as a shock to most readers, because his poetry has lived a long time on the subsidizing strategies of sense without making much sense at all – Ashbery writes poems that promise everything and deliver nothing. He's the original bait-and-switch merchant, the prince of Ponzi schemes. Over and over, you're lured into a poem, following along dutifully in your poetry reader's way; then the trap door swings open and you're dumped into a pit of malarkey – or a pile of meringue. And that has been the pleasure.
  . . .
  Ashbery had, and still has intermittently, a beautiful gift for language – very few poets since Shakespeare have so expanded the working vocabulary of poetry. Ashbery pilfers his words wherever he finds them (he's been kicked out of most of language's expensive shops and most of the thrift stores, too), and he carefully developed a style

where the dizzying shifts of idiom distracted the reader with sublime little jolts or twitches of words unexpected – the banquet of meaning was indefinitely delayed. At worst this was like starving in a room of plastic fruit, but at best the permissions of the poetry were so delicious you hardly minded that an hour later you couldn't remember a line (once we had throwaway lines – we have progressed to throwaway poems). You read every poem with hope, and ended most of them feeling swindled – yet how grateful you were, at times, for being swindled.

    ...

    Ashbery at his most irritating, his most frivolous and trivial, is also Ashbery in the fullest command of his talents (he doesn't have the talents a conventional poet requires). His gifts are impossible to adapt to the fulfillments of garden-variety poetry – he has to keep meaning permanently off balance (Ashbery writes the way Groucho Marx walked). Charming and witty and silly he can be till the cows come home, but he writes as if emotion were written in a language he can't understand – the language of cows.

    Ashbery is still capable of vintage nuttiness ("Today a stoat came to tea / and that was so nice it almost made me cry"), but now the nuttiness is mixed with passages strangely romantic ("My mistress' hands are nothing like these, / collecting silken cords for a day when the wet wind plunges"), or politically wholesome ("In the end it was their tales of warring stampedes / that finished us off. We could not go them one better / and they knew it, and put our head on a stamp" – *our head*?), or simply, sweetly banal ...

    However dull I thought Ashbery could be, I never thought he could be dull in the ordinary ways. Bring back the meringue! Bring back the malarkey!' – William Logan, *New Criterion*, 2000

'It is probably too soon to assess the overall trajectory of Ashbery's poetic career. But as this dazzling new collection makes clear, his ability to produce memorable poems uniquely his own remains undiminished.' – Marjorie Perloff, *Thumbscrew*, 2001

OTHER TRADITIONS (2000)

'The chapters are chronicles of disappointment, madness and suicide, all leavened by Ashbery's wit, his obvious pleasure in revealing the eccentricities of his subjects. The critical readings of the poems themselves are tougher going, as Ashbery attempts what may be impossible: the explication of the indeterminate.' – Taylor Antrim, *New York Times Book Review*, 2000

'*Other Traditions*, Ashbery's small book of essays about the work of several lesser-known poets (John Clare, Thomas Lovell Beddoes, Laura Riding, Raymond Roussel, John Wheelwright, and David Schubert) is a pure pleasure to read. Ashbery is a keen and knowledgeable commentator, paying graceful homage to these artists' work, to his own history as a poet and reader, and to the rich mysteries of poetry itself. In a brief amount of space, Ashbery manages to touch on an impressive amount of material. He explores the historical and aesthetic contexts in which the poets lived and wrote; provides thoughtful, absorbing readings of their work; and discusses their impact on him as a poet. One hopes the book, a quiet triumph, will garner these poets more critical understanding and attention in the future. Ultimately, *Other Traditions* is an exploration of Ashbery's own reading mind and his philosophy on poetry as experience: "no poem can ever hope to produce the exact sensation in even one reader that the poet intended; all poetry is written with this understanding on the part of poet and reader."' – Lisa Beskin, *Boston Review* 2001

'Whether it is due to bad luck on the poet's part or simply a lack of merit, the strength of minor poetry, Ashbery would say, lies precisely in its imperfection. [His] Norton Lectures attempt to solve that puzzle, namely, the degree to which originality is the product of a peculiar kind of inability... *Other Traditions* is an entertaining and shrewd little book. To begin with, the life stories of the six poets he discusses are all amazing. Ashbery is an accomplished raconteur and the lectures are full of delightful anecdotes ... The lectures also provide abundant hints about Ashbery's own method. As he readily admits, poets when writing about other poets frequently write about themselves.' – Charles Simic, *New York Review of Books,* 2000

'Over the years the Charles Eliot Norton lectures at Harvard have been delivered by some of the most eminent figures in world literature (Italo Calvino, Czeslaw Milosz, Nadine Gordimer). Nearly all have been published, but few are likely to be as winning, not to say winsome, as *Other Traditions* ...' – Michael Dirda, *Washington Post Book Review,* 2000

'[Ashbery] untangles their lives from their work, their obscurity from their talent and their importance to us from their obscurity.' – Susan Salter Reynolds, *Los Angeles Times Book Review,* 2000

As Umbrellas Follow Rain (2001)

'"Red Skelton asked me if I had a book coming out. He seemed drowned / in lists of trivia and itching-powder dreams / you know, the kind that make you wake up / and then sort of fall back asleep again. / His brother was cleaning up after the elephants ..." Each of these thirty short lyrics displays the quiet, attentive mastery that has become Ashbery's trademark since *April Galleons*, when he seemed to put away his avant-garde party suit permanently and adopted the "French Zen" persona he credited his old friend Frank O'Hara with founding. One poem has the speaker ruminating nostalgically on the now-extinct "pancake clock" ("It had tiny Roman numerals embedded in its rim"), while another, "Random Jottings of an Old Man", starts as a Seuss-like spectacle of evicting an unwanted poetry-producing houseguest, and morphs into a wistful, Proustian revelry of sounds and senses: "The pianola never recovered from the loss". If only for this new emotion he's invented "flagrant" longing for "multiple directions" Ashbery's new book is great: accessible, yet challenging our habits of feeling.' – *Publishers Weekly,* 2002

Chinese Whispers (2002)

'It's unlike John Ashbery to make things clear, but he does give hints, like titling his new collection "Chinese Whispers", the British name for that game in which a message gets whispered around until it doesn't make sense. You couldn't ask for a more helpful metaphor for the way Ashbery works, given his fondness for pat phrases pulled out of context and for setting his poems in a decentralized universe: they go wherever, objects and observations bobbing along in the flow, descriptions demonstrating the mind's innate disregard for fixed categories and even meaning. "In the pagan dawn three polar bears stand / in the volumetric sky's grapeade revelation". And yet understanding (more or less) what Ashbery is up to is not the same as enjoying him. There is something touching and admirable in his dedication to his mode, which never gives in to the reader's craving for coherence, but it is the rare poem in this volume that carries emotional weight. Ashbery's openly elegiac moments may be more affecting for seeming incidental, but reaching them requires slogging through rubble-slides of inscrutable whimsy. His fans may like those parts best. Others may find their minds wandering as much as Ashbery's, though not in the same direction.' – Matthew Flamm, *New York Times Book Review*, 2002

'Ashbery's most recent style equal parts cracked drawing room dialogue, 4-H Americana, withering sarcasm and sleeve-worn pathos has been perfected over five or so books and adapted by generationally diverse poets from James Tate to Max Winter. The late Kenneth Koch's description of Ashbery as "lazy and quick" remains thoroughly apropos; these 61 page-or-two poems can seem brilliantly tossed off, much like those in his 2000 collection, *Your Name Here*. The title is appropriate too: "Chinese Whispers" is the British name for the game of "Telephone", where children (or adults) gather in a circle and whisper a "secret" word or phrase into the ear next to them. The last person says it out loud; the results are often "off" in funny, surprising and telling ways. The surprise, in poem after poem, is that high and low comedy and offhanded delivery can read like simultaneous expressions of pain and regeneration and that they do not dull after multiple permutations are spun out: "The beginning of the middle is like that. / Looking back it was all valleys, shrines floating on the powdered hill, // ambivalence that came in a flood sometimes, though warm, always, for the next tenant/ to abide there". As with all Ashbery's work, these poems leave plenty of room for readers to abide.' – *Publishers Weekly*, 2002

'Since winning the Pulitzer Prize, the National Book Award, and the National Book Critics Circle Award in 1975 for *Self-Portrait in a Convex Mirror*, Ashbery has been regarded as one of our major poets. This thoughtful new collection may not be any great advance – with Ashbery's elliptical style, how far can one go? – but it does maintain his momentum. The eye is immediately caught by some lines in an early poem – "Our lives ebbing always toward the center, / the unframed portrait" – which feel like a key to Ashbery's aesthetic; he doesn't want us to look only at the centre, at the shapes that predominate, but at the details along the edge. Thus, at first reading, his poems can seem like a string of out-of-sequence images, but they do bleed a definite atmosphere. Often, that atmosphere is disquieting or at least restless, but in these autumnal pieces a sense of calm predominates. True, the tale "jerks / back and forth like the tail of a kite", and frogs and envelopes mutter, "That was some joust!" But the energy crackles only momentarily; here, things repeatedly fall, ebb, dissipate, or descend. Not that these are dreary pieces; there is a light touch and consistent pacing throughout, making this a satisfying read. Given Ashbery's stature, this is recommended for all contemporary poetry collections.' – *Library Journal*, 2002

'Ashbery, prolific, incisive, and bewitching, is not only a great poet, he's a philosopher and a tease. His balletic leaps from the abstract to the concrete, the inanimate to the animate, the intimate to the elusive provoke and unsettle until the reader surrenders to his elegant charm and wise humour, his sly toying with the oddities and hidden significance of colloquialisms and social convention, and his offhanded yet wistful inquiries into the nature of time and the hunger for meaning that drives our dream-drenched lives. Gallantly confiding and satirically funny, the poet pretends that he's above it all, but for all his glimmering and grace, sauciness and savoir faire, he, like everyone else, is forever fishing for clues and playing detective, anxious to tease out something timeless from the transient babble and whirl of our routines. And what he discovers and revels in is a glistening twilight beauty, lovely and ephemeral, and a deep resolve to stick around to see the sun rise and set again, to share stories, to cherish simple things, to stay attuned and spellbound.' – Donna Seaman, *Booklist*, 2002